The Office and Authority of the Local Prior in the Order of Saint Augustine

The Office and Authority of the Local Prior in the Order of Saint Augustine

Robert F. Prevost, OSA
Pope Leo XIV

Foreword by Thomas Joseph White, OP

 THE CATHOLIC UNIVERSITY OF AMERICA PRESS
WASHINGTON, D.C.

Copyright © 2025
Pontifical University of St. Thomas Aquinas (Angelicum)
All rights reserved
The paper used in this publication meets the minimum requirements
of American National Standards for Information Science—Permanence of
Paper for Printed Library Materials, ANSI Z39.48-1992.

Cataloging-in-Publication Data is available from the Library of Congress

ISBN (cloth): 978-0-8132-4062-6
ISBN (ebook): 978-0-8132-4063-3

Text designed by Burt&Burt / Interior set in Dante MT

The Office and Authority of the Local Prior in the Order of Saint Augustine

Vidimus et approbavimus,
Romae, apud Pontificiam Studiorum Universitatem S. Thoma Aq. In Urbe:

    P. Iosephus Castano, O.P.
    P. Albertus Gauthier, O.P.

Imprimatur
    † Ennio Appignanesi, Archiep. Tit. Lorii

    Romae, die 6 mensis Februarii 1987.

PONTIFICIA STUDIORUM UNIVERSITAS A S. THOMA AQ. IN URBE

ROBERT F. PREVOST, O.S.A.

THE OFFICE AND AUTHORITY OF THE LOCAL PRIOR IN THE ORDER OF SAINT AUGUSTINE

Dissertatio ad Lauream
in Facultate Iuris Canonici
apud Pontificiam Universtitatem S. Thomae
De Urbe

ROMAE 1987

CONTENTS

Abbreviations	xii
Foreword by Thomas Joseph White, OP	xiv
Introduction	1

CHAPTER ONE
THE SUPERIOR'S ROLE OF SERVICE TO THE COMMUNITY
11

CHAPTER TWO
THE AUTHORITY OF THE LOCAL PRIOR
35

Potestas	40
«Religious» authority	43
Power of governance	51
Personal authority	55
The exercise of the Prior's authority	59

CHAPTER THREE
THE OFFICE OF THE LOCAL PRIOR
65

Definition	65
Ecclesiastical office	67
Nomination	68
Term of office	70
Requisites	75
Conferral of office	78
Termination of office	81
Expiration of term of office	81

CONTENTS

Resignation	82
Transfer	84
Removal	85
Privation of office	86
Vacancy of office	87

CHAPTER FOUR
THE MUNUS DOCENDI
89

The Community as an educational environment	91
The Prior's role in formation	95
In houses of formation	96
Ongoing formation	100
Preaching the Word of God	104
In the apostolate	107
Lay fraternities	110

CHAPTER FIVE
THE MUNUS SANCTIFICANDI
113

The «cura animarum»	114
Prayer life of the community	118
Liturgy of the Hours	119
Devotional practices and retreat	121
The Eucharist	125
Community celebration	127
Mass intentions	128
The Sacrament of Penance	129
Care of the sick	136
For the deceased	139

CHAPTER SIX
THE MUNUS REGENDI
141

The Local Prior and his Council	143
Membership	144
Procedure	145
Matters requiring the consent/advice of the Council	153
The Local Chapter	155
Membership	157
Authority	159
Procedure	163
Matters to be discussed by the local Chapter	166
Administration of temporal goods	171
Safeguarding the life of the community	176
Conclusion	187
Bibliography	193
Sources	193
Authors and books	194
Articles	198
Subject Index	205
Scripture Index	210
Canonical Index	211

Abbreviations

AAS *Acta Apostolicae Sedis*. Official Commentary. Rome: Vatican City. From 1909 ff.
Acta OSA *Acta Ordinis Sancti Augustini*. Official Commentary. Rome: Curia Generalizia. From 1956 ff.
AG *Ad gentes divinitus*. Decree on the Missionary Activity of the Church.
can. *Codex Juris Canonici* (1983).
CLSA Canon Law Society of America.
CpR *Commentarium pro Religiosis et Missionariis*. Rome. From 1920 ff.
DH *Dignitatis humanae*. Declaration on Religious Freedom.
ES *Ecclesiae Sanctae*. Norms for the application of various decrees of Vatican II, AAS 57(1965)5-71.
ET *Evangelica testificatio*. Apostolic exhortation of PP. Paul VI to the members of every religious family in the Catholic world. June 29, 1971. AAS 63(1971)497-526.

ABBREVIATIONS

LG	*Lumen gentium.* Dogmatic Constitution on the Church.
MR	*Mutuae relationes.* Directory on relations between bishops and religious in the Church. Sacred Congregation for Religious and Secular Institutes and Sacred Congregation for Bishops. May 14, 1978: AAS 70(1978)473-506.
OT	*Optatam totius.* Decree on Priestly Formation.
PC	*Perfectae caritatis.* Decree on the Renewal of Religious Life.
PL	*Patrologia Latina,* ed. J.-P. Migne. 221 volumes. Paris, 1844-1864.
PO	*Presbyterorum ordinis.* Decree on the Ministry and Life of Priests.
SC	*Sacrosanctum Concilium.* Constitution on the Sacred Liturgy.
SCRSI	Sacred Congregation for Religious and Secular Institutes.
UR	*Unitatis redintegratio.* Decree on Ecumenism.
Vfr.	*Liber Vitasfratrum.* Jordan of Saxony, OSA.
v. can.	Codex Juris Canonici (1917).

Foreword

Thomas Joseph White, OP
Rector, Pontifical University of St. Thomas Aquinas,
Angelicum, Rome

Robert Prevost studied at the Angelicum in Rome from 1981 to 1985, during which time he acquired a licentiate in canon law (*Juris Canonici Licentiatus*) and then successfully defended his doctorate in the same field (*Juris Canonici Doctor*). Although the thesis was submitted in 1985 and received high marks, it was not officially published by the Angelicum until 1987, presumably due to the ministerial work that Prevost undertook in Peru in 1985 as a newly ordained priest in the Order of Saint Augustine.

The influence of ecclesiastical graduate studies in Rome on the lives of those who later become popes ought not to be overstated, but neither should its importance be underestimated. The most recent previous pontiff to have undergone formal training in canon law was Giovanni Battista Montini (Saint Pope Paul VI), who completed a degree in this subject as part of his training to become a member of the international diplomatic corps of the Holy See. Montini subsequently steered the Church through a challenging period, overseeing the completion of the Second Vatican Council and its initial reception throughout the Catholic

Church. His canonical training probably influenced him in a myriad of ways through this process, and yet simultaneously, research into Montini's early study does not allow one to predict and explain later outcomes. He, as a former student, clearly came to have new insights and moral inclinations in his leadership of the Church that were not manifest earlier in his ecclesial career.

Similarly, we can observe that the doctoral research of Karol Wojtyła, completed in the 1940s at the Angelicum on the theological virtue of faith in the thought of Saint John of the Cross, is indicative of some themes that remained steadfast in the character of the author throughout his life.[1] However, the dissertation in question is hardly predictive of the whole wellspring of teaching and activity that would characterize the pontificate of Saint Pope John Paul II. Instead, the early academic work of such figures is part of a much larger story. However, it does tell us something, namely, about each of them becoming a certain kind of truth-centered person through their research and the formation of their intellectual habits. It is persons, after all, who govern the Church in and through living ideas, rather than ideas that govern, mediating through persons.

Unlike Montini and Wojtyła, Prevost was a member of a religious order, one of medieval origin, the Order of Saint Augustine. Accordingly, the doctorate of Prevost focuses on a different subject matter: *The Office and Authority of the Local Prior in the Order of Saint Augustine*.[2] Founded in the mid-thirteenth century, this

---

[1] The original title of this work, completed in 1948, was *Doctrina de fide apud S. Ioannem a Cruce*, published in English as *Faith According to Saint John of the Cross*, trans. Jordan Aumann, OP (Ignatius Press, 1981).

[2] The original publication is Robert F. Prevost, *The Office and Authority of the Local Prior in the Order of Saint Augustine* (Pontifical University of St. Thomas, 1987). Candidates for the doctorate in Roman pontifical universities are typically required to produce a local publication of their doctoral thesis after it is approved and to distribute it

community is an order of mendicant friars, marked by vows of poverty, chastity, and obedience. It is dedicated to the observance of a common life of liturgical prayer, theological study, priestly ministry, and evangelization. As such, it bears similarities to other communities of friars, such as the Franciscans, the Carmelites, and the Dominicans.[3] The Augustinian Order takes its original inspiration from the writings of Saint Augustine, and thus is governed in part by the ancient *Rule of Saint Augustine*, which served as a basis for the religious life of this and several other medieval orders, including the Dominicans. The Augustinian Friars in Rome maintain a prestigious institute for the study of patristic theology (the *Istituto Patristico Augustinianum*), but they do not have a faculty of canon law. Hence, it is hardly surprising that an Augustinian friar should undertake the canonical study of his own Order's constitutions at the Angelicum, with canonists from an adjacent religious order which is similarly marked by governmental reference to the *Rule of Saint Augustine*.

Prevost took courses with and wrote under the guidance of José Manuel Castaño, OP (1926–2005), a respected canonist of his time. Castaño was an expert in particular on law pertaining to both marriage and consecrated religious life. In the 1980s, he was a lecturer in canon law both at the Pontifical Lateran University in Rome and at the Pontifical University of Saint Thomas Aquinas (Angelicum), where he also served as dean of the Faculty of Canon

---

to the libraries of the Roman pontifical universities prior to the official reception of doctorate. This dissertation version remains in the library of Villanova University and a handful of other institutions worldwide.

3 On the history of the Order, see David Gutiérrez, *Los Agustinos en la edad media: 1256–1356, Historia de la Orden de San Agustín* vol. I/1 (Institutum Historicum Ordinis Fratrum S. Augustini, 1980).

Law.[4] This context is of relevance for a variety of reasons. Castaño regularly lectured on Church-state relations (the interaction of civil and canon law) and the canon law of matrimony as well as that pertaining to consecrated religious life. He was one of many canon lawyers who advised Pope John Paul II on the revision of the 1917 Code of Canon Law that took place in light of the Second Vatican Council, which issued in the 1983 Code of Canon Law. Naturally, then, Castaño was a close observer of the revisions that took place in the Code pertaining to consecrated and religious life.[5] It should be noted, accordingly, that Prevost began working on his doctorate with Castaño in this field in 1983, the same year the new Code of Canon Law was promulgated. His interpretations of the Code were aided, then, by the guidance of a person who had a privileged analysis of the text under consideration.

Prevost's thesis seeks to analyze the modern Constitutions of the Order of Saint Augustine in light of the then-newly promulgated 1983 Code of Canon Law, so as to consider how they are to be interpreted in the postconciliar epoch. In 1968, the Augustinian Order had already completed a revision of its own Constitutions in light of the Second Vatican Council, as was required of every major religious institute at the time. However, these modern constitutional revisions took place before the promulgation of the 1983 Code. Thus, there remained the outstanding challenge of interpreting the constitutions of the Order of Saint Augustine in light of the 1983 Code and its norms regarding religious life.

---

[4] See Angelo Urru, *La Facoltà di diritto canonico della Pontificia Università di San Tommaso d'Aquino in Roma: cento anni di storia* (Pontifical University of St. Thomas, 1998); Efrem Jindrácek, "L'insegnamento domenicano a Roma (1909-2009)," *Angelicum* 19, no. 4 (1942): 289–311.

[5] See in particular, the 1983 *Code of Canon Law*, Part III, section II, canons 607–709. For an official English translation, see www.vatican.va. See also, *Code of Canon Law*, Latin-English Edition (CLSA, 2001).

Prevost's thesis sets out to do this not in a comprehensive way, which would have been too extensive a subject, but instead concentrates prudently on a precise but important topic, the role of the prior in the governance of the local priory, in accord with both the Order's norms and the general law of the Church.[6]

From Context to Content: On Authority and Spiritual Life in the Community of the Catholic Church

At this point the reader may well wonder whether this subject is of interest to those unfamiliar with canon law in the Catholic tradition. The answer is, I think, undoubtedly affirmative. Rightly understood, the Catholic Church's canon law is indicative of the life of the Church and her convictions regarding both the mystery of God and the nature of human rights and responsibilities. It indicates fundamental structures found in the world of nature and grace, and thus is something profound at heart, and of universal interest. Indeed, we can say that, precisely speaking, the law of the Church seeks to indicate the nature of the human person and his or her responsibilities, privileges, and rights, both in relation to God and to other human persons. In this sense, canon law is implicitly theological and ontological, and its subject matter points us toward the individual and collective moral agency of persons in the Catholic Church. It is also practical, however. Treating a range of important topics, from the governance of the Church as a whole, to the nature of the sacraments, to justice in human

---

6 Religious orders, including the Order of Saint Augustine, are typically governed by a Major Superior, under which there are Provinces with Provincial Superiors, and finally priories or houses, under the jurisdiction of Local Superiors. Prevost intentionally wrote about the latter only.

society, and the aims of priestly ministry, this body of law has a wide-reaching application. Its prescriptions and prohibitions touch upon the very constitution of the Catholic religion, both in its essence and in its concrete daily life. As such, canon law is, when rightly understood, a daily companion of Catholic theological, moral, and philosophical doctrine. It derives from their principles, or is their architectural offspring, employed by the Church for the governance of her ordinary life in time.

This last observation is of importance when evaluating key themes in Prevost's work. It is best understood as a work that seeks to indicate and analyze the objective structure of the life of the Catholic Church, particularly with regard to the religious practices of a specific community of ordained priests and their common commitments. This has suggestive importance when considering the later biography of the author, but only up to a point. On the one hand, it is the excellent work of a young priest, and it does focus on themes that have relevance for his later life as a prior, provincial, and major superior in the Order of Saint Augustine, as well as for his work as a bishop, cardinal, and pontiff. However, the themes as enunciated by a doctoral student of canon law also should not be made to bear too great a weight in seemingly predicting or casting expectations upon subsequent developments or decisions of Prevost as a religious superior or bishop.

Additionally, we should note, as it could go without saying, that the work in question is not part of the Magisterium of the Catholic Church. It should not be confused with documents having an authoritative value when estimating the teaching legacy of Pope Leo XIV. Certainly, it does not fall within the oft-misunderstood papal charism of infallibility, nor does it call for the "religious submission of the intellect and will" that Catholics are meant to give the ordinary authoritative teaching of the Roman pontiff.[7] This all being said, if these pages do not tell us where Pope Leo is going, they at least give us some background on where he is coming from, so to speak, on themes that will perdure in his pontificate. Indeed, there are themes of great value and of universal interest in the thesis, and I will mention here only some of these, leaving readers to explore both these and others at their own leisure.

Structure

The thesis is composed of six parts that develop organically and logically from one another. The introduction and first chapter are concerned with the nature of authority in the Church and on the role of the superior in the life of the community. The second chapter treats governance in religious life in general, and the power of jurisdiction in the Church, specifically relating to the priest who is a prior in a religious community. The third chapter examines the office of the prior according the Constitutions of the Order of Saint Augustine. The fourth, fifth, and sixth chapters then examine sequentially the *munus docendi*, the *munus sanctificandi*, and the *munus regendi*. These are the three modes of authority envisaged by the Second Vatican Council as constitutive of priestly authority in the Church: the gift of teaching, of sanctification (particularly through the administration of the sacraments), and of prudential government. If we were to summarize the whole simply, we could say that the thesis treats the Augustinian religious superior as an authority whose office is to serve the common good of the

---

7 See *Code of Canon Law*, canon 751. Even personal theological or pastoral works written by a pope during his pontificate do not necessarily fall under this canon, as Pope Benedict XVI famously pointed out at the beginning of his *Jesus of Nazareth* series. Pre-papal works certainly do not.

religious community, in accord with its objective needs, the rule of life, the respect of persons, and the life of the virtues, with charity being principal among them. In doing so, the prior as a priest has the responsibility to exert the three *munera* in a way that conforms to and is at the service of his religious institute. Thus, in the Augustinian life, he is responsible as a priest-superior to teach the truth of the Gospel, to celebrate the sacraments and assure their apostolic vitality, and to govern prudently in accord with the rule of the institute and the law of the Church. At the heart of this vision is an Augustinian conception of the spiritual life—where the superior, who depends upon God's grace—is called upon to make a personal sacrifice of his life to God for the service of the community, and in doing so is meant to be inwardly conformed to the charity of Jesus Christ. Understood in this light, we can summarize briefly six themes that characterize the thesis, one for each chapter.

Authority and the Common Good

How did the young Fr. Robert Prevost view authority in the Church? A central theme of the introduction and first chapter of the thesis pertains to the common good as a measure for the exercise of ecclesiastical obedience. On this view, authority in the Church, as well as obedience to legitimate authority on the part of subjects, is characterized by the shared pursuit by all of the common good of the Church and of the local religious community. The notion of the "common good" (*bonum commune*) derives particularly from the thought of St. Thomas Aquinas, but it is of systematic importance in the modern articulation of Catholic social thought, in authors like Pope Leo XIII and in documents of the Second Vatican Council.[8] The notion also appears in the 1983 *Code of Canon Law*.[9] The simplest way to think of the common good is to consider that there are many essential goods that we cannot enjoy individually but only collectively. Human beings cannot enjoy being married or being members of a human family only individually but instead only participate in these goods collectively. The same can be said of other goods such as universities, national states, congregations of religious orders, or the Catholic Church as a whole.

Authority, the thesis underscores, is exerted as a service of the superior who seeks to take account of the objective parameters of the common good as a communion of persons who pursue a common set of activities. The law of the community is measured by the common good in question and the means or joint activities by which the good is pursued. The superior, then, is a person who seeks to facilitate the common pursuit of the good on the part of all the members of the community, taking into account their individual gifts, limitations, needs, and so forth, as well as the way that each one can contribute to the whole. This vision of obedience is personalistic and intellectual in character. It is

---

[8] See for example, St. Thomas Aquinas, *Summa Theologiae* I-II, q. 90, a. 2, where Aquinas asks whether every law is directed to the common good, and answers affirmatively. See *Summa Theologica*, trans. L. Shapcote (Benziger Bros., 1947). Leo XIII makes appeal to the notion of the common good systematically in several of his encyclicals on Catholic social doctrine, including *Immortale Dei* (1885) and *Rerum Novarum* (1891). The Second Vatican Council makes extensive reference to the common good, including in the documents *Gaudium et Spes*, *Dignitatis Humanae*, and *Lumen Gentium*. For references to these documents of the Catholic Magisterium, see the official translations at www.vatican.va.

[9] See, e.g., *Code of Canon Law*, canon 223, §§1–2: "In exercising their rights, the Christian faithful, both as individuals and gathered together in associations, must take into account the common good of the Church, the rights of others, and their own duties toward others. In view of the common good, ecclesiastical authority can direct the exercise of rights which are proper to the Christian faithful."

personalistic because the observance of a common set of norms is intended to facilitate personal growth in communion with God, the life of virtue, and the love of God and neighbor. The common life of the members is oriented toward personal flourishing in communion. It is intellectual in nature because it presupposes that the superior who commands and the subject who obeys are joined together in a common exercise of understanding, referring themselves to the truth about God and humanity revealed in the person of Christ and in the teachings, sacramental practices, and ethical norms of the Catholic Church.

Thus, obedience is not blind or merely voluntaristic. Instead, our freedom is augmented through obedience precisely because it is guided by a sustained reference to the truth and because it aims at personal growth in love. Obedience, on this view, cultivates character or virtue in the service of the love of God and of the truth about the human person. The superior is bound when he commands by reference to the truth about divine and human love, and the superior seeks to facilitate his own freedom and that of others in reference to this truth. The human conscience has a necessary and vital role to play in this process, as each one is called upon by the mission of the Church to reflect on the commonly held truth and practice of the faith and to seek together the common good of the Church by facilitating in oneself and in others a deeper life in Christ.

Ecclesial Identity of Religious Life

The second chapter of the thesis touches upon a series of challenging historical and theoretical topics. It notes first that the authority of religious superiors is not formally identical with that of the apostolic hierarchy of the Catholic Church, and that there are various opinions on the ontological origins and theological status of the authority of religious orders and their founders and rules of life, as related to their participants. By contrast, the priesthood of any given religious superior is directly under the jurisdiction of the apostolic hierarchy, and functions according to the triple *munera* of teaching, sanctifying, and governing, in keeping with the universal mission of the Catholic Church. Consequently, the Catholic priest-superior who is in a religious order must maintain the governance of the institute both in accord with its particular law, in keeping with its distinct charism, and in accord with the universal agency of the priesthood, subject to the apostolic hierarchy and the episcopacy of the Catholic Church. Far from thinking of this priestly identity of the religious superior as something alien to the religious life, one should instead consider it as essential to the life of a clerical religious institute. Just as the religious congregation functions for the pursuit of the common good of the Church, both in its members and in those to whom it ministers, so those religious who are priests serve the greater order of the Church through religious observances that intensify and perfect their life of priestly ministry. This takes place both through the contemplative dimensions of religious life—in liturgical prayer, meditation, study, and conversion of life—as well as through the external ministries of the religious institute that perform both spiritual and temporal works of mercy on behalf of others. In sum, the priest-superior is a representative both of the charism of the institute and of the hierarchical Church. He seeks to govern the institute in view of the conversion of life of both himself and its members. This occurs through both a life of contemplation and apostolic ministry. This is the context in which the superior should seek to exert the three apostolic *munera*: teaching, sanctification, and apostolic governance.

Spiritual Authority

The third chapter of the thesis notes that the prior of the Augustinian community possesses canonical and jurisdictional power in virtue of the office that is assigned to him by the provincial (his ordinary superior) and his provincial council. However, the author also notes that canonical power is distinct from personal authority that is moral and spiritual. The latter stems from the moral credibility, spiritual integrity, and prudential competence of the superior. Evidently, subjects find it easier to obey a person who is in possession of a jurisdictional mandate when the person in question is also characterized by spiritual understanding and moral wisdom. The capacity to govern in light of these higher qualities is something that the Church should seek to cultivate in its leadership to the extent possible. Likewise, those assigned to lead others are greatly helped in this task to the extent that their own interior life, Christian prudence, and human moral competency are well-formed.

Laws that govern the exercise of office, such as that of the prior or provincial, are designed to allow a timely rotation of leadership personnel. This method allows the Church in her religious orders to circumnavigate the problem of excessive reliance upon or submission to individual personalities. It invites various contributions successively over time from persons of distinct and complementary gifts. It also protects good leaders and superiors from unsustainable or imprudent forms of commitment and continuation. The exercise of leadership itself, then, takes place within a communitarian logic and a historical unfolding of shared responsibility and ongoing prudential conversation and recalculation. This wider context of communitarian distribution of leadership provides institutes with a greater flexibility and strength in meeting the demands of both adaptation to new circumstances and sustained fidelity across time.

Intellectual Life: Learning, Preaching and Teaching the Gospel

The fourth chapter of the thesis considers the prior's role in the exercise of the teaching office of the Church, understood by analogy to the episcopacy and papacy and in subsidiary service to the latter. The Augustinian prior must be a kind of *magister* in the sense articulated by Augustine: a person who conveys genuine learning in the Catholic tradition so as to elicit from others their own search for the truth. The Church receives genuine divine revelation from God and thus shares in divine truth, but she also conveys this truth through a common life, one shared by individuals who seek truth out in their natural freedom and mutual capacities for learning. The prior must, therefore, acquire a real and profound sense of theological learning and must exert his teaching within the context of religious life. This notion has several consequences. First, the prior like other priests must train to acquire accurate and qualified understanding of the intellectual patrimony of the Catholic tradition. In doing so he has to have a sense of his responsibilities and capacities, but also of his limitations, within a communal context. Second, his teaching is exerted in an analogical sense, across a spectrum of forms: preaching, theological instruction, and sound counsel and advice.

Third, his responsibility as prior is not only one of spiritual instruction but also of the assurance of intellectual and spiritual formation. This is acutely the case when he is responsible for the formation of future priests and consecrated religious. The superior of a priory of formation for candidates to the priesthood must be especially attentive to the central role of study in the Augustinian life, and of the norms and requisite aims of priestly formation on the part of the Catholic Church. Even outside the seminary context, the prior in an Augustinian priory needs to attend to the role of study in the Augustinian life, so that the friars nurture their interiority and their apostolic commitment by a constant return to the intellectual life and the study of theology. Fourth, the prior must have knowledge not only of theology but also of the constitutions and norms of the Order, so that he can teach these to others and govern the life of the community effectively in light of the Order's internal law. Here law is understood also as having an intellectual grounding in the truth about the Church and her religious life. Finally, the cultivation of a life of learning and study within the Order is oriented not only toward the search for God and the contemplative life but also toward the apostolic teaching and preaching of the Catholic faith to others. The prior's respect for a life of dedication to study in the Order can bear fruit for the larger ecclesial community, since this way of life facilitates a deeper meditation on and effective communication of the sacred teaching of the apostolic faith and the resources of the Catholic intellectual tradition.

Sacramental Life and the Centrality of the Eucharist

In the fifth chapter, Prevost characterizes the prioral-priestly role of sanctification in terms of the *cura animarum*, the care of souls. The prior should be concerned to facilitate a priestly life of sanctification on behalf of the religious community through the medium of the common life. His principal concern in this regard is with the holiness of the brothers. Here the famous saying from canon law holds especially true: *suprema lex salus animarum*. The supreme law of the Church is ordained to the salvation of souls, and their growth in sanctification.

Accordingly, the prior has a responsibility to uphold and facilitate the integral celebration of the liturgical prayer and sacramental life of the Catholic Church, since, after all, it is primarily through the liturgy and the reception of the sacraments that the members of the Church are directed immediately toward God. Canonical religious life thus entails the liturgy of the hours, which is the collective practice of prayer expressed through the recitation or singing of a precise schedule of psalms and hymns, accompanied by readings from sacred scripture and tradition. Daily meditation, devotional practices, annual retreats, and spiritual chapter talks of instruction all form part of the life of the priory, and these too are to be facilitated or provided by the prior.

The celebration of the Eucharist is of central importance to the life of the Church and of every religious community. The Mass is a privileged place of encounter with God, and it is the instrumental occasion for every person's spiritual conformity to the mystery of Christ. So too, then, in religious life, the Mass is at the center of the identity and spiritual practice of the religious community. The prior must above all be responsible for the life of daily celebration and corporate participation in the sacred worship of the eucharistic liturgy. The practice of sacramental communion, however, has as its necessary complement in religious life the regular practice of the sacrament of penance. So too, then, the community should have access to regular occasions for confession. Here the superior must show respect for the conscience of the members of the Order.

Ordinarily the superior should not act as the confessor or spiritual director (i.e., one who has competence in "the internal forum") for those he governs (having public authority in "the external forum"), and he is forbidden to seek any manifestation of the internal state of conscience from those he governs. Nevertheless, the superior is one of the persons involved in making sure that the priests of the community do have canonical faculties to hear confessions from the bishop of the diocese, in accord with the exigencies of the sacrament that contribute to its validity.

Finally, as part of the *munus sanctificandi* the prior must be vigilant to seek the well-being of the sick, and to serve the suffering or dying members of the community with vigilance. He must take care of the dying not only as they prepare for death but also by seeing that the community prays for them after death and offers Mass on their behalf. Praying for the dead is a constitutive obligation of the religious life, and one in which living members of the community seek to assist the souls of their departed brethren by their intercession and by celebration of the sacrifice of the Mass on their behalf.

In this perspective on the priestly life of the superior, the conception of leadership that prevails is undoubtedly theocentric. The common good that characterizes religious life is centered on God, and it is principally for this reason that it is subject to the law of the Church. The superior who seeks the salvation and sanctification of the membership of his community must seek to govern them liturgically and sacramentally in view of their union with God, especially through a public and personal life of prayer, contemplation, and love of God.

FOREWORD

The Governance of Persons in View of Communion and Mission

As the final chapter of the thesis notes, the most tangible responsibility of the prior is for the concrete care of the priory in its daily life. Here references are made to the House Council and the House Chapter as governing bodies of the community. The prior presides over each, and each has a distinct administrative function. The work of the Council is more hierarchical and restricted, while the Chapter is inclusive of the whole community. The former has more governmental weight, but both the prior and the Council need to consult with and listen to the Chapter. Here also is noted the place of the treasurer, who maintains practices of economic probity, responsibility, and transparent reporting. In other words, the governance of the community is cooperative and entails a system of checks and balances, common deliberations, and collective accountability in finances. The prior does officiate and must frequently make decisions over and above the directions indicated by the Chapter, but he is bound to consult and can at times be required by law to receive a vote of approval for his decisions.

Prevost also notes the importance and challenge of the discipline of errant members of the community who are neglecting or acting in disaccord with their religious vows. Correction and guidance from superiors toward such members of the community is to be exerted in view of their conversion, well-being, and moral progress, as well as for the well-being and protection of the community and the Church.

Throughout this process of governance, the prior should maintain consistent respect for procedures of government. The details matter. It is important to oversee elections carefully so that any voting that takes place is always valid, in accord with the rights of the community and the norms of the constitutions. When the Council or Chapter requires consultation by law, the prior should consult. Advising and mutual deliberation are a part of the life of the Church, including for authorities, who can seek to develop their deliberative prudence in the greater service of the Order. Likewise, the prior has a unique, genuine, and irreplaceable executive power which he must exert with responsibility, even after the deliberations of his Council and in light of them. In other words, in the end someone must be in charge and must make final decisions that others are bound to obey. This central leadership of the priory is essential precisely so that the unity, integrity, and harmony of the life of the community can be maintained consistently, for the good of all.

Conclusion

To repeat, it is not really feasible to predict or foretell from the youthful doctoral work of a future pope how and in what way that pontiff might govern. Human life is in many ways historically open-ended, interesting, and surprising, not governed by a simple history of ideas. Nevertheless, the formation of our ideas does matter, and they can have historical legacies and consequences. Accordingly, there are pertinent observations one can make about the thesis of Robert Prevost that should have some bearing upon a truly Catholic conception of the papacy. Clearly the notion of the Augustinian prior and his priestly ministry that is envisaged in this thesis has its context in a larger whole, that of the Church. Consequently, the Augustinian notions of governance and the vision of the *munera* of the priesthood that it explores are exemplified in other more overarching ways if one expands the realm of reflection to consider the role of the major superior, the bishop, or the pope. Each of these figures is responsible for the common good, in ever expanding and more extensive ways, and each is bound to participate in the authority of Christ and his Church by accord with the threefold *munera* of teaching, sacramental sanctification, and governance. Truth be told, one could reconceptualize the thesis in question by thinking of the role of the papacy in the universal Church rather than the prior in the local Augustinian community, and certainly not all but many of the spiritual and canonical norms would remain, and only gain importance of universal extension and intensive significance.

Evidently the author of the thesis at age thirty did not have this horizon in view, but one can respectfully ask whether divine providence is not at work when a person preparing himself for the participation in the common life of his religious community in fact considers elements of communal existence—an existence that will have great pertinence for all of the offices that he will subsequently accept in unforeseeable circumstances under obedience to others. I will not attempt to envisage the larger story of how the early work of Fr. Prevost was preparatory for or indicative of themes that might emerge in his service to the Church as Pope Leo XIV. There are clearly, however, in this early work central themes regarding the life of the Church, the apostolic tradition, and ecclesial authority in the service of the common good that may well indicate directions and themes in the subsequent life and teaching of the author. Historians and theologians alike may enjoy considering parallelisms that occur between this Augustinian vision of the prior and the subsequent unfolding of an Augustinian pontificate. Hopefully, the publication of this work by The Catholic University of America Press in its original English (and other presses in other languages) will lead to constructive debate about and comprehension of the relationship between the two.[10] May it inspire all priors, pastors, bishops, and anyone who holds authority in the Church to exert that authority for the sake of the common good: to find unity with one another through a shared life of charity, a common pursuit of the truth, and a life ordered toward union with God.

---

[10] I would like to thank the staff of CUA Press, especially its director Dr. Trevor Lipscombe, for the speed and professionalism with which it has produced this volume. For all our collaborations and all that you do to promote the intellectual life of the Church, thanks are due to Dr. Trevor Lipscombe, Brian Roach, Dr. Trevor Crowell, Libby Vivian, John Martino, Dr. Carole Monica Burnett, Kayla Cooper, Rachel Daly, and Lucia Tosatto.

Introduction

«Authority as service», «authority and obedience», «the role of the superior and the renewal of religious life»; these and many other similar topics have been the theme for literally hundreds of journal articles and books written since the Second Vatican Council.[1] Vatican II was a catalyst for much of this activity in calling for an authentic renewal of religious life.[2] In another sense, though, the Council's decree *Perfectae caritatis* was not the beginning, but a response (as was the Council itself) to a realization on the part of the Church that the world was changing and that there was need for a suitable corresponding renewal within the Church in order for it to continue its mission in the world.[3]

Religious orders were by no means exempt from the changes that were taking place in the world. It was clear, well before the Council, that the adaptation of religious life to the modern world was a necessary process that had to take place. Pope Pius XII,

---

[1] M. AUGÉ, «Autorità e obbedienza nella vita religiosa: rassegna bibliografica (1966-1976)» in *Claretianum* 18(1978)5-34, lists over 380 books and articles on the topic.

[2] See the Council decree *Perfectae caritatis*.

[3] JOHN XXIII, Constitutio apostolica *Humanae salutis,* December 25, 1961: AAS 54(1962)5-13.

already in 1950, had encouraged religious to blend the old with the new in seeking new possibilities for their way of life.[4]

The Council, then, in *Perfectae caritatis*, set forth general principles through which the consecrated life, by means of renewal, could contribute more effectively to the good of the Church.[5] Subsequently, in 1966, another document was published, *Ecclesiae sanctae*,[6] which established some specific norms for the implementation of various conciliar documents, including the Decree on the Renewal of Religious Life. Here it was mandated that every religious institute call a special general chapter for the purpose of reviewing and revising its constitutions.[7]

Much before this time, however, the Order of Saint Augustine had begun work on rewriting its Constitutions. In 1959, the General Chapter mandated the formation of a special commission that would take on this important task.[8] Work continued on various proposals through the following eight years. While the first drafts prepared were done along the lines of the Constitutions of 1926, still in effect at that time, the final version was the result of many modifications. At the Special General Chapter of 1968, held at Villanova, Pennsylvania,[9] after many years of revisions, rewriting and new formulations, the new Constitutions of the

---

4 PIUS XII, Allocutio *Annus sacer*, December 8, 1950: AAS 43(1951)26-37.

5 PC, no. 1.

6 *Ecclesiae sanctae*, August 6, 1966: AAS 58(1966)757-787. The part which deals with implementation of PC is in ES, II.

7 ES, II, Pars I\u1d43 no. 3: «Ad accommodatam renovationem promovendam in singulis Institutis, congregetur intra duos vel ad summum tres annos speciale Capitulum generale, ordinarium vel extraordinarium.»

8 See Decretum, October 5, 1959: *Acta OSA* 5(1960)24-26.

9 This chapter was convoked by the Prior General, Agostino Trapè, on March 19, 1968. See *Acta OSA* 13(1968)13-20.

Augustinian Order were approved.[10] Vastly different from the preceding legislation, these Constitutions no longer were based upon the Code of Canon Law, but were the product of a much different approach, drawing heavily upon the monastic principles of St. Augustine, the apostolic traditions of the Order, and the teaching of the Second Vatican Council.

Contemporaneously, the Church was engaged in the process of revising its principal legislation, the Code of Canon Law. In 1959, Pope John XXIII announced the formation of an apostolic commission for the revision of the *Codex Iuris Canonici*. Pope John saw the renewal of canon law as a key element in the Church's striving to fulfill its mission in modern times.[11] The process for revising the Code took much longer, however, than did that of the Order's Constitutions, for obvious reasons, and twenty-five years to the day after Pope John had announced the plan for revision of the Code, Pope John Paul II promulgated the new *Codex Iuris Canonici*. One of the major effects of the long-awaited revised Code can be expressed in the Pope's own words:

> It is naturally to be hoped that the new canonical legislation will prove to be an efficacious means in order that the Church may progress in conformity with the spirit of the Second Vatican

---

10 See *Acta OSA* 13(1968) Fasciculus specialis. These Constitutions underwent minor revision at the General Chapter of 1977, and again in 1983 (this latter time, especially for adaptations required due to the promulgation of the new Code). These were published in 1978, and the changes from 1983 can be found in *Acta OSA* 28(1983) Fasciculus Specialis, pp. 114*-120*. Unless otherwise indicated, all references to the Constitutions will be from these last two sources.

11 JOHN XXIII, Allocution, January 25, 1959: AAS 51 (1959) 65-69. In the same homily, Pope John announced the Synod of Rome, the Ecumenical Council and the revision of the Code. He called this revision the «crowning» of the other two events (see p. 68).

Council and may every day be ever more suited to carry out its office of salvation in this world.¹²

One side of the picture has now been sketched: renewal in the Church and in the Augustinian Order as an attempt to aid in the work of proclaiming Christ's message of salvation in the modern world. However, all of the dialogue, and at times painful struggle, surrounding the renewal of the exercise of authority in religious life has another facet: the experience of the human person in today's society. Values have changed, there is a new understanding of the dignity of each person, and a new age of personalism has been born. Obedience as blind submission to the will of another is no longer accepted, and authority at all levels has been challenged, with claims that promote the values of human liberty and democracy but do not accept or understand the Church's standpoint on authority and obedience.

Pope Paul VI addressed himself to this issue on various occasions, always recalling the value of authority and obedience in light of the gospel. In an address before the Sacred Roman Rota, Pope Paul made several observations on this topic:

> No one today ignores the accentuated tendency to depreciate authority in the name of freedom. The Council underlined this fact in a very meaningful document, the one on the topic of religious freedom, when it observed that «they are not few, those who under the pretext of freedom, resist every dependence and little appreciate the duty to obey.»¹³ It is the diffused, so-called

---

12 JOHN PAUL II, Constitutio apostolica *Sacrae Disciplinae Leges*, January 25, 1983: AAS 75, Pars II (1983) xiii: «Quibus omnibus consideratis, optandum sane est, ut nova canonica legislatio efficax instrumentum evadat, cuius ope Ecclesia valeat se ipsam perficere secundum Concilii Vaticani II spiritum, ac magis magisque parem se praebeat salutifero suo muneri in hoc mundo exsequendo.»

13 *Dignitatis humanae*, no. 8.

«charismatic» tendency which becomes anti-hierarchic: the difficult-to-define function of the spirit is underlined to the detriment of authority. In this way, a mentality spreads which presents disobedience as being justifiable and legitimate, as caring for the freedom that the children of God must enjoy.[14]

Continuing, the Pope outlined several objections which lie at the basis of this attitude; two of these are worthy of note here. First of all, this appeal to freedom is done in such a way that it is opposed to law, any law whatsoever. To support this, the gospel is used. In effect, the gospel does proclaim the value of freedom of the spirit against, for example, the legalism of the pharisees. Jesus, not wanting to be a political and domineering Messiah, chose to be called Son of Man and came to serve and to give his life for others. But, the Pope emphasizes, the gospel teaching has another dimension as well. The same Jesus who preached love and who proclaimed freedom gave moral prescriptions and practices, obligating his disciples to remain faithfully observant.[15] Freedom and law are not terms which contrast with one another. They are values which must be integrated with each other. The presence of a juridical order and authority underlines the necessity of effective care for the common good, part of which is the fundamental notion of the exercise of freedom. The law of the New Testament

---

14 PAUL VI, Discourse, January 29, 1970: AAS 62(1970)111-118. (Also, *Communicationes* 2[1970]28-35.) On p. 113: «Nessuno ignora oggi l'accentuata tendenza a svalutare l'autorità in nome della libertà: lo ha sottolineato il Concilio in un documento molto significativo, quello appunto sulla libertà religiosa, quando ha osservato che "non sembrano pochi coloro che, sotto pretesto della libertà, respingono ogni dipendenza e apprezzano poco la dovuta obbedienza" (DH, no. 8). E' la diffusa tendenza cosiddetta carismatica, che diventa antigerarchica: si sottolinea esclusivamente la difficilmente definibile funzione dello spirito a scapito dell'autorità. In tal modo, si diffonde una mentalità che vorrebbe presentare come legittima e giustificata la disobbedienza, a tutela della libertà di cui debbono godere i figli di Dio.»

15 Ibid., p. 114.

does not deprive man of his freedom; it is the intrinsically just guide of freedom.

A second objection of those who proclaim the primacy of freedom is the proclamation of freedom over and against authority, doing so in such a way as to claim that the gospel does away with authority. But, the gospel does not only not abolish authority, but it institutes it; the gospel established authority. Authority is placed at the service of the good of others, this is true; not, however, because and in as much as it is derived from the community, but because it is received from above for governing and judging, originating in a positive intervention on the part of the Lord.[16]

These thoughts of Pope Paul VI, as well as many other interventions on the part of the Church, present one side of the very painful struggle that has gone on over the past twenty or more years. Society has indeed changed, and many new values have been proclaimed, not always, however, ones which have been easily integrated into religious life. Frequently, the relationship between the individual and the common good has become the opposite of what it was formerly. Instead of the individual's molding his personality to serve the common good (a notion that has had its own exaggerations in the past), the «community» becomes the context within which the individual can be fulfilled, seeking self-interests and personal values. An extreme form of this has been called «ontological individualism»; more than a value, it becomes a fundamental way of understanding reality.[17] The purpose of any structure, of any community, is to provide a means for the fulfillment of personal goals.

---

16 Ibid., p. 115.
17 ROBERT BELLAH, «Religion and Power in America Today» in *Catholic Theological Society of America Proceedings* 37(1982)21.

Structures and authorities in the religious life have in no way been left out of the struggle that results as these systems—one proclaiming that community and its goals are primary, and the other declaring the primacy of the individual and the rejection of authority—have collided. Problems have been serious because of the abuses of power and authority that at times took place before the time of renewal in the Church had begun. It was only logical that there would be reactions to the opposite extreme. In the midst of all this, serious attempts have been made to find authentic, meaningful expressions for the exercise of authority in religious life. The work of renewal is by no means completed. But with the «tools» more or less in order (the final one being the new Code), the work of implementation can continue.

This study on the role of the local Prior in the Order of St. Augustine is a small expression of the work and struggle which has gone on over the past twenty years. It is an attempt to take one of the most important authority figures in the Augustinian Order (important, not because of the extent of his authority, but because it is, in effect, on the level of the local community that Augustinian life is really lived) and present it under its juridical aspects.

Motivation for such a study is very simple: the struggle to find the best way to live authority and obedience in religious life is not over. More concretely, however, the incentive for doing this research came out of a request made to the Order's General Chapter of 1983. In a letter of the Prior General, Father Theodore Tack, to the whole Order, in which the principal arguments to be discussed at the Chapter were presented,[18] he stated:

---

18 T. TACK, Letter, May 14, 1983: *Acta OSA* 28(1983) Fasc. spec., pp. 58-61.

> It would be well to point out from the beginning that the great majority of the suggestions or observations received have concerned the government and structure of the Order.[19]

He then went on to point out four particular points which had emerged as meriting the attention of the Chapter that was to be celebrated later that year. One of these was «the role and authority of the local Prior».[20] Committees were formed, but at the Chapter no final document was approved. While there are apparently various reasons for this, there was no official statement made as to the future of such a study.

At any rate, the topic seemed important enough to this writer that it merited some serious study. While the Constitutions, under the section «The Office and Authority of the Local Prior»,[21] have only seven numbers on the topic, in reality the question of the Prior's role is much more complex. This study covers primarily one aspect: the juridical dimension of the office of Prior. Nevertheless, in an attempt to integrate the ministerial, «sacramental» reality of the Prior's role with the juridical structures as they exist, certain theological aspects are presented.

This study is not intended to be historical in its approach. It is an analysis of what the Prior's role is today. However, at certain points, in order to clarify the intent or the value of certain legislation, reference is made to the former Constitutions, to the old Code, to the history of the Order, and so on. The primary mode of presentation, though, is based upon a systematic analysis of those numbers of the Constitutions and those canons of the

---

19 Ibid., p. 58.
20 Ibid.
21 *Constitutiones*, chapter 15, nos. 310-316.

new Code which regulate or determine the office and duties of the local Prior.²²

The last three chapters (in effect, the second half) of this study are entitled according to the three *munera* of teaching, sanctifying, and governing. This was not done merely because it was thought to be a convenient tool for organizing the material. These three functions, offices, highly talked about since the Vatican Council, were used because of the conviction that the Prior's role is an ecclesial ministry. One of the insights of the Council was the very important role that the consecrated life has to play within the Church, not merely because it provides priests and religious to serve in the apostolate, but because in its very essence, it gives witness to and causes the sanctification of the Church.²³ Priors (and all other authority figures) therefore have a special role to play, not only within the local community—in organizing, coordinating, leading—but in a mission which has great value for the whole Church.

One final word: what is written here is based primarily upon canon law and the Constitutions, norms which are written for a rather broad range of circumstances and which must be applied in communities around the world. But the actual unfolding of the Prior's role is done in a specific local community, a specific culture, in specific situations. Application of general laws and guidelines must take place in the concrete circumstances of any community. Reference is occasionally made to the determinations that are to

---

22 On the whole, the content of this study was determined by *Constitutiones*, no. 274: «Praeter leges communes Ecclesiae religiosos afficientes atque praescripta a S. Sede nobis data, Ordo noster regitur: a) Regula S.P. Augustini; b) Constitutionibus Ordinis; c) ordinationibus Capitulorum Generalium et Prioris Generalis; d) consuetudinibus legitime praescriptis et non obsoletis.»

23 See *Lumen Gentium*, no. 44. Also, J. CASTAÑO, «Il contesto ecclesiale della vita consacrata» in AA.VV. *Il nuovo diritto dei religiosi* (Rome: Ed. Rogate, 1984), pp. 41-60.

be made by Provincial Statutes, but that is not enough. Priors, and their communities, will have to work together to concretize the way in which they will best be able to offer their service within the local community, as well as in the Order and for the Church.

CHAPTER ONE

THE SUPERIOR'S ROLE OF SERVICE TO THE COMMUNITY

Consideration of the local superior's role may well begin from the basis provided in the Rule and in the Constitutions, as well as with the first two canons from the chapter «De institutorum regimine» under the title «De institutis religiosis» in the Code of Canon Law.[1] As this chapter will show, there is actually a harmonious pattern between the Augustinian sources and the Church's legislation on the role of the superior. Themes of equality among the Brothers, service according to the evangelical model, care for the spiritual welfare of the community, and the giving of example in living the consecrated life are prominent in both the Rule and Constitutions, as well as in the Code of Canon Law.

A very important emphasis is made in number fifteen of the Constitutions:

> Just as the office of Prior «in the Order is not an office of power, but of fraternal love, not of honor but of obligation, not of

---

1 CIC, Liber II, Pars III, Sectio I: «De institutis vitae consecratae.»

domination, but of service,»² so must obedience be carefully observed by the Brothers in the spirit of faith and love . . .³

This echoes St. Augustine's own words, in Chapter Seven of the Rule (which speaks of governance and obedience):

> The superior for his part must not think himself fortunate in his exercise of authority but in his role as one serving you in love.⁴

Augustine's concept of authority and obedience in religious life was that they were to be means which, when necessary, would aid the community in its striving to live a life of perfect charity. Authority in the monastery is not an end in itself. The presence of a superior is to provide a service which renders the goal of religious life more readily attainable.

«The main purpose for your having come together is to live harmoniously in your house, intent upon God in oneness of mind and heart.»⁵ Beginning his Rule of life in this way, Augustine clearly establishes that everything which in some way makes up or has a part in the living of the common life must be directed according to this precept. Writing in another place, Augustine expresses that the purpose of the governing authority, in the monastery is to watch over the common life. Making the analogy of ships in a port, Augustine explains that those who choose to enter the religious life have in one sense a kind of freedom from

---

2 JORDAN of SAXONY, *Liber Vitasfratrum* (1357; crit. ed., New York: Cosmopolitan Science and Art, 1943), p. 91.

3 *Constitutiones*, no. 15: «Sicut officium Prioris 'in Ordine non est officium potestatis, sed caritatis, non honoris, sed oneris, non dominii, sed servitii' ita oboedientia in spiritu fidei et amoris a Fratribus intense coli debet . . . »

4 *Regula S. P. Augustini*, c. 7: «Ipse vero qui vobis praeest, non se existimet potestate dominantem, sed caritate servientem felicem.»

5 *Regula*, c. 1: «Primum, propter quod in unum estis congregati, ut unanimes habitetis in domo et sit vobis anima una et cor unum in Deum.»

many preoccupations. There are, however, dangers that a ship can encounter upon entering a port, and care must therefore be taken that these ships not collide into each other at the piers. «Let equality based on impartiality, and constant charity be observed. And when a strong wind enters the port from the open sea, a prudent skipper should intervene.»[6] Fraternal charity should be enough to maintain the peace and unity of the community. But when there are difficulties, there should be an authority which can prudently take action which will resolve the situation. A part of the service of the superior is making sure that the Rule is observed, and that corrections are made if and when they are necessary:

> But it shall pertain chiefly to the superior to see that these precepts are all observed and, if any point has been neglected, to take care that the transgression is not carelessly overlooked but is punished and corrected.[7]

Further indication of the superior's role is given by Augustine in the following paragraph of the Rule:

> He must show himself an example of good works towards all. Let him admonish the unruly, cheer the fainthearted, support the weak, and be patient towards all.[8]

These responsibilities of a superior are found in canon 619 of the new Code as well, and, in fact, both of these texts have as their

---

6 *Enarratio in psalmum* 99, 10. PL 37, 1277: «... servetur ibi parilitas aequabilitatis, constantia caritatis; et quando forte ventus ex illa parte qua patet, irruerit, sit ibi cauta gubernatio.»

7 *Regula*, c. 7: «Ut ergo cuncta ista serventur et, si quid servatum non fuerit, non neglegenter praetereatur, sed emendandum corrigendumque curetur, ad praepositum praecipue pertinebit...»

8 *Regula*, c. 7: «Circa omnes seipsum bonorum operum praebeat exemplum, corripiat inquietos, consoletur pusillanimes, suscipiat infirmos, patiens sit ad omnes...»

common source Paul's First Letter to the Thessalonians, where the same affirmation is also found.[9]

A closer look at canons 618 and 619[10] reveals that there is actually a series of exhortations and theological principles which provide a good outline for the consideration of the ministry of a superior in the religious life. They relate what might be considered a fundamental attitude or posture of the superior toward his community. It has even been suggested that these two canons would make good material for a retreat for religious superiors.[11]

In these two canons, the notion given by the Second Vatican Council regarding authority in the religious life is made law, and they thus provide a good concrete example of the incorporation into the Code of the spirit of the Council.[12] Canon 618 is taken almost verbatim from the Council document on renewal in the religious life, *Perfectae caritatis:*

> Superiors are to exercise their power, received from God through the ministry of the Church, in a spirit of service. Therefore, docile to the will of God in carrying out their duty, they are to govern their subjects as children of God and, promoting their voluntary obedience with reverence for the human person, they are to listen to them willingly and foster their working together for the good of the institute and of the Church, but with the superiors' authority to decide and prescribe what must be done remaining intact.[13]

---

9 1 Thess. 5:14.

10 For the text of these two canons, see footnotes 13 and 34, respectively.

11 V. DAMMERTZ, «La nuova figura del superiore» in AA.VV., *Il nuovo diritto dei religiosi* (Rome: Ed. Rogate, 1984) p. 134.

12 See *Principia quae*, document of the Synod of Bishops on the principles of revision for the Code of Canon Law, October 7, 1967: *Communicationes* I(1969)77-85.

13 Can. 618: «Superiores in spiritu servitii suam potestatem a Deo per ministerium Ecclesiae receptam exerceant. Voluntati igitur Dei in munere explendo dociles, ipsi

Some rather significant ideas are presented in this canon, and it therefore merits particular attention.

Superiors are to exercise their power, received from God through the ministry of the Church, in a spirit of service.[14] The idea that a superior's role is one of service is certainly not new. It is founded in the gospel, and is also central to the Augustinian concept of authority. It is, nevertheless, a renewed emphasis on the fundamental purpose of authority that was all too frequently overlooked or ignored in the experience of far too many members of religious institutes. Instead of being a servant of others, the superior was a dominating ruler who was in many cases insensitive to those entrusted to his care.[15] Superiors are once again being reminded of the example of Jesus, who in humility made himself the servant of others. Of the many scriptural citations that could be made to illustrate the evangelical spirit of service, perhaps none is more striking than the account in the Gospel of John, wherein Jesus is described washing the feet of his disciples:

> After he had washed their feet; he put his cloak back on and reclined at table once more. He said to them: «Do you understand what I just did for you? You address me as 'Teacher'

---

subditos regant uti filios Dei, ac promoventes cum reverentia personae humanae illorum voluntariam oboedientiam, libenter eos audiant necnon eorum conspirationem in bonum instituti et Ecclesiae foveant, firma tamen ipsorum auctoritate decernendi et praecipiendi quae agenda sunt.» Cf. PC, no. 14c. The English texts of canons are from the CLSA translation.

14 Ibid.

15 Until the time of the Second Vatican Council, the authority that a superior exercised was known as «dominative power», *potestas dominativa*. (In addition, superiors in clerical, exempt orders possessed the power of jurisdiction: see v. can. 501, §1.) Because the name «dominative power» carries with it unfavorable connotations, it has for the most part gone out of use. It no longer appears in the Code (see can. 596). Chapter two of this study gives more detail on these various concepts of power and authority in the religious life.

and 'Lord', and fittingly enough, for that is what I am. But if I washed your feet - I who am teacher and Lord then you must wash each other's feet. What I just did was to give you an example: as I have done, so you must do.[16]

The Apostles, as leaders of the early Church, were to consider their role as one of service, servants of Christ and servants of the Christian community. It is the apostolic model of service which must serve as the «canon»,[17] the «regula», the guiding line for all forms of authority in the Church.

The same doctrine is preached by Saint Augustine, as has already been mentioned in reference to the Rule. Elsewhere Augustine writes: «We are put in charge and we are servants; we possess authority, but only if we serve.»[18] There is no room in Augustine's concept of authority for one who is self-seeking and in search of power over others. The exercise of authority in any Christian community requires the setting aside of all self-interest and a total dedication to the good of the community. This is the attitude which must be adopted as the starting point for an authentic understanding of the role of the local superior.

The following phrase of canon 618 states that *the superior is to be docile to the will of God in carrying out his duty*.[19] Obviously, since the service which a superior offers within the community is the

---

16 John 13:12-15. Other gospel texts on the subject of service can be found in Luke 12:41-43, and Mark 10:35. See also the Letter to the Philippians 2:5-11. «Your attitude must be that of Christ: Though he was in the form of God, he did not deem equality with God something to be grasped at. Rather, he emptied himself and took the form of a slave . . . »

17 The etymology of the word «canon»: from the Latin, «canon» which means measuring line, rule, model; from the Greek «Kanon», rod, rule. *(American Heritage Dictionary* [New York: American Heritage Publishing Co., 1969], p. 197.)

18 «Praepositi sumus, et servi sumus; praesumus, sed si prosumus.» Guelferb. 32,3; Misc. Agost. 1(1930)565.

19 Can. 618: « . . . Voluntati igitur Dei in munere explendo dociles . . . »

result of a power which is received from God, there must be an openness on the part of the superior to listen and to learn. There is the assumption made here that the will of God can be known in some way before a decision is made, and it therefore follows that a superior must be willing to take the time to discern what course of action seems to be most in congruence with the divine plan.

> It follows that the substance of the office of the superior is to obey; to obey the will of God and to put great effort into trying to know it, to formulate it and to specify it for his subjects. This general will of God, antecedent to any decision by the superior, can be known by reading the signs of the times, by looking for God's designs in the ordinary events of his providence. It can also be known through the inspirations of the Holy Spirit.[20]

The discernment of God's will and the receiving of insights as gifts from the Spirit are in no way reserved to the superior, although there may indeed be a special «grace of the office» which the superior does receive. Because of this, it is essential that the search for or discernment of God's will be undertaken within a context of dialogue. The superior and the community which he serves must work together in order to arrive at decisions which reflect a real cooperation with what the plan of the divine will would be in the given situation.

Superiors are to govern their subjects as children of God.[21] Along with the next phrase of the canon, which will emphasize the owed respect towards the human person, this phrase is seeking to give a particular direction to the way in which a superior governs within the community. The equality and the fraternity

---

[20] LADISLAS ÖRSY, «Government in Religious Life» in *The Way*, Supplement, 2(1966)95.

[21] Can. 618: «... ipsi subditos regant uti filios Dei ...»

of all the members of the community, by virtue of the baptism and profession of vows which is common to them all, requires that a superior love the members of his community with the same kind of love as that with which God loves all his children. This should not be misconstrued to indicate some kind of paternalism, whereby the superior who erringly considers himself to be above his community condescends to serve, or worse, expects to be served by the other religious of that community. The superior is expected to be a living witness to the love of God offered freely and generously to the community, and to each individual who makes up a vital part of that community.

With reverence for the human person, superiors promote voluntary obedience.[22] Reverence for the human person, *reverentia*, is a concept which includes such values as respect, recognition of the dignity and maturity of the other, recognition of the talents, the intelligence and the capabilities of the religious in the house. Each person is, in a very real way, a reflection of God's glory in the world, and more specifically, in the particular community. The local superior must be able to recognize this, and must seek to bring out the talents of each, reflections of God's grace, so as to help the individual contribute in the best way possible to the good of the community, the Order, and the Church. It is in and through this reverence for the human person that the superior is to promote voluntary obedience. An ideal is proposed here which is paradoxical. Instead of proposing a style of obedience which flows from a passivity, or an elimination of the individual's will, the Church speaks of voluntary obedience, an active obedience in which the person is positively and actively involved.

---

22 Can. 618: «... ac promoventes cum reverentia personae humanae illorum voluntariam oboedientiam ... »

The religious, in being given the due respect and recognition, is invited to join into a decision-making process where there is a creative combination, a balanced approach to a certain dependence upon the will of the superior and the creative contribution of the community member. «A discerning superior will find a balance between imposing his own will on another person and letting him formulate a responsible decision.»[23]

Superiors are to listen to their subjects willingly.[24] Mention has already been made of the importance of dialogue between the superior and the members of the community. The Code makes this explicit here, and determines, in effect, that a superior must make himself available to the community, whether as individuals or as a group, to learn what the needs of the community are. Only in this way will he be able to serve in a way which corresponds to the reality of the given situation. Also to be considered is the superior's willingness and ability to create an atmosphere of trust and confidence. He will have no one to listen to if he is unable to create such a trusting environment. The members of the community must feel free to come to him and discuss those issues which are of particular importance to them, and at the same time, the superior must respect their freedom of conscience. He must never attempt to pry information from a member of the community, nor can he pass on information concerning the conscience of a person, even to a higher authority (the Provincial, for example) without the explicit permission of the individual concerned, «a permission which is not to be requested lightly, is never presumed, and is invalid if it is obtained with subtle constraint.»[25] While the

---

23 L. ÖRSY, op. cit., p. 100.
24 Can. 618: «... libenter eos audiant...»
25 ÖRSY, p. 101. Also, see below, p. 130.

superior is obliged to listen, he is free not to respond. There will be cases where there will be no response to a given situation, or where the giving of a response would be imprudent or unjust.[26] It is essential, however, that the individual know that he has been listened to, and not just tolerated and then dismissed as though what he had to say were not important.

Superiors are to foster their working together for the good of the institute and of the Church.[27] The role of superior implies that the person chosen for such a task be capable of offering his community a certain dynamic spirit which seeks to animate and direct the activity of the community and of its individual members for the Order and for the Church. The specific way in which this aspect of the superior's role will be exercised will depend greatly upon the personality and particular gifts of the superior, as well as on the nature of the community and its apostolate(s). In every case, however, certain common factors will be present. The community will have a sense of its contribution to the mission of the Church, something which is intrinsic to Augustinian life:

> Obliged as we are by the nature of our apostolic fraternity and by the «demands of love» and seeing as we do the presence of Christ in others, we cannot do less than extend to the entire ecclesial community and to all men, by means of the apostolate, what God has deigned to effect in us and in our community . . . .[28]

---

26 DOMINGO J. ANDRÉS, *El Derecho de los Religiosos* (Madrid: Publicaciones Claretianas y Commentarium pro Religiosos, 1983), p. 95.

27 Can. 618: «... eorum conspirationem in bonum instituti et Ecclesiae foveant...»

28 *Constitutiones*, no. 39: «Fraternitate apostolica et 'necessitate caritatis' compulsi, quod Deus dignatus est operari in nobis et in nostra Communitate, non possumus cum tota Communitate ecclesiali et cum omnibus hominibus nostra actuositate non communicare, Christum in eis intuentes.»

THE SUPERIOR'S ROLE OF SERVICE TO THE COMMUNITY

There will be an active responsibility on the part of each and every member of the community in working for the common good. The superior will help instill a sense of «ownership» in the community so that even in cases where the men work in «individual» apostolates, they will have a comprehension of the way in which they are contributing to the Order and to the Church, and an ever-increasing desire to fulfill that which is defined as the very purpose of the Order: «to seek and worship God together with one heart in brotherhood and spiritual friendship and in our working to serve the people of God.»[29]

The last clause of canon 618 is an affirmation which has been made repeatedly by the Holy See since the beginning of the period of renewal in religious life that followed the Vatican Council: *«but with the superiors' authority to decide and prescribe what must be done remaining intact.»*[30] After all of the above discussion on dialogue and cooperation between the superior and the members of the community, someone might find difficulty in understanding the inclusion of this part of the canon. The authority of a superior must be personal, however, according to the mind of the Holy See. The Council Fathers themselves made this clear in *Perfectae caritatis*,[31] which, as was stated earlier, was the source for canon 618. Later, in an apostolic exhortation of Pope Paul VI, *Evangelica testificatio*,[32] the importance of the personal authority of superiors was again highlighted. Writing about the renewal of religious

---

29 *Constitutiones*, no. 16: «Finis Ordinis in eo est simul concorditer in fraternitate et amicitia spirituali Deum quaeramus et colamus atque in servitium populi Dei laboremus.»

30 Can. 618: « . . . firma tamen ipsorum auctoritate decernendi et praecipiendi quae agenda sunt.»

31 PC, no. 14.

32 June 29, 1971; AAS 63(1971)497-526.

life, Pope Paul insisted upon the necessity of dialogue between superiors and the members of the community, and of working to find consensus when the entire community is involved. But these processes, he states, must be concluded with the decision of the superior, whose presence and recognition is necessary in every community.³³

Continuing with its style of «spiritual introduction» in the section on superiors, the Code gives what is a series of exhortations to those who are called upon to be official leaders of communities:

> Superiors are to devote themselves to their office assiduously and, together with the members entrusted to them, they should be eager to build a community of brothers in Christ in which God is sought after and loved before all else. Therefore, they are to nourish the members frequently with the food of the word of God and lead them to the celebration of sacred liturgy. They are to be an example to the members in cultivating virtues and in the observance of the laws and traditions of the particular institute; they are to meet the personal needs of the members in an appropriate fashion, look after solicitously and visit the sick, admonish the restless, console the faint of heart, and be patient toward all.³⁴

---

33 ET, no. 25: «Itaque auctoritas et cuiusque libertas nedum inter se repugnent, in voluntate Dei implenda una simul procedunt, quae fraterno more exquiratur per colloquium, fiducia nixum, inter superiorem eiusque fratrem, cum de re personali agitur, aut per consensionem indolis generalis, cum res ad totam spectat Communitatem . . . Hoc opus communis perscrutationis finiendum est, si casus fert, iudicio ac voluntate superiorum, quorum praesentia, ut talis agnita, cuivis Communitati est prorsus necessaria.» For further discussion on the question of the personal authority of the local superior, refer to chapter two of this study.

34 Can. 619: «Superiores suo officio sedulo incumbant et una cum sodalibus sibi commissis studeant aedificare fraternam in Christo communitatem, in qua Deus ante omnia quaeratur et diligatur. Ipsi igitur nutriant sodales frequenti verbi Dei pabulo eosque adducant ad sacrae liturgiae celebrationem. Eis exemplo sint in virtutibus colendis et in observantia legum et traditionum proprii instituti; eorum necessitatibus personal-

While there is no one single source for this canon, various elements can be found in the documents of the Council, in the old Code, and in postconciliar decrees.[35] This canon can be divided into eleven precepts which describe various aspects of the responsibility of the superior, and which, just as in the case of the previous canon, can be used as points of reflection for a superior to analyze and evaluate the service he is asked to give to the community.

Superiors are to dedicate themselves diligently to their office.[36] Even if he has other duties, the superior must be dedicated to his community, not leaving the requirements of this office as secondary to various other activities in which he may be involved. Frequently, especially in smaller communities, the Prior will have other responsibilities, often on a «fulltime» basis: pastor of a parish, teacher, director of retreats, etc. There can be at times the tendency to allow these other demands, all of which are legitimate in themselves, and even necessary at times, to draw the superior away from many of the tasks which are required of him in serving the community. This requires special effort on his part, then, to find a just balance between the many demands that are made upon his time and energies. A particularly Augustinian theme is sounded here. Augustine wrote frequently about the difficulties of active ministry, about the «burden» involved in such work, and about the inevitable tension that exists for the monk who is called to active ministry due to the pressing needs of the Church.[37] The very nature of the Order as it was founded in the

---

ibus convenienter subveniant, infirmos sollicite curent ac visitent, corripiant inquietos, consolentur pusillanimes, patientes sint erga omnes.»

35 Cf. for example, PC,. no. 6a, Se, 15a; LG, no. 44a; ES II, 16,1; v. cann. 593,595, §§ 1,2.

36 Can. 619: «Superiores suo officio sedulo incumbant . . . »

37 Cf. GEORGE LAWLESS, «Augustine's Burden of Ministry» in *Angelicum* 61(1984)295-315.

thirteenth century includes active ministry,[38] and there is thus a need to blend this aspect of service in the apostolate with the values of religious life that develop out of the more contemplative aspects of the Order. The local superior must be especially sensitive to such issues as it is he who is expected to offer guidance and leadership in such matters to the rest of the community. It is specifically because he is superior that he must be prepared to emphasize the importance of those aspects of community life which are frequently disregarded because of the many demands made on the Brothers in the apostolate.

Superiors, together with the members entrusted to them, should be eager to build a community of brothers in Christ, in which God is sought after and loved before all else.[39] Here again, the Code resonates with a fundamental element of the spirituality of Augustinian religious life. In the first chapter of the Rule, Augustine wrote: «The main purpose for your having come together is to live harmoniously in your house, intent upon God in oneness of mind and heart.»[40] Life in the community is built upon the monastic ideal of Augustine, which he modeled upon the primitive Christian community in Jerusalem.[41]

---

38 *Constitutiones,* no. 10: «Religio enim nostra Ordo est fraternitatis apostolicae seu Communitas Fratrum, quae cum populo Dei vivit, praebens exemplum, testimonium nempe caritatis et paupertatis evangelicae et sanam doctrinam . . . »

39 Can. 619: «Superiores . . . una cum sodalibus sibi commissis studeant aedificare fraternam in Christo communitatem, in qua Deus ante omnia quaeratur et diligatur . . . »

40 *Regula,* c. 1: «Primum, propter quod in unum estis congregati, ut unanimes habitetis in domo et sit vobis anima una et cor unum in Deum.»

41 Acts 4:32ff. Augustine frequently related the model of the early church at Jerusalem to the monastic ideal which he taught and lived. The verses, Acts 4:32-35, can be found more than 80 times in his writings, in whole or in part. See L. VERHEIJEN, *La Règle de saint Augustin, vol. II: Recherches historiques* (Paris: Études Augustiniennes, 1967), p. 90. Also, G. LAWLESS, «Psalm 132 and Augustine's Monastic Ideal» in *Angelicum* 59(1982)527.

THE SUPERIOR'S ROLE OF SERVICE TO THE COMMUNITY

> St Augustine ... intended to renew the ideal of the sharing of goods that existed among the early Christians as a very suitable way to attain perfectly Christian love by living in a fraternal community in which we would all be «intent upon God in oneness of mind and heart.»[42]

Every dimension of the common life which strengthens unity among the Brothers is an aid in fostering the search for God. «But we cannot seek God unless we have Christ, the Incarnate Word, as the way.»[43] Every member of the community must play an active role in the realization of the communion of mind and heart in and through which the Brothers seek God. The superior has the role of a kind of catalyst, but can do nothing if there is not an active cooperation on the part of each and every member of the community.

Canon 619 goes on to give two very important aspects of the superior's role of spiritual leader of the community. *Superiors are to nourish the members frequently with the food of the word of God, and they are to lead them to the celebration of the sacred liturgy.*[44] Since both of these concepts are effectively the topics of subsequent chapters in this study,[45] little will be said here. Let it suffice to point out that the role of superior is much more than merely an administrative role, or one of a mere coordination of community activities. His responsibility also includes the spiritual welfare of the members

---

[42] *Constitutiones*, no. 66: «Praeterea, ... S.P. Augustinus ... ideale communionis bonorum inter christianos primitivos vigens renovare intendit utpote aptissimum ad christianam caritatem perfecte assequendam, in Communitate fraterna, in qua omnibus nobis sit 'anima una et cor unum in Deum' (*Regula*, c. 1) ... »

[43] *Constitutiones*, no. 32: « ... Sed non possumus Deum quaerere si Christum, Verbum incarnatum, non habemus viam ... »

[44] Can. 619: « ... Ipsi igitur nutriant sodales frequenti verbi Dei pabulo eosque adducant ad sacrae liturgiae celebrationem ... »

[45] See chapters four and five, respectively.

of his community, and thus the Scriptures and the celebration of the liturgy are essential dimensions in the playing out of the superior's service within the community.

Superiors are to be an example to the members in cultivating virtues.[46] The Order's Constitutions place the same expectation on the local superior: «By his fidelity and obedience to the will of God, the Prior should be a model for the flock committed to him.»[47] This same number of the Constitutions then refers to a verse in the First Letter of Peter: «Be examples to the flock, not lording it over those assigned to you.»[48] The concept is clear enough. The members of the community have the right to expect that their superior offer them a kind of model, not in an idealistic way that would have no grounding in reality, but in a way which inspires the community to live out the values which each member embraced in his profession of vows as an Augustinian. Here too it is essential to keep in mind the advice given in the Constitutions regarding the Prior's fulfillment of his office: «For the successful carrying out of his office he should trust more in God than in his own talents and ability . . . »[49] The virtue of humility is indispensable for any superior. Without it, the man who is chosen to exercise leadership in the community will never be able to gain the confidence and trust of those who are entrusted to his care. The superior does not have to be a saint. He does, however, have to be honest enough to recognize and admit his own strengths and weaknesses, and

---

46 Can. 619: « . . . Eis exemplo sint in virtutibus colendis . . . »

47 *Constitutiones,* no. 311: «Sua erga Dei voluntatem oboedientia atque fidelitate, gregis sibi commissi forma factus ex animo, Prior iura et obligationes totius Communitatis diligenter dignoscere satagat . . . »

48 1 Peter 5:3.

49 *Constitutiones,* no. 312: «In officio adimplendo, potius quam in suis viribus et ingenio spem in Deo reponat . . . »

from this basis, relying on the grace of God, he must seek to live out the values which are proper to the religious life. Such an example will be a strong invitation to the other members of the community to follow in like manner the leadership being offered by the superior. The Prior who does not provide this kind of model for his community can be nothing but detrimental for the life of the community.

Continuing in this same line of thought, canon 619 states: *Superiors are to be an example to the members in the observance of the laws and traditions of the particular institute.*[50] The Prior must therefore know, be thoroughly familiar with, the history and Constitutions of the Order, as well as the statutes of his particular Province. He must have an appreciation for the spirituality of the Order, so that he can effectively inspire the same in the members of the community. Once again, there is no limit to the value that such example can provide within the life of the community.

This particular counsel is a good indication of one of the major differences between the old and new Codes, and that is the recognition and encouragement of the particular nature, purpose and traditions of any given institute of consecrated life. The old Code basically forced all religious institutes into a kind of uniform appearance which greatly limited the possibilities of individual expression on the part of the many and varied groups which exist in the Church under the single heading «religious life». On the other hand, the new Code frequently refers to the particular law of the institute, and insists that each group be faithful to its specific «patrimonium».[51]

---

50 Can. 619: « . . . Eis exemplo sint . . . in observantia legum et traditionum proprii instituti . . . »

51 See can. 578.

Superiors are to meet the personal needs of the members in an appropriate fashion.[52] This element of the canon brings into focus another dimension of the particular kind of service which the superior is called upon to give. Individual members of the Order are to be valued as such, and no longer should there be need for the complaint that in religious life all the members are treated as if they were the same, with no regard for the individuality of each person. Thus, the needs of each are to be considered, and it is the superior's responsibility to see that these needs are met in a way that is in keeping with the values of the religious life. This concept resonates well with Augustine's own understanding of the monastery, as he makes this very point in the Rule:

> Food and clothing shall be distributed to each of you by your superior, not equally to all, for all do not enjoy equal health, but rather according to each one's needs. For so you read in the Acts of the Apostles that «they had all things in common and distribution was made to each one according to each one's need.»[53]

> If those in more delicate health from their former way of life are treated differently in the matter of food, this should not be a source of annoyance to the others or appear unjust in the eyes of those who owe their stronger health to different habits of life. Nor should the healthier brothers deem them more fortunate for having food which they do not have.[54]

---

52 Can. 619: «... eorum necessitatibus personalibus convenienter subveniant...»

53 *Regula*, c. 1: «... distribuatur unicuique vestrum a praeposito vestro victus et tegumentum, non aequaliter omnibus, quia non aequaliter valetis omnes, sed potius unicuique sicut cuique opus fuerit. Sic enim legitis in Actibus Apostolorum, quia 'erant illis omnia communia et distribuebatur unicuique sicut cuique opus erat' (Act. 4:32,35).»

54 *Regula*, c. 3: «Qui infirmi sunt ex pristina consuetudine, si aliter tractantur in victu, non debet aliis molestum esse nec iniustum videri, quod facit alia consuetudo

THE SUPERIOR'S ROLE OF SERVICE TO THE COMMUNITY

The Constitutions also speak to this point, recognizing the fact that each Brother should be treated as a mature individual who has freely chosen the Augustinian way of life.[55]

Besides physical needs, the superior must be available to the members of his community in providing for the requirements that they may have in other aspects of their lives. Opportunities for intellectual development, for example, must be given those religious who have been gifted with the capacity and desire to do advanced studies. To those members of the community who may experience the need, psychological counselling should be made available within an atmosphere of acceptance and encouragement. The same is true for spiritual direction. The new Code makes further emphasis on this point, insisting that the institute must «furnish for its members all those things which are necessary according to the norm of the constitutions for achieving the purpose of their vocation.»[56] It is the right of the individual member to receive from the Order those things which he requires in order to live out the commitment he has made in professing solemn vows in the Order. The local superior, therefore, as the one directly responsible for the life of the brethren, must see to it that these needs are met. Discussion on this point has frequently been fueled by a questioning of what is a «need» and what is a «want». There is obviously the necessity here for serious dialogue between the Prior and the individual concerned. Let the superior take his role

---

fortiores. Nec illos feliciores putent, quia sumunt quod non sumunt ipsi, sed sibi potius gratulentur, quia valent quod non valent illi.»

[55] *Constitutiones*, no. 68: «Communitatis est providere Fratribus necessaria et convenientia iuxta normas Domus et Provinciae, ita ut tamquam homines maturi semper appareant, qui libere hoc genus vitae profitentur . . . »

[56] Can. 670: «Institutum debet sodalibus suppeditare omnia quae ad normam constitutionum necessaria sunt ad suae vocationis finem assequendum.»

in this regard very seriously, trying always to do what is best both for the individual and for the community as a whole.

Next in the list of precepts given by canon 619, *superiors are to care for and visit the sick*,[57] is an affirmation that is as obvious as it is important. It is a concrete example of the preceding phrase which exhorts superiors to meet the needs of the individual members. It is also one of the directions given by Augustine in the Rule.[58] Echoed here as well is the Gospel account of the final judgment: «I was ill and you comforted me.»[59] While each member of the community should make special effort to care for any of the Brothers who is sick, the superior has received a special mandate of service, so that it is he who is primarily responsible to see to it that the sick person is given proper care. The Constitutions emphasize the importance of care for the sick and the superior's role in caring for them:

> So that they may bear their difficulties more patiently and more fruitfully, we should show the greatest concern and fraternal love in the care of the sick and the aged, for in them we serve Christ. Priors should see that all their spiritual and material necessities are generously provided for, and without denying, because of poverty, whatever the doctor judges necessary for the sick.[60]

---

57 Can. 618: «... infirmos sollicite curent ac visitent...»
58 *Regula*, c. 5.
59 Matthew 25:36.
60 *Constitutiones*, no. 122: «In curam infirmorum et senium, cum Christo serviamus in illis, quam maximam sollicitudinem et fraternam caritatem impendere debemus, quo sua incommoda patientius et fructuosius tolerare possint. Priores igitur invigilent ut omnia necessaria sive spiritualia sive materialia eis benigne subministrentur, nec denegetur, ratione paupertatis, quod, medicorum iudicio, infirmis opus fuerit...» See chapter five, regarding the care of the sick and the sacrament of Anointing of the Sick.

THE SUPERIOR'S ROLE OF SERVICE TO THE COMMUNITY

One of the more difficult, and often unpleasant duties of the superior is summed up in the following words of canon 619 in the expression that he is to *admonish the restless*.[61] The kind of correction that the superior is expected to give is one that, when it is necessary, will be firm so as to be effective. The words used, *corripiant inquietos*, which are rather strong in meaning, might also be translated «correct the unruly», «restrain or chide the restless», or «reprimand those who neglect their duties». Consideration is due to those who are for some reason unhappy or discontent with their life in the community or in the work they have been assigned. However, the result of such a situation can frequently have a disruptive and even divisive effect in the community by causing great harm to the morale of the other Brothers in the house. Thus, it becomes the superior's responsibility to seek to aid the Brother who is unable to live harmoniously within the house. While this is a personal obligation of the Prior,[62] a reminder might well be given about the expectation made upon all the Brothers regarding fraternal correction: in fact, in the Rule, Augustine places the first responsibility on the Brother who knows of the difficulty to try and help the erring individual. Only afterwards, if he has not succeeded, is he to bring the situation to the attention of the superior.[63]

Closely related to the preceding prescription is the superior's role of *consoling the faint of heart*.[64] There is no doubt as to the importance the Prior can have in the life of the community in his seeking to offer support and comfort to those members who, for

---

61 Can. 619: «... corripiant inquietos ...» Also; *Regula*, c. 7.

62 Refer to chapter six of this study, where there is a section on the Prior's role in caring for the discipline of the community.

63 Cf. *Regula*, c. 4.

64 Can. 619: «... consolentur pusillanimes ...» Also see *Regula*, c. 7.

any number of reasons, may be suffering in a particularly difficult period of their lives. Whatever be the cause for this «faintness of heart», the concern—which in order to be effective must be authentic—offered by the Prior to the individual, will be a great aid, not only to the individual but also to the life of the entire community. To be able to offer such concern and support, the superior must be a person capable of establishing good personal relationships. If he does not know how to relate to others, it will be impossible for him to exercise this important aspect of his ministry within the community.

Never to be forgotten by the superior is the last counsel given by canon 619: *be patient towards all.*[65] A very simple piece of advice, and yet it is an attribute which may make a great difference in the effectiveness of a Prior's service to his community. Through his patient manner, a superior will be able to develop a basis of trust and understanding within the community, without which the life of the community will remain at a very superficial level. By practicing the virtue of patience, the superior will develop a certain comprehension of each of the members of the community, which will be most useful as he develops the essential relationships with the Brothers who are placed in his care. Certainly, patience does not mean over-toleration or complacency, characteristics which can lead to a destructive pattern of a lack of leadership on the part of the superior. While the superior must be patient in his ministry, he must also be prepared to take decisive action when such is called for.

Canon 619 ends at this point, but in the Rule Augustine adds another point of reflection. Speaking of love and of fear, he writes

---

65 Can. 619: «...patientes sint erga omnes.» Also see *Regula*, c. 7: «patiens sit ad omnes.»

that though both are necessary, the superior should strive to be loved rather than feared, ever mindful that he must give an account of the Brothers to God.[66] Deepest commitment to observance of the religious life comes when it is founded on love and not on fear. It is love that causes the spiritual life to be fruitful and lasting.[67] And finally, the superior must carry out his responsibility not primarily because he must answer for his actions to the community itself, but because he is responsible before God for the Brothers entrusted to his care. It is from this perspective that the Prior must understand the import of his role.[68]

Saint Augustine, in concluding the Rule, recommends that it be read weekly, serving as a mirror, so that no point in it might be neglected.[69] In much the same way, the superior would do well to consider frequently the counsels given in chapter seven of the Rule and in canons 618 and 619, so as to examine and evaluate his service to the community. In this way, he will be able to see where he has truly given what has been asked of him, and where he may still need to give more generously in his ministry of service to those who are entrusted to his care.

---

[66] *Regula*, c. 7: «Et quamvis utrumque sit necessarium, tamen plus a vobis amari appetat quam timeri, semper cogitans Deo se pro vobis redditurum esse rationem.»

[67] See A. TRAPÈ, «Introduzione» in S. Agostino, *La Regola* (Milan: Ancora, 1971), pp. 167-169.

[68] See Chapter Five of this study, on the *munus sanctificandi*, where the Prior's role as «steward», caring for the Brothers in the name of another, and his role in guiding the spiritual life of the Brothers are discussed in further detail.

[69] *Regula*, c. 8.

CHAPTER TWO

THE AUTHORITY OF THE LOCAL PRIOR

In a recent document published by the Sacred Congregation for Religious and Secular Institutes, entitled «Essential Elements in the Church's Teaching on Religious Life as Applied to Institutes Dedicated to the Works of the Apostolate»,[1] several key points were made regarding the role of government in the consecrated life.[2] While the document discusses the role of superiors on all levels of government (general, intermediate and local), there are several concepts which are directly applicable to the local Prior and the authority which he exercises in virtue of his office. Because members of religious institutes have chosen to live a life of vowed obedience, «they therefore require a form of government that expresses [the value of the consecrated life] and a particular form of religious authority.»[3] Furthermore, this authority does not derive from the members of the institute, but is «conferred

---

1 SCRSI, May 31, 1983. This document was published in English in the *Osservatore Romano*, June 25, 1983.

2 The document, in outlining these «essential elements», lists nine characteristics: consecration by public vows, communion in community, evangelical mission, prayer, asceticism, public witness, relation to the Church, formation, and government.

3 «Essential Elements», II, 49.

by the Church at the time of establishing each institute and by the approving of its constitutions.»[4] This authority is «invested in superiors for the duration of their term of service at the general, intermediate or local level.»[5] And finally, the document affirms that «strictly speaking, this religious authority is not shared. It may be delegated according to the constitutions for particular purposes but it is normally *ex officio* and is invested in the person of the superior.»[6]

In the following section of the document, which gives various norms, primarily taken from the new Code of Canon Law, affirmation is once again made of several of these points on authority in the religious life. «Authority to govern in religious institutes is invested in superiors who should exercise it according to the norms of common and proper law (can. 617). This authority is received from God through the ministry of the Church (can. 618). The authority of a superior at whatever level is personal and may not be taken over by a group. For a particular time and for a given purpose, it may be delegated to a designated person.»[7]

Any discussion of a superior's authority must also take into consideration its complementary dimension, the vow of obedience. Pope Paul VI, in his Apostolic exhortation on the Renewal of religious life, *Evangelica testificatio*,[8] emphasized this very point:

> Authority, therefore, and obedience, serving the common good, are exercised as two complementary aspects of the same act of

---

4 Ibid.
5 Ibid.
6 Ibid.
7 Ibid., III, 43.

8 «Evangelica testificatio», June 29, 1971. AAS 63 (1971)497-526. «Uniuscuiusque religiosae familiae in catholico orbe sodalibus: de religiosa vita secundum Concilii oecumenici Vaticani II renovanda praeceptiones.»

sharing in the oblation of Christ. Those who act endowed with
authority should comply with the Father's most loving design
in their brethren; while religious, by accepting their precepts,
follow the example of our Master and are joined to His work
of salvation. Thus authority and each person's liberty need not
be in opposition. Together they result in fulfilling the will of
God, which is sought fraternally through a trustful dialogue
between superior and brother when the matter in question
is personal, or through the agreement of a general nature
when the matter affects the whole community. In this quest, a
religious should avoid both needless agitation of spirit and the
desire to allow the seductive power of current opinion to prevail
over the deepest concept of the religious life. Everyone, but
especially superiors and those who exercise any responsibilities
among their brethren or sisters are in duty bound to revive in
the communities that certitude of faith by which they should
be governed. The aim of the foregoing quest is to have this
certitude more clearly perceived and carried into the practice
of daily life—as occasion demands, but under no circumstances
may it lead to controversy. This task of communal discernment
must end, if disaster threatens, by the judgment and will of
superiors whose presence, acknowledged as such, is indispens-
ably necessary for any kind of community.[9]

---

9 ET, no. 25: «Auctoritas ergo et oboedientia, bono communi servientes, tamquam duae rationes complentes eiusdem actus participandi Christi oblationem exercentur: ii, qui auctoritate praediti agunt, oportet in fratribus consilio Patris, amoris pleno, obsecundent; religiosi autem, eorum praeceptionibus obtemperantes, exemplum Magistri nostri sequuntur atque operi salutis sociantur. Itaque auctoritas et cuiusque libertas nedum inter se repugnant, in voluntate Dei implenda una simul procedunt, quae fraterno more exquiratur per colloquium, fiducia nixum, inter superiorem eiusque fratrem, cum de re personali agitur, aut per consensionem indolis generalis, cum res ad totam spectat Communitatem. In hac vestigatione religiosi abstineant tum nimia animorum concitatione, tum sollicitudine efficiendi, ut vis attractiva opinionum, quae in dies ventilantur, praevaleat altissimo sensui vitae religiosae. Unusquisque, praesertim vero superiores et quotquot inter fratres suos aut sorores munera gerunt, officio tenentur

In the Constitutions, an entire section is dedicated to religious obedience.[10] While it is not necessary to examine all seven numbers, certain points are fundamental in providing this discussion with its particularly Augustinian dimension.

> Through religious obedience we offer the dedication of our wills as a sacrifice to God; we are joined to His salvific will; and we more fully imitate Christ who for us became obedient unto death (cf. Phil. 2,8). Religious, under the inspiration of the Holy Spirit, submit themselves in faith to their Superiors, who act in the name of God. Through their Superiors they are guided to the service of all the brethren by reason of his submission to the Father. This obedience grounded in faith and strengthened through humility and self-sacrifice, is an effective expression of love toward God; it is not a loss of freedom but rather its fulfillment.[11] Submission to God is a free act; a free submission, where not necessity, but love is the servant . . . Let love make you a servant, because the truth has set you free.»[12] In keeping with this thought the Rule extols the dignity of obedience when it invites us to obey «not as slaves living under the law but as men living in freedom under grace.»[13]

---

refovendi in Communitatibus fidei certitudinem, qua hae regantur oportet. Vestigationi enim illi propositum est, ut eiusmodi certitudo penitius percipiatur atque in vitae cotidianae usum transferatur secundum temporis necessitatem, nullatenus tamen ut ea in controversiam adducatur. Hoc opus communis perscrutationis finiendum est, si casus fert, iudicio ac voluntate superiorum, quorum praesentia, ut talis agnita, cuivis Communitati est prorsus necessaria.» The English translation is from *Religious Life: A Mystery in Christ and the Church*, ed. by Rose Eileen Masterman (New York: Alba House, 1975), pp. 42-43. The Latin «si casus fert», found in the last sentence of the paragraph, would be better translated «if the case calls for it», or at most, «if danger is present.» There is not the sense of «disaster» in the expression.

10 *Constitutiones*, nos. 75-81.

11 See PC, no. 14.

12 Augustine, *Enar. in Ps.* 99, 7: PL 37,1275; see also LG, no. 43.

13 *Constitutiones*, no. 75: «Oboedientia religiosa nostrae voluntatis dedicationem velut sacrificium Deo offerimus, eius salvificae voluntati coniungimur et Christum ple-

Together with St. Augustine we must value the importance of religious obedience for our fraternal community. Truly, «a coordinated balance between authority and obedience among those who live together»[14] is a necessary condition for domestic peace in the entire community . . .[15]

Priors therefore should take care to exercise the authority which they have received with their office in the service of the Brothers. They should gladly and sincerely listen to them while maintaining at the same time due authority; encourage their initiatives for the good of the Order; and impose only just and reasonable commands, so that the obedience of the Brothers may be truly active and reasonable . . .[16]

All of the above serves as introduction and as a basis upon which this chapter will be developed. While from a juridical point of view it is necessary to talk about such things as power and authority structures, these must never be looked upon as more than what

---

nius imitamur, qui factus est pro nobis oboediens usque ad mortem (cf. Phil. 2,8). Religiosi, Spiritu Sancto movente, Superioribus, vices Dei gerentibus, in fide sese subiciunt et per eos in ministerium omnium in Christo Fratrum ducuntur, sicut ipse Christus, ob suam erga Patrem submissionem, Fratribus ministravit. Quae oboedientia fide innixa, humilitate et sui oblatione confirmata, amoris erga Deum est efficax expressio, libertatis perfectio, non amissio. 'Libera servitus est apud Deum; libera servitus, ubi non necessitas, sed caritas servit . . . Servum te faciat caritas, quia liberum veritas fecit.' Hac de re oboedientiae dignitatem extollit Regula, cum nos invitat ut oboediamus 'non sicut servi sub lege, sed sicut liberi sub gratia constitui'.» See *Regula*, c. 8.

14 Augustine, *De civ. Dei*, 19,14, PL 41,643.

15 *Constitutiones*, no. 76: «Una igitur cum S.P. Augustino oboedientiae religiosae momentum pro nostra fraterna communitate aestimare debemus. Nam 'ordinata imperandi oboediendique concordia cohabitantium', condicio est necessaria ut pax domestica oriatur in tota Communitate . . . »

16 *Constitutiones*, no. 78: «Curent igitur Priores auctoritatem, quam ex officio receperunt, in servitium Fratrum exercere, libenter et sincere eos audire, firma tamen manente sua auctoritate, eorum incepta in bonorum Ordinis promovere, iusta et rationabilia tantum praecepta imponere, ita ut eorum oboedientia vere activa et rationabilis esse possit . . . » Cf. PC, no. 14. For a fuller treatment of obedience in the thought of St. Augustine, see R. Lazcano, «Notas sobre la obediencia y la caridad en san Agustín», in *Revista Augustiniana* 25(1984)219-236.

they are: aids to the peaceful and harmonious living of the Brothers in community so that the values of Augustinian religious life can be realized.

1. Potestas

Discussion on the subject of *potestas*, power in the religious life (or for that matter, in the Church) is potentially unsettling for some. While the need for some kind of authority is understood and accepted, the notion of power is one which is not so easily integrated with gospel values.

> You know how among the Gentiles those who seem to exercise authority lord it over them; their great ones make their importance felt. It cannot be like that with you. Anyone among you who aspires to greatness must serve the rest; whoever wants to rank first among you must serve the needs of all.[17]

No one will dispute that service must be the essence of authority in the Church and in religious life. Yet it cannot be ignored that over the centuries there has developed in the Church a legal structure that employs as one of its concepts the notion of *potestas*. The limits of this study prevent any in-depth presentation of the development of this juridical notion and its assimilation into canon law.[18]

---

17 Mark 10:42-44; also Matthew 20:25-27; Luke 22:25-27.

18 For a greater understanding of the concept of «power» in the Church and in religious life, two main lines of development would have to be followed, not to mention the need for investigation into several related areas. For the interested reader, certain highlights of these are presented here. Already in the time of the the New Testament, there were members of the Christian communities who were chosen to exercise a certain authority within the community. At the same time, the community was urged to obey these authorities. (cf. 1 Thes. 5:12-13; Heb. 13:17) Thus in addition to the authority given to the Apostles, the «Twelve» (which in itself forms another «institution» of Church ministry; cf. Matt. 10:1-4; Mark 3:14-18; Lk 6:13-16; John 20:24; 1 Cor. 15:5), there were other ministers in the local churches. «Presbyters» appear in Acts 11:28-30; 16:4;

1 Peter 5:1; James 5:14. See also Heb. 13:7,17,24; 1 Thes. 5:12; 1 Tim. 3:1-7; 5:17. While no technical description is given in the New Testament for these ministries, it is certain that in each community ministers were appointed who were to provide some kind of order and leadership within the local church. (In the Johannine communities the theology of authority in the Church developed somewhat differently; there is a structure of ministry, but it is not a teaching authority. But by the end of the second century, there were no Johannine communities; they were either part of the «Great Church», or they had become gnostic sects. (cf. A. LEMAIRE, *Les ministères aux origines de l'Église* [Paris: Les Éditions du Cerf, 1971]; G. KONIDARIS, «De la prétendue divergence des formes dans le régime du christianisme primitif: ministres et ministères du temps des Apôtres à la mort de saint Polycarpe» in *Istina* 10[1964]59-92; E. SCHILLEBEECKX, *Ministry: Leadership in the Community of Jesus Christ* [New York: Crossroad, 1981].) Every authority in the Church was considered as having as its foundation the apostolic authority given by Christ to the Apostles. By the third century the concept of apostolic succession was already well accepted. The surest test of authenticity of a doctrine was whether a church had been founded by, or was continually linked with, the apostles. Authority, always understood as being linked with the apostles, was seen as *diakonia*, translated then into Latin as *ministerium*, service. In the Fathers of the Church, there is repeated insistence on this aspect of service. St. Augustine, in letter 140, defines the bishop as «servus Christi servorumque Christi». (See V. GROSSI and A. DI BERARDINO, *La Chiesa antica: ecclesiologia e istituzioni* [Roma: Borla, 1983]; J.N.D. KELLY, *Early Christian Doctrines* [New York: Harper and Row, 1978]; Ch. MUNIER, «Autorità nella Chiesa» in *Dizionario Patristico e di Antichità Cristiane*, vol. 1 [Rome: Marietti, 1983], cols. 450-457.) Running parallel to this development of what might be called «official» ministry in the Church was another type of authority, one which had a more charismatic style. This can be found in the ascetic movement of the fathers of the desert. Several points can be highlighted in order to appreciate some of the characteristics of authority that were present in these early roots of the monastic tradition. Among those who went out to the desert, there was a common attitude about spiritual authority, a common response to masters of the ascetic life. «But no one took power for granted. A claim to the title of ἀββᾶς, spiritual father, depended on a wide range of qualifications, recognized throughout the desert» (P. ROUSSEAU, *Ascetics, Authority, and the Church in the Age of Jerome and Cassian* [Oxford: Oxford Univ. Press, 1978], p. 22). Leaders were considered as belonging to an historical tradition, not only in the history of the Church, but also in the longer and more general history of God's dealings with mankind. Furthermore, the personal experience of the master was very important. The mark of distinction which differentiated the master from the others was his greater age. A very important principle was that the master would never teach others what he himself had not already done. Thirdly, the master had an insight, a capability to speak with authority that derived from a spiritual perception which then prompted the trust of his disciples. And finally, there was a quality of inspiration, the supposed inspiration of the master by God which was the essential basis for trust in the teaching of the fathers. «An apparently intimate relationship with God, a complete dependence upon him, did more than anything else to give experienced ascetics a permanent standing in the eyes of other men» (Ibid., p. 29). As a gradual movement took place from the heremitic or solitary lifestyle to one that had more of a communal dimension, the charismatic authority was

maintained, but changes were slowly taking place in the interpretation and exercise of authority. There was an increase in formality, which reflected the growing complexity of relationships among the ascetics. Authority became more institutional. Readiness to conform remained the willing response to a charismatic leader; obedience was prompted by the belief that submission to the guidance of the father would guarantee fulfillment of God's will. There was, however, a gradual hardening of attitudes: «Superiors were becoming more impersonal and remote; and the awareness was growing that outward conformity might be achieved without an interior submission» (ibid., p. 55). As the sacramental priesthood becomes part of the ascetic life, a further transition begins to evolve. The priesthood (sacramental) became, at first, a support for the charismatic authority, and then a substitute. In the end, «functions traditionally reserved for spiritual leaders endowed with charismatic power were gradually taken over by men whose qualifications were almost entirely clerical. It was clerics, now, who gave spiritual assurance, when famous holy men were no longer able to 'speak the word'; it was clerics who possessed visionary power ... «The manner in which authority had been passed down traditionally, from one generation to the next within the ascetic group, was now becoming» confused with the continuity of a clerical system» (Ibid., p. 63). (For the concept of authority in the ascetic movement, see also B. BAROFFIO, «La paternità dell'abate nel monachesimo primitivo» in *Renovatio* 12[1977]67-79.) Another important transition point in this development is found in the influence that the Egyptian ascetics had on the West. By the end of the fourth century, the monks of Egypt «became something of a tourist attraction» (Rousseau, p. 79). St. Augustine gives further testimony to this influence when he speaks of the *Life of Antony* in the *Confessions* (Book VIII, 14, 15, PL 756). But in the West, the ascetic movement took on a different direction, and there are many examples of men who, while being devoted to the monastic life, lived in a manner that was very much given to the carrying out of pastoral duties. Augustine and Martin of Tours are just two examples of «monk-bishops», and there are many other examples of men who were recruited from monasteries to become priests or bishops. One of the results that came about as the Eastern cenobitic ideal was adopted in the West, however, was that the style of religious, charismatic authority was institutionalized. Jerome, in one of his letters, expressed that the «ascetic life had now become completely identified with, or absorbed into, the public life of the Church» (Jerome, ep. xxii, 23; see Rousseau, p. 111). Augustine, in the Rule, speaks of two authorities in the monastery, the *praepositus* and the *presbyter*. The *praepositus* is the laymonk who is concerned with the daily direction of the community. The *presbyter* must take action when there are particularly grave faults committed by members of the group, or when matters of doctrine are in question *(Regula*, c. 7; LUC VERHEIJEN, «Saint Augustin: Un moine devenu prêtre et évêque» in *Estudio agustiniano* 12[1977]314). One more important influence is key to this study, and that regards the terminology that has been adopted by the Church in its juridical understanding of its authority. In the eleventh and twelfth centuries, as canonists began the systematization of the laws of the Church, they turned to Roman law as one of their sources. In addition, the various ecclesiastical laws promulgated prior to this time were heavily influenced by Roman law. Thus, it was during this period that the distinction first came about between *potestas iurisdictionis* and *potestas ordinis*. Jurisdiction (from *ius dicere*) was a power conferred by the Church, a power to govern. Eventually, distinctions were made

However, the fact remains that by law the Prior is given a certain power, and therefore some consideration of this topic must be made.

a) «Religious» authority

In canon 596, the existence and extent of the power of superiors is presented. Although the translation of the Code by the Canon Law Society of Great Britain and Ireland uses the word «authority» in its translation of the first paragraph, the original text reads *potestas*, and the American translation (which follows) translates the word more literally using the word «power»:

> Superiors and chapters of institutes enjoy that power over members which is defined in universal law and the constitutions.[19]

This power is to be exercised according to the norms of universal law and proper law,[20] and within the limits of the superior's office.[21] This authority is found in all institutes of consecrated life, and is

---

between public and private power, power of jurisdiction and the *potestas dominativa*, etc. (See A. BERGER, *Encyclopedic Dictionary of Roman Law* [Philadelphia: American Philosophical Society, 1953], pp. 523, 533, 640; R.J. COX, *The Juridic Status of Laymen in the Writing of the Medieval Canonists* [Washington, DC: The Catholic University of America Press, 1959], pp. 14-17; H. BERMAN, *Law and Revolution: The Formation of the Western Legal Tradition* [Cambridge: Harvard University Press, 1983], pp. 199-204; V. ARANGIO-RUIZ, *Istituzioni di diritto romano*, 14th ed. [Naples: Ed. Dott. Eugenio Jovene, 1983], pp. 480ss.) It is from these various influences that much of today's juridic structure of authority is drawn. Thus, even the word *potestas* must be understood as part of a long development, and not merely as a form of leadership which in and of itself may well be unacceptable in light of the evangelical model of authority as service.

19 Can. 596, §1: «Institutorum Superiores et capitula in sodales ea gaudent potestate, quae iure universali et constitutionibus definitur.»

20 Can. 617: «Superiores suum munus adimpleant suamque potestatem exerceant ad normam iuris universalis et proprii.»

21 Can. 622: «Supremus Moderator potestatem obtinet in omnes instituti provincias, domos et sodales, exercendam secundum ius proprium; ceteri Superiores ea gaudent intra fines sui muneris.»

distinct from that ecclesiastical power of governance traditionally referred to as the power of jurisdiction.[22]

The source from which canon 596, §1 was taken is apparently canon 501, §1 of the old Code.[23] There has been, however, a change in the terminology used to indicate that authority which is exercised by religious superiors and chapters. In the old Code, this power was called *potestas dominativa*, dominative power.[24] Also called domestic or paternal authority, it was similar to the authority inherent in any private society. It was considered as deriving from the natural law by virtue of the vow of obedience, and was compared to the power that a parent has over his own children.[25] Such terminology is for the most part no longer in use today.[26] This power is referred to rather as the authority proper to the particular institute as determined by the constitutions and common law, or, as religious authority.

In addition to the change in terminology, a certain evolution has taken place in the understanding of what this authority is and from what source it derives. In the past, this power was not considered as belonging to «the Keys», nor was it looked upon as

---

[22] The fact that this distinction exists is made evident by can. 596, §2 (see below, p. 51, which indicates that superiors in clerical religious institutes of pontifical right also possess the power of governance.

[23] V. can. 501, §1: «Superiores et Capitula, ad normam constitutionum et iuris communis, potestatem habent dominativam in subditos...»

[24] See the commentary on v. can. 501, §1 of A. LARRAONA, «Commentarium codicis: can. 501» in *Commentarium pro Religiosis* (CpR) 7(1926)30-33.

[25] F. CAPPELLO, *Summa Iuris Canonici*, vol. 2 (Rome: Pont. Universitas Gregoriana, 1945), pp. 15-18; M. RAMSTEIN, *A Manual of Canon Law* (Hoboken, NJ: Terminal Printing and Publishing Co., 1948), p. 308; S. WOYWOOD, *A Practical Commentary on the Code of Canon Law* (New York: Joseph F. Wagner, 1952), p. 213.

[26] There are some authors who continue to use the expression *potestas dominativa*: E. GAMBARI, *Consacrati e inviati* (Milan: Ancora, 1979), p. 544; L. BOMBIN, «L'obbedienza religiosa nel diritto canonico» in AA. VV., *Autorità e obbedienza nella vita religiosa* (Milan: Ancora, 1978), pp. 299-332.

descending from Christ by means of a special gift to the Church. The explanation was given that this power was born radically from the will of those who profess the vow of obedience and who donate themselves to the religious institute with the promise and obligation to obey according to its Rule.[27] This «dominative power» was private in nature in that it was comparable to the authority of a father of a family or a leader in an «imperfect society».[28] Even before the Vatican Council, however, authors began to refer to the «dominative power» as a public power, especially in light of a decision of the Commission for the Interpretation of the Code in 1952,[29] according to which the prescriptions of canons 197, 199 and 206-209 (which referred to the power of jurisdiction) were to be applied as well to dominative power.[30] There was the realization that the authority of a superior or a chapter in a religious institute is much more similar to the *potestas iurisdictionis* than it is to

---

27 Suarez, T.15, tr.8, Lib.4, cap.12, nn. 1-5; in no.3: «Deinde haec potestas [dominativa] nascitur radicaliter ex ipsis subditis . . . »

28 Political doctrine establishes four basic requirements in order for a society to be called «perfect»: «1) ut *finem* habeatur *supremum* in proprio ordine, seu quod hic finis non sit per ordinem ad alium finem *medium;* 2) quod dentur *omnia media* ad proprium finem consequendum *necessaria*, et quidem *ut propria* seu non ab alio recepta; 3) quod *plenitudo auctoritatis* (iuris) in proprio ordine stet, et 4) denique quod sit *plena autonomia* (quid internum) et *absoluta independentia* (quid externum)» (J. CASTAÑO, *Ius Ecclesiae constitutionale,* vol. 2 [Rome: Pont. Universitas a S. Thoma, 1976], p. 39).

29 AAS 44(1952)497. Already A. LARRAONA had advanced the theory of the *potestas dominativa* as a public power. See «De potestate dominativa publica in iure canonico» in *Acta Congressus Iuridici Internationalis, 1934,* vol. 4, pp. 145-180. Speaking of this power, he says that it is not merely private, but «ius regendi societatem iuridicam necessario—voluntariam et universalem ab Ecclesiae Suprema Auctorita[t]e erectam et approbatam, ut statum publicum religiosum plene, statum vero clericalem religioso adiunctum magna ex parte contineat et moderetur, fideles qui religionem amplectuntur singillatim et quatenus corpus constituunt, ad christianae caritatis perfectionem efficaciter dirigendo» (p. 161).

30 The decision of the Code Commission in 1952 was incorporated into the new Code, can. 596, §3: «Potestati de qua in §1 applicantur praescripta cann. 131, 133 et 137-144.»

the authority of a father of a family, which is entirely private in nature. Thus, the *potestas dominativa* came to be considered as semi-public.[31] Moreover, today religious authority, or the power proper to the institute, is recognized as being of public character since it is exercised in the name of the Church. This understanding of religious authority is much more in keeping with the emphasis placed today on the ecclesial dimension of any religious institute.[32]

Another dimension of this «religious authority» which the local Prior as well as any superior holds arises in consideration of its «source» or origin. The theory of Suarez was that this power arose from the will of the religious themselves in their profession of the vow of obedience. The Church gave official recognition to this power in its approval of the institute and its constitutions.[33] More recently, on the other hand, along with the altered perspective on the public nature of this authority, came a new understanding of its origin. No longer was the source of this power seen as being born in the will of the members of the institute; it was, rather, granted by the Church in the act of approving the foundation of an institute and its rule or constitutions. Pope Pius XII, in a talk to the general superiors on February 11, 1958,[34] stated:

---

31 *Comentarios al Codigo de Derecho Canonico,* vol. 1 (Madrid: Biblioteca de Autores Cristianos, 1963), p. 71.

32 See for example can. 573, §2: «Quam vivendi formam in institutis vitae consecratae, a competenti Ecclesiae auctoritate canonice erectis, libere assumunt christifideles, qui per vota aut alia sacra ligamina iuxta proprias institutorum leges, consilia evangelica castitatis, paupertatis et oboedientiae profitentur et per caritatem, ad quam ducunt, *Ecclesiae eiusque mysterio speciali modo coniunguntur*». (emphasis mine).

33 Suarez, T.15, tr.8, lib.4, cap.12, n.3: «Deinde haec potestas [denominativa] nascitur radicaliter ex ipsis subditis, requirit autem acceptationem auctoritate Apostolica factam.»

34 AAS 50(1958)153-161.

In this dimension of our ministry we have taken you on, beloved sons, as participants in our highest duty, delegating to you, by means of the Code of law, part of our supreme jurisdiction, establishing the foundation of your power, which is called «dominative», when we approve your rules and institutes. Because of this, we are particularly interested that you exercise this authority according to our desire and that of the Church.[35]

Since that time, there has been increasing acceptance of the notion of the Church as source of the religious superior's authority, and in the new Code this theory has been included. Canon 618, which is taken primarily from the Council document *Perfectae caritatis*, states that «superiors are to exercise their power, received from God through the ministry of the Church, in a spirit of service . . . »[36] What is noteworthy is the addition of the words «received from God through the ministry of the Church». They are not found in the paragraph of *Perfectae caritatis* from which canon 618 is taken.[37] This modification adds much greater emphasis to the ecclesial dimension of the ministry of the religious superior, a theme more clearly addressed in the document issued jointly by the Congregation for Religious and Secular Institutes and the

---

35 Ibid., p. 154: «In hac igitur parte Nostri muneris, vobis, dilectissimi Filii, sive recto tramite, aliquid vobis per Codicem Iuris delegantes Nostrae supremae iurisdictionis, sive per ipsa Nobis probata Regulas et Instituta vestra illius potestatis vestrae, quam «dominativam» appellant, fundamenta ponentes, vos socios Nostri supremi officii assumpsimus. Hinc fit ut Nostra plurimum intersit, ut ad mentem Nostram et Ecclesiae hanc vestram auctoritatem exerceatis.»

36 Can. 618: «Superiores in spiritu servitii suam potestatem a Deo per ministerium Ecclesiae receptam exerceant . . . »

37 PC, no. 143: «Superiores vero, rationem pro animabus sibi commissis reddituri, voluntati Dei in munere explendo dociles, in spiritu servitii pro fratribus auctoritatem exerceant . . . » It is also worthy of note that the Code speaks of «potestas» in place of «auctoritas».

Congregation for Bishops, *Mutuae relationes*.[38] It is, in fact, this document's treatment of the superior's authority which provides the foundation for canon 618, and for the theory of the Church's being the source of religious authority.[39] By emphasizing this doctrine, the Code clearly is seeking greater and closer cooperation between religious institutes and the universal ministry of the Church.[40] Nevertheless, all authors are not in agreement. There are still those who claim that the source of religious authority is found in the institute itself, by virtue of the vow of obedience.[41] The Church's role is looked upon as giving official recognition to an authority that is born within an association of persons united for the realization of certain goals.[42]

While the role of the vow of obedience certainly cannot be excluded in any consideration of the superior's authority, in light of *Mutuae relationes* and canon 618, the religious authority proper to the institute is better understood as deriving from the Church. The vow of obedience that each member professes incorporates him into the institute and makes him subject to that authority.

---

38 SCRSI and S.C. pro Episc., *Mutuae relationes*, May 14, 1978, AAS 70(1978)473-506.

39 MR, no. 13: «Superiores munus suum serviendi et dirigendi explent intra religiosum Institutum secundum propriam ipsius indolem. Eorum autem auctoritas a Spiritu Domini procedit in conexione cum sacra Hierarchia, quae canonice Institutum erexit eiusque specialem missionem autentice approbavit.»

40 The document MR directly addressed the relationship between bishops and religious, and gave norms for the coordination of the apostolic work of each group. Another question which branches out of this discussion is that of «exemption», but it is impossible to treat the matter in this study. Mentioned in can. 591, as well as in LG 45, CD 35,3, and in MR 22, «exemption» has undergone a certain transition in the way in which it is interpreted today. See J. GARCÍA MARTÍN, «Exemptio religiosorum iuxta Concilium Vaticanum II» in CpR 60(1979)281-330; 61(1980) 9-36; 97-130; 62(1981)193-206; 289-302.

41 See for example, L. BOMBIN, op. cit., p. 306: «I superiori non hanno il loro potere dal Signore; non lo ricevono direttamente da lui, anche se spesso si sentono dire delle frasi in questo senso.»

42 Ibid. «... l'autorità negli istituti di perfezione è un'autorità eminentemente 'sorgiva', cioè un'autorità nata, sorta all'interno di un'associazione di persone ...»

In the eyes of the Church, the two go hand in hand; there is no mistaking, however, the Church's wish to clarify its position as minister of the authority exercised within institutes of religious life.[43]

Since this power is received through the ministry of the Church, it cannot therefore be exercised outside of that communion which exists between all the members of the Church. Depending on how one understands certain ecclesiological questions, the transmitting and reception of religious power is subject to various interpretations. Some scholars believe that there is no authority in the Church which does not derive from Peter, and by means of Peter.[44] Others are not only in disagreement, but find the view that all power in the Church derives from the Keys as totally unacceptable.[45] These are doctrinal issues which

---

[43] Another related discussion which probably has much to do with this question of the source of religious authority is that of «status» in the Church. «Status» in a juridical sense refers to a stable mode of living which has been established by a competent juridical authority. In the Church, by divine institution, the faithful are divided into laity and clergy. From these two groups, certain ones are called, and by means of the profession of the evangelical counsels, they become members of this third status. (cf. cann. 207, §§1,2; 588, §1.) The consequence of establishing the consecrated life as a distinct status within the Church is that as a distinct juridical category, it carries its own specific rights and obligations apart from those of either the laity or the clergy. It could be argued that the Church, in officially recognizing the consecrated life as a distinct status, has also wanted to emphasize its direct relationship not only in the establishment of religious institutes, but also in the ongoing ordering of the consecrated life: it is thus essential that the Church be directly responsible for the authority which fosters this ordering. (For further discussion on the question of status, see: *Dictionarium morale et canonicum*, vol. 4, s.v., «Status» by A. PUGLIESE [Rome: Officium Libri Catholici, 1968], p. 354; J. CASTAÑO, «Lo 'status consecratorum' nell'attuale legislazione della Chiesa» in *Angelicum* 60[1983]190-223.)

[44] See, for example, J. BEYER, *I Superiori locali e la loro missione* (Milan: Ancora, 1983), p. 7: «Il superiorato è una missione ecclesiale. Non vi è alcun potere—e un superiore locale ha una autorità, un potere—che non derivi da Pietro per mezzo di Pietro.» Also E. GAMBARI, op. cit., p. 552.

[45] R. KRESS, «Membership and Leadership in the Church» in *The Jurist* 42(1982)29-69. The Roman Catholic explanation not only has the custom of summing up «all

are worthy of much further study, but which are unfortunately outside the scope of the work at hand. Let it suffice to say that there seems to be room for recognizing more than one immediate source of authority in the Church. If indeed the state of the consecrated life does not pertain to the hierarchical structure of the Church,[46] it could be logically concluded that the authority in religious institutes has a source other than that of the papacy. For example, since *Lumen gentium* speaks of religious life as a special gift, or charism, which pertains to the holiness of the Church,[47] is it not possible to perceive the authority of a particular institute as part of the gift of the Spirit to the institute? In order to foster and preserve the gifts of that institute, the Church could then make the same affirmation which is found in the Code:

> It belongs to the competent authority of the Church to interpret the evangelical counsels, to regulate their practice by laws, to constitute therefrom stable forms of living by canonical approbation, and, for its part, to take care that the institutes grow and flourish according to the spirit of the founders and wholesome traditions.[48]

By so doing, the Church might be able to encourage greater freedom among religious institutes so that they could develop

---

Church authority, office and leadership in the office of the papacy. Much worse, it has located them there originally, making the papacy the enabling and originating source of all other leadership, official-executive and other, in the Church» (p. 34).

46 LG, no. 44.

47 LG, no. 44: «Status ergo, qui professione consiliorum evangelicorum constituitur, licet ad Ecclesiae structuram hierarchicam non spectet, ad eius tamen vitam et sanctitatem inconcusse pertinet.»

48 Can. 576: «Competentis Ecclesiae auctoritatis est consilia evangelica interpretari, eorundem praxim legibus moderari atque stabiles inde vivendi formas canonica approbatione constituere itemque, pro parte sua, curare ut instituta secundum spiritum fundatorum et sanas traditiones crescant et floreant.»

appropriate ways of exercising authority in light of their particular charism.⁴⁹

b) Power of governance

For Priors in the Augustinian Order, there is another classification of authority granted by the Church. Canon 596 states in the second paragraph:

> Moreover, in clerical religious institutes of pontifical right [superiors] also possess ecclesiastical power of governance for both the external and internal forum.⁵⁰

This *potestas ecclesiastica regiminis* is the same as that referred to in canons 129 to 144, and is also called the power of jurisdiction.⁵¹ While the Code gives no definition of this power, jurisdiction can be considered as a public power «to rule or direct members of the society with legislative, executive and judicial functions.»⁵² In the case of the local Prior, it is executive power which he possesses.⁵³ The Constitutions reiterate the Prior's possession of ecclesiastical

---

49 While this particular discussion may not be directly related to authority structures in the Augustinian Order, there are related questions which will be subsequently discussed. Furthermore, in order to present a minimum of the factors required in order to understand religious authority, it is pertinent that these questions at least be raised.

50 Can. 596, §2: «In institutis autem religiosis clericalibus iuris pontificii pollent insuper potestate ecclesiastica regiminis pro foro tam externo quam interno.»

51 See can. 129, §1: «Potestatis regiminis, quae quidem ex divina institutione est in Ecclesia et etiam potestas iurisdictionis vocatur, ad normam praescriptorum iuris, habiles sunt qui ordine sacro sunt insigniti.»

52 J. CUNEO, «The Power of Jurisdiction: Empowerment for Church Functioning and Mission Distinct from the Power of Orders» in *The Jurist* 39(1979)187.

53 Ordinary legislative power in the Order is possessed by Chapters (see *Constitutiones*, nos. 243,276,282). A local Prior can impose precepts (no. 286), but this is in virtue of the executive power of governance (see cann. 48 and 49).

power.⁵⁴ This authority is ordinary and proper as it is possessed in virtue of the Prior's office and exercised in his own name, and the power can be delegated.⁵⁵

The power of governance is in the Church by divine institution,⁵⁶ and the understanding of this power is that it derives from the «power of the keys» conferred by Christ to Peter.⁵⁷ The concept of power in the Church was altered by the Vatican Council, and instead of speaking of the powers of orders and jurisdiction, the Council chose to speak of the *munera* of sanctifying, teaching and governing. Speaking of the episcopal office, *Lumen gentium* offers the following interpretation of sacred power in the Church:

> Now, episcopal consecration confers, together with the office of sanctifying, the duty also of teaching and ruling, which, however, of their very nature can be exercised only in hierarchical communion with the head and members of the college.⁵⁸

> Those who, under the authority of the bishop, sanctify and govern that portion of the Lord's flock assigned to them render the universal Church visible in their locality and contribute efficaciously toward building up the whole body of Christ.⁵⁹

---

54 *Constitutiones*, no. 243: «... Capitula et Superiores, in suo quisque gradu, potestatem et iurisdictionem ecclesiasticam habent ad normam iuris communis, Constitutionum et Statutorum Provincialium exercendam...»

55 Cann. 131 and 137.

56 Can. 129, §1 (see footnote 51).

57 A. DE PASQUALE, «La Gerarchia – Principi generali» in *Il Diritto nel Mistero della Chiesa*, vol. 2 (Rome: Libreria Editrice della Pontificià Universita Lateranense, 1981), p. 117.

58 LG, no. 21: «Episcopalis autem consecratio, cum munere sanctificandi, munera quoque confert docendi et regendi, quae tamen natura sua nonnisi in hierarchica communione cum Collegii Capite et membris exerceri possunt.»

59 LG, no. 28: «Qui sub auctoritate Episcopi portionem gregis dominici sibi addictam sanctificant et regunt, Ecclesiam universalem in suo loco visibilem faciunt et in aedificando toto corpore Christi validam opem afferunt.»

Thus, there is a three-fold concept of power which is proposed by the Council, and these functions can only be exercised in communion with the hierarchy of the Church. There is a clear emphasis on the ecclesial dimension of any exercise of the power of governance, for the person who is entrusted with this authority has an increased participation in the Church's mission and ministry. «Jurisdiction is the principle which unites the person (bishop, priest, minister, person with a particular share in mission or function) to the community and to the rest of the ecclesial communion.»[60] The ministry of the local Prior has, therefore, a dimension which is united with the ministry of the entire Church by virtue of the fact that he is given a share in the duty of governing.[61]

The presence of the power of governance in the Order raises several questions. One of these is the classification of the Order as a «clerical institute».[62] Although the definition of a clerical institute has changed in the new Code, the Augustinian Order remains, as it was under the old, within this category:[63]

---

60 J. CUNEO, op. cit., p. 209.

61 The change in name to *potestas regiminis* in the Code is a further reflection of the Council's understanding of this power: «Rectius quidem vocatur *potestas regiminis*, quia haec locutio magis congruit historiae, et quia magis convenit cum assertis in Constitutione dogmatica *Lumen gentium* et in decretis Concilii Vaticani II, in quibus distinguuntur munus docendi, munus sanctificandi et munus regendi,» *Communicationes* 9(1977)234.

62 According to can. 596, §2 (see footnote 50), only the superiors and chapters in clerical institutes of pontifical right are given a share in the *potestas regiminis*. That the Order is of pontifical right is evident from its very founding, which was an act of the Apostolic See (cf. *Const.*, no. 4); can. 589: «Institutum vitae consecratae dicitur iuris pontificii, si a Sede Apostolica erectum aut per eiusdem formale decretum approbatum est . . . »

63 In the old Code, an institute was called clerical if a majority of its members were priests; cf. v. can. 488,4[b]: «*Religionis clericalis,* religio cuius plerique sodales sacerdotio augentur, secus est laicalis.» The Schema of 1980 stated that «instituta vitae consecratae, suapte natura, neque clericalia neque laicalia sunt» (*Schema Codicis Iuris Canonici*, Libreria Editrice Vaticana, 1980, can. 516, §1). The new Code, on the other

CHAPTER TWO

> An institute is said to be clerical if, by reason of the purpose or design intended by its founder or in virtue of legitimate tradition, it is under the supervision of clerics, it assumes the exercise of sacred orders, and it is recognized as such by church authority.[64]

In the case of the Augustinian Order, there is a certain amount of difficulty in clearly determining whether the Order was founded with the intention of its being a clerical order. Due to a lack of documentary evidence about the composition of the Order in its earliest period, around 1256 and before, it may be that the percentage of lay brothers was high. However, «it is equally probable that the percentage declined rapidly, both because of the increasing emphasis on studies and because the apostolate of the mendicants was directed chiefly toward the pastoral ministry.»[65] And by the end of the thirteenth century, the Order was certainly clerical, with as many as seventy-five percent of the members as priests or aspirants to the priesthood.[66] Thus, there seems to be little question that, almost from the very beginning, the government of the Order was in the hands of clerics. There can therefore be no doubt that in light of the definition given in the new Code

---

hand, states that «status vitae consecratae, suapte natura, non est nec clericalis nec laicalis» (can. 588, §1).

64 Can. 588, §2: «Institutum clericale illud dicitur quod, ratione finis seu propositi a fundatore intenti vel vi legitimae traditionis, sub moderamine est clericorum, exercitium ordinis sacri assumit, et qua tale ab Ecclesiae auctoritate agnoscitur.»

65 A. ENNIS, «The Historical Development of the Constitutions of the Order as Seen Chiefly through an Analysis of the Ratisbon Text of 1290» in *Second Annual Course on Augustinian Spirituality*, Rome, 1976, pp. 140-141. For a thorough treatment of the history of the Order from its founding through its first hundred years, see: D. GUTIÉRREZ, *Los Agustinos en la edad media: 1256-1356*, Historia de la Orden de San Agustin, vol. I/1 (Rome: Institutum Historicum Ordinis Fratrum S. Augustini, 1980).

66 D. GUTIÉRREZ, op. cit., p. 83.

the Augustinian Order is a clerical institute.[67] Its superiors are consequently granted the ecclesiastical power of governance.

2. Personal authority

Already in Chapter One,[68] reference was made to the fact that the Church insists upon the presence of a superior in every community. While great emphasis is placed upon the necessity of seeking consensus among the members of a community, in the last analysis there must be an authority figure whose decision will be recognized and accepted by the group.[69] Again, at the beginning of this chapter, reference was made to a recent document

---

67 A number of other questions arise at this point, but inasmuch as they are not part of the central issue of this study, they cannot be treated at length. Of these, the topic of exemption comes up once again. In the old Code, the granting of the power of jurisdiction to religious superiors and chapters was limited to clerical, exempt institutes (cf. v. can. 501, §1). The extension of this power to other superiors raises once again the meaning of exemption under the new legislation (See footnote 40 of this chapter). Another much discussed topic today branches off of the whole discussion of the Augustinian Order as a clerical institute. This would be the question of the lay brother as superior. In revising the 1968 Constitutions in 1977, the General Chapter adopted the proposal that all Brothers be eligible for all offices. The requirement of sacramental priesthood was looked upon as being extrinsic to the nature of the Order, and therefore, the SCRSI was petitioned to allow this change so as to eliminate the distinction between priests and lay brothers in this regard; the permission was denied since such an alteration would be contrary to canon law (see Litt. SCRSI, 15 May 1978, in *Acta OSA* 23[1978]24-25). Since that time, the new Code has been promulgated, but basically, the possibility is still contrary to the law: cf. can. 129, §1: «Potestatis regiminis, quae quidem ex divina institutione est in Ecclesia et etiam potestas iurisdictionis vocatur, ad normam praescriptorum iuris, habiles sunt qui ordine sacro sunt insigniti.» There have been cases where lay brothers were granted permission to exercise the office of Prior, but each case is an exception to the rule. While the new Code does give greater possibility for the exercise of the power of governance (the cooperation in its exercise; cf. can. 129, §2) to non-clerics, the requirement of priesthood remains a requisite for the office of Prior, not by choice of the Order, but by virtue of the common law of the Church. See AA.VV., *Il fratello religioso nella comunità ecclesiale oggi* (Rome: Ed. CIPI, 1983), esp. C. COUNIHAN, «Il Religioso fratello Agostiniano», pp. 151-165.

68 See pp. 45-47.

69 ET, no. 25 (See p. 22).

published by the Congregation for Religious and Secular Institutes on the essential elements of the religious life, in which the same affirmation is made: «strictly speaking, this religious authority is not shared. It may be delegated according to the constitutions for particular purposes but it is normally *ex officio* and is invested in the person of the superior.»[70]

There is full agreement between the Church's legislation in this regard and the Constitutions of the Order:

> Since no human society can be without an appropriate structure, our Order, from the beginning, chose for itself a structure that conforms to its nature, one, that is, in which fraternal equality governs the relationships between Superiors and the other brethren and in which no one is superior to the others, except by reason of an office or duty assigned to him for a time.[71]

In order to establish a house of the Order, it is required that there be a single local Prior.[72] Nevertheless, this attribute of the superior's authority merits a certain amount of consideration in order to attain a clear understanding of what the superior's presence in the community represents.

In the new Code, provision is made for the exercising of authority in a situation where several persons are granted, as a

---

70 «Essential elements», II, 49.

71 *Constitutiones*, no. 240: «Cum nulla humana societas congruenti structura carere possit, Ordo noster, iam ab initio, sibi formam elegit suae naturae consentaneam, in qua scilicet fraterna aequalitas relationes inter Superiores et alios Fratres moderatur, nec quisquam aliis superior est, nisi ratione officii seu muneris pro tempore eidem commissi.»

72 *Constitutiones*, no. 244: «Unio Fratrum in eodem loco vel in locis vicinioribus eamdem vitam participantium, sub unius Prioris Localis moderamine, Domum Ordinis constituit.»

group, the power to fulfill some function in the Church. This possibility is recognized in the case of parochial ministry:

> When circumstances require it, the pastoral care of a parish or several parishes together can be entrusted to a team of several priests *in solidum* with the requirement, however, that one of them should be the moderator in exercising pastoral care, that is, he should direct their combined activity and answer for it to the bishop.[73]

There is, therefore, by law, the possibility of holding the power of governance as a group. Some religious might therefore want to ask if it would not be possible for a similar governmental structure to be established in a religious community. Instead of a local superior, there would be a board of three persons, for example, who would coordinate and direct the activity of that particular community. To this possibility, the Congregation (SCRSI) has already spoken. Requested about whether the ordinary form of government, whether on the general, provincial or local level, could be collegial, so that the superior, if there is one, would be merely an executor, the Congregation issued a negative response emphasizing once again that the superior's authority must be personal.[74]

---

73 Can. 517, §1: «Ubi adiuncta id requirant, paroeciae aut diversarum simul paroeciarum cura pastoralis committi potest pluribus in solidum sacerdotibus, ea tamen lege, ut eorundem unus curae pastoralis exercendae sit moderator, qui nempe actionem coniunctam dirigat atque de eadem coram Episcopo respondeat.»

74 *Experimenta*, SCRSI, Feb. 2, 1972: AAS 64(1972)393-394. «An, contra can. 516 [VCIC], regimen collegiale ordinarium et exclusivum admitti fas sit, sive pro toto Instituto religioso, sive pro provincia, sive pro singulis domibus, ita ut Superior, si habetur, sit merus executor ... Ad mentem Concilii Oecumenici Vaticani II (PC 14) et Adhortationis pontificiae *Evangelica testificatio*, n. 25, ratione habita legitimarum consultationum necnon limitum a iure sive communi sive particulari receptorum, Superiores auctoritate frui debent personali.»

While many different styles of leadership can be utilized within a community, in the end there must also be an individual who retains the authority to make decisions and to guide the life of the religious. Many religious, perhaps reacting to the abuses that were experienced by some in the past, look upon such authority as an effort on the part of the Church to impose a hierarchical or monarchical model within the religious life. This is not the case, however, and there are many good reasons for this insistence upon the personal authority of the superior. One of the most important aspects of living the religious life is the communion, the unity, that is shared by the members, as a means of seeking God. The human reality, however, can make this a rather difficult task, and at times there is a need for intervention on the part of a superior to address those difficulties. The trust level between the individual concerned and the superior will more likely be greater where there is an individual superior (the local Prior) who has sought to establish such a basis on a personal level. This is less likely to happen between an individual and a collegial authority. Likewise, in order to provide more adequately for a person's needs, an individual superior can offer a greater accessibility, so that the individual religious will feel free to approach the local Prior and to express those needs or concerns which are at issue. In other words, personal contact, often on a one-to-one basis, is necessary for the life of the community, and for the individuals of the community.

Authority is an instrument, an aid which is provided for the sake of fulfilling the purpose of religious life. Its correlative, obedience, has, at least in the Augustinian context, much the same orientation. While obedience has a definite communal dimension (the word means «to listen to»), on the practical level it is rather contrived to think of obeying a team, a collegial authority. This is not, however, meant to lessen the importance of the involvement of the whole community in deciding certain issues, nor to underestimate the value of the Council in aiding a Prior in the governance of the community.[75] But apart from the ideal, it seems that in living the daily reality of religious life, the individual superior is much more capable of fulfilling the many and varied responsibilities that make up part of the service of authority.

3. The exercise of the Prior's authority

The office of Prior in the Order «is not an office of power, but of fraternal love, not of honor, but of obligation, not of domination, but of service.»[76] Nevertheless, as has been demonstrated above, there is a certain power attached to the office of local Prior. In what manner is this power to be exercised? As there are various forms or styles of leadership, each superior will have to find that style with which he can best serve the community. This being a juridical study, however, it is not possible to present theories from the social sciences regarding the various aspects and styles of leadership.[77] Of primary interest here are the dimensions of the community's life within which the Prior is expected to exercise his power, to carry out his pastoral ministry.

---

75 Regarding the role of both the House Chapter and the House Council, refer to chapter six of this study.

76 Vfr. 2,4, p. 91: «... non est officium potestatis, sed caritatis, non honoris, sed oneris, non dominii, sed servitii ... » See also *Constitutiones*, no. 15.

77 C.I. BARNARD draws a distinction between various aspects of «executive activity»: leadership, communication, decision-making, authority, responsibility; all very important aspects of a Prior's ministry. *The Functions of the Executive* (Cambridge: Harvard Univ. Press, 1938), pp. 6, 21, 259.

Brief mention has been made of the Council's use of the concept of *munus*. Although there are at least two senses of the word in the documents of the Council,[78] the ministry of leadership within a religious community, by means of analogy, has been made equivalent to the *munus pastorale* in its three-fold function of teaching, sanctifying and governing.[79] This comparison is found in the document *Mutuae relationes*, published by the Congregation for Religious and Secular Institutes and the Congregation for Bishops.[80] Each aspect of the Prior's office in the exercise of authority is thus analogically compared with the *munus pastorale* entrusted to a diocesan bishop. In terms of the threefold function of this ministry, the document reads:

> As regards the *duty of teaching*: Religious Superiors have the competency or authority of *spiritual directors* according to the evangelical tradition of their Institute. Therefore, in this context they must impart to their Congregation as a whole or to each one of its communities, a real *'spiritual direction'*, in agreement with the authentic teaching of the Hierarchy, and fully aware of the fact that they are performing a duty of grave responsibility within the form of life laid down by the Founder.[81]

---

78 In LG, no. 21, the *munus sanctificandi*, together with the *munera docendi* and *regendi*, is conferred in episcopal consecration. But in LG, no. 27, reference is made to the *munus regendi*, also called the *munus pastorale*, in the ministry of a diocesan bishop. In other words, in addition to the sacramental conferral of a certain authority, there is the question of «office» involved. What is the difference between the *munus* sacramentally conferred and a function which is attributed to a certain office? The same question leads to the necessity of distinguishing between a power given on the one count, and a service rendered within a specific community on the other.

79 The *munus pastorale* is described in LG, no. 27, CD, nos. 3,8,9,12,16. In the case of religious authority, it is obvious that (following the thought from the footnote above) of major concern is the office, or duty, of carrying out this ministry, rather than the conferral of a power (which in the case of bishops takes place in episcopal ordination), although an authority is definitely conferred with the office.

80 MR, no. 13.

81 MR, no. 13(a): «quoad *munus docendi*: Superiores Religiosi competentiam habent et auctoritatem *magistri spiritus* secundum evangelicam proprii Instituti conformatio-

As to the office of sanctifying: Superiors have a special competency, as well as the responsibility, of 'perfecting', in various ways, the life of charity, within the rule of the Institute, either in what refers to the initial and ongoing formation of their brethren, or to the communal and personal fidelity in the practice of the Evangelical Counsels according to the Rule. This duty, conscientiously performed, is considered by the Supreme Pontiff and the Bishops as a valuable help in the fulfillment of their fundamental ministry of sanctification.[82]

As to *the office of governing*: Superiors must organise the life of the community, distribute offices to its members, take care of the special mission of the Institute, develop it and work at its effective insertion into the ecclesial activity, under the direction of the Bishop.[83]

There is, then, an internal organization in religious institutes (CD 35, §3) which has its proper field of competency and a measure of real *autonomy*, even though in the Church this autonomy can never become *independence* (CD 35, §§3,4). The right degree of this autonomy and its concrete delimitation of

---

nem; quare in eius ambitu veram explere debent *spiritualem directionem* totius Congregationis et singularum Ipsius Communitatum; quam quidem ipsi perficient in sincera concordia cum authentico Hierarchiae magisterio, scientes sibi grave mandatum exsequendum esse in ambitu evangelicae formae a Fundatore statutae.»

[82] Ibid., (b): «Quoad *munus sanctificandi:* Superiores peculiarem competentiam atque mandatum habent *perficiendi,* distinctis tamen muneribus, in iis quae ad incrementum vitae caritatis secundum Instituti propositum spectant, sive circa sodalium formationem, et initialem et continuam, sive circa communitatis et singulorum fidelitatem erga evangelica consilia iuxta Regulam exsequendam. Hoc vero munus, si recte expletum erit, putabitur a Romano Pontifice et ab Episcopis tamquam pretiosum auxilium in praecipuo eorum sanctificationis ministerio.»

[83] Ibid., (c): «Quoad *munus regendi:* Superiores servitium explere debent propriam Communitatis vitam ordinandi, Instituti membra disponendi eiusque peculiarem missionem curandi et augendi atque providendi, ut idem actuose inseratur ecclesiali actioni sub Episcoporum ductu.»

competency are contained in the common law and in the rules
or constitutions of each Institute.⁸⁴

Using the analysis of the authority of religious superiors as it is outlined in *Mutuae relationes*, Chapters Four, Five and Six of this study will present the duties of the local Prior as they are specified in common law and in the Constitutions. A perfectly clear distribution of the various responsibilities is perhaps not possible, nor even desirable, since realistically speaking there will be much interplay between many of the activities that are entrusted to the Prior. In addition, the fact that the three-fold description of *munus* is in many senses inadequate for describing the overall pastoral function of the Prior (or for that matter, of the Church) results in a certain artificiality in trying to conceive of the exercise of authority within these categories.⁸⁵ Nevertheless, such an approach

---

84 Ibid. «Exstat igitur 'ordo Institutorum internus' (cf. CD 35,3), qui proprium competentiae campum habet, ad quem genuina quaedam *autonomia* spectat, quae tamen in Ecclesia numquam ad *independentiam* redigi potest (cf. CD 35, 3 et 4). Congruus vero autonomiae gradus eiusque definita competentiae descriptio in iure communi atque in Regulis, seu Constitutionibus, uniuscuiusque Instituti continentur.»

85 N. MOERSDORF, «Munus regendi et potestas iurisdictionis» in *Acta Conventus Internationalis Canonistarum*, Rome, 1968, pp. 199-211. «His omnibus perpensis dici potest distinctionem trium munerum Christi et Ecclesiae nec adaequatam nec completam esse . . . » (p. 203). The problem is further complicated by the presence of a number of doctrinal difficulties. There are theological disputes about the nature and source of various powers in the Church. The difference between what we have called «religious» authority and the power of governance is not clear. It has even been proposed that the two are actually one and the same power (see A. GUTIÉRREZ, «I canoni riguardanti gli Istituti di vita consacrata e le società di vita apostolica» in *Vita Consacrata* 20[1984]70). The doctrinal dispute about the various powers in the Church, and the difference between the ecclesiastical power of governance and the «religious» authority, or the power proper to the institute, is not about to be resolved. (See *Communicationes* 14[1982]150ss.) In discussing the *potestas regiminis*, the Commission for the revision of the Code decided they could not decide the doctrinal issues related to the distinction or relationship between these powers or authorities. The question becomes even more complicated for the fact that in the Augustinian Order superiors possess both «religious» authority and the power of governance. So here, the analogy of *Mutuae relationes* is strengthened by a superior's real participation in the three *munera* of teaching, sanctifying and governing.

can still be helpful not only for organizational purposes, but also because it provides a means whereby the ecclesial context of the Prior's role can be conceptualized.

Chapter Three, in the meantime, will provide a detailed analysis of the office of Prior: its conferral, requisites, termination of office, and so forth.

Thus, it becomes very difficult to answer such questions as when is a Prior acting in virtue of «religious» authority, and when in virtue of the *potestas regiminis*. Except for the clearest of cases (perhaps delegation of the license to hear confessions is one of these), there will not be a great deal of clarity in this regard until there is a greater clarification of the theological issues involved. (See D.J.A. GUTIÉRREZ, «Notas directivas para obispos y religiosos» in *Revista española de Derecho Canónico* 34[1978]548-657; J.A. SOUTO, «El *munus regendi* como función y como poder» in *Acta Conventus Internationalis Canonistarum*, Rome, 1968, pp. 239-247).

CHAPTER THREE

THE OFFICE OF LOCAL PRIOR

After having given consideration to the role of service and leadership that a local superior is asked to fulfill, and to the authority that the Prior exercises, discussion must turn to more specific questions about the office of the local Prior and some of the fundamental mechanics that are determining factors on the juridical level of this office. These include such matters as the way in which the individual is chosen or nominated, requisites for office, and the term of office.

1. Definition

Frequently, the terms «local Prior» and «local superior» are used interchangeably. There is, however, need to make a technical distinction which is based upon the way in which the community is formed.

«A religious community must live in a house legitimately constituted under the authority of a superior who has been designated according to the norms of law.»[1] In the Augustinian Order, there are two types of communities which can be

---

1 Can. 608: «Communitas religiosa habitare debet in domo legitime constituta sub auctoritate Superioris ad normam iuris designati . . . »

established. In the vast majority of cases, houses of the Order are constitutionally established.[2] To do so, there must be at least three members who possess active voice assigned there, so that a local Chapter can be held. If this criterion is not met, the community is called a residence of the Order.[3] It is at this point that the distinction must be made. If the community is not constitutionally established as a house of the Order, its superior is not a Prior, and his authority is limited to that which is granted him by the Province Statutes. Thus, while the local superior who is not a Prior does have a certain moral authority, his juridical authority must be granted to him by each Province in the statutes.[4]

A word is also in order as to the necessity of having a superior in each community. The Constitutions, in defining a house of the Order, state: «The union of Brothers who share the same life in a single place, or in several places close by, constitutes a House of the Order, under the direction of a single local Prior.»[5] It is clear that, according to number 244 of the Constitutions and canon 608, the local Prior is a constitutive element of the community. A constitutional religious house cannot exist without a Prior. Such an authority is to be present so that there is one who is guardian

---

[2] The requirements for the establishment of a house are given in the *Constitutiones*, no. 246: «Ad erectionem uniuscuiusque Domus requiritur:
- a) petitio facta Priori Generali a Capitulo Provinciali vel a Provinciali de consensu sui Consilii;
- b) consensus Ordinarii loci scripto datus;
- c) licentia Prioris Generalis scripto danda.»

[3] *Constitutiones*, no. 245: «Domibus non minus quam tres Fratres voce activa fruentes assignentur, ita ut Capitulum Locale celebrari possit; secus Residentiae Ordinis vocantur . . . »

[4] *Constitutiones*, no. 245: «Eorum Superiores non sunt Priores sensu stricto et ea tantum auctoritate gaudent quam Statuta Provincialia eis conferant.»

[5] *Constitutiones*, no. 244: «Unio Fratrum in eodem loco vel in locis vicinioribus eamdem vitam participantium, sub unius Prioris Localis moderamine, Domum Ordinis constituit.»

of the communion of Brothers who live together in the same community.

2. Ecclesiastical office

An ecclesiastical office is defined in canon law as «any function constituted in a stable manner by divine or ecclesiastical law to be exercised for a spiritual purpose.»[6] By virtue of this definition, there would seem to be little question that the office of local Prior or of local superior in the Augustinian Order is an ecclesiastical office. What this implies then is that all of the legislation in the Code on ecclesiastical offices must be considered in order to determine what parts of it directly relate to the office of local Prior. This legislation is found in Title IX of the first book of the Code, covering canons 145 to 196. Generally speaking, the two areas which are of immediate concern are the provision of ecclesiastical offices, and the loss of the same.

---

6 Can. 145, §1: «Officium ecclesiasticum est quodlibet munus ordinatione sive divina sive ecclesiastica stabiliter constitutum in finem spiritualem exercendum.» The source of this canon is found in *Presbyterorum ordinis,* no. 20. This document revised the notion of ecclesiastical offices, making significant changes in the former law. V. can. 145, §1 stated: «Officium ecclesiasticum lato sensu est quodlibet munus quod in spiritualem finem legitime exercetur; stricto autem sensu est munus ordinatione sive divina sive ecclesiastica stabiliter constitutum, ad normam sacrorum canonum conferendum, aliquam saltem secumferens participationem ecclesiasticae potestatis sive ordinis sive iurisdictionis.» From the time of PO, then, there is no longer the distinction between ecclesiastical offices in the wide sense and the strict sense. Secondly, the participation in either the power of orders or the power of jurisdiction has been eliminated, a distinction which practically speaking eliminated the possibility of non-clerics holding an ecclesiastical office. Obviously, if an office is conferred, some kind of authority is given so that the office holder is able to perform that function established by either divine or ecclesiastical law, but it is not necessarily *potestas ordinis* or *potestas regiminis.*

3. Nomination

«An ecclesiastical office cannot be validly acquired without canonical provision.»[7] «Provision of an ecclesiastical office occurs by the free conferral of a competent ecclesiastical authority . . . »[8] These two canons are applied by the Constitutions of the Order in the nomination of the Prior: «The Prior is appointed by the Provincial with the consent of his Council.»[9] This is normally done after the Ordinary Provincial Chapter, which is held once every four years. Once the Chapter is concluded, the Prior Provincial convokes his Council for the purpose of arranging the local communities and nominating the Priors and other officials.[10] In providing for the office of local Prior, the Provincial proposes a candidate to the Council who must either approve by absolute majority or reject the candidate, in which case the Prior Provincial will nominate another individual.[11] A local Prior therefore cannot be validly named until the Prior Provincial receives the consent (absolute majority) of his Council.

A word might be said about the fact that in the Augustinian Order the local Prior is not elected by the membership of the

---

7 Can. 146: «Officium ecclesiasticum sine provisione canonica valide obtineri nequit.»

8 Can. 147: «Provisio officii ecclesiastici fit: per liberam collationem ab auctoritate ecclesiastica competenti . . . »

9 *Constitutiones*, no. 314: «Prior a Priore Provinciali, de consensu sui Consilii, post Capitulum Provinciale Ordinarium nominatur . . . »

10 *Constitutiones*, no. 361: «Capitulo absoluto, Prior Provincialis suum Consilium convocet, cui hac vice adnumerandus est Prior Provincialis in Capitulo praecedenti absolutus, ut infra tempus a Statutis Provincialibus determinatum ordinet Familias locales, eligat Priores et alios officiales, ratione habita Statutorum Provinciae et programmatis a Capitulo confecti.»

11 *Constitutiones*, no. 363. «Electiones vel confirmationes, in providendo officiis, fiant per maioritatem absolutam suffragiorum inter singulos candidatos a Priore Provinciali propositos . . . »

community. There are cases in which a Provincial might ask a given community to propose or suggest a name or series of names for the office of Prior in that particular house. The Provincial is not, however, obliged to follow these requests. He would do well to keep in mind, however, the recommendation given by the Constitutions: «The progress and renewal of the Order depends much on the worthiness of Superiors and, therefore, in the [choosing] of Superiors two things need to be harmonized: the widest participation of the brethren, and the spirit of obedience.»[12] There is a great need of sincere and thorough cooperation between the Provincial and the individual community before a local Prior is appointed. Although the «power» or authority of the Superior comes from the Church through the legitimate appointment made by the Provincial, the members of a community will be much more readily disposed to giving «authority» over to that person if they feel that they have had some kind of participation in the selection of that leader.[13] Thus, the blending or harmonizing

---

12 *Constitutiones*, no. 292: «Cum Ordinis progressus atque renovatio a Superiorum idoneitate multum dependeat, duo simul in electionibus Superiorum componi debent: maxima Fratrum participatio et oboedientiae spiritus . . .» The English translation of the Constitutions translates «electionibus» as «election», but at least in the case of the local Superior it would seem that «choosing» is a more accurate translation. There is no reason to believe that this principle does not apply to the selection of the local Prior just as well as to the other officials who are elected by the membership.

13 Two points must be specified here: first, regarding the «source» of the authority of the local Prior, see the discussion on this question in Chapter Two. Then, in terms of the distinction between «power» and «authority»: while they can be used synonymously, the two can also be used to identify two different realities. «Power» or «potestas» is conferred in an official, or canonical way. «Authority» can refer to that respect or esteem which is given by a group to a person in whom they recognize the talent of leadership. In Italian, there are two words which help make the distinction: «autorità» and «autorevolezza». Van Bavel, in commenting on the Rule of Saint Augustine, states: «The Rule connects a person's being a superior with the esteem which others have for him. We sometimes do not pay sufficient attention to this important connection and to the substantial interaction between these two. No one can be a superior unless others esteem and value him as such. Thus a person may well be appointed leader of a group

of active participation and the spirit of obedience will be much more easily brought about by an encouragement of the Brothers' cooperation in the selection of possible candidates for the office of Prior.

4. Term of office

Provision is made in the new Code for assigning a specific length of time for the Prior's term of office; however, such specification is to be made by the constitutions or directory of the particular institute.[14] The Code also indicates that proper law should establish a time interval so that superiors do not remain too long in offices of governance without interruption.[15] The intention behind this would be to avoid the practice of having individuals continuously holding positions of authority: the religious life is one of vowed obedience, not of governing. This law is given both for the good of the individual and of the institute. It is not just to expect the same

---

and charged with responsibility for it, but, unless there are also people who accept this leadership, nothing will come of it in everyday life. Only when a summons is answered does it really become a summons; otherwise it will remain an empty word. In this sense our esteem makes another our superior. Conversely, this means too that the members of a group can emasculate the function of leadership and make the leader's task impossible. No one is our superior by nature, but, because of our commitment, we make another person our superior; thus our free choice and co-operation are presupposed. To esteem another more highly than ourselves (Phil. 2:3) is of importance not only in our relationship to the superior; it is also a basic law in our ordinary day-to-day contact with one another.» (T.J. VAN BAVEL, "Introduction and Commentary" to *The Rule of Saint Augustine*, trans. R. Canning [London: Darton, Longman and Todd, 1984], p. 108)

14 Can. 624, §1: «Superiores ad certum et conveniens temporis spatium iuxta naturam et necessitatem instituti constituantur, nisi pro supremo Moderatore et pro Superioribus domus sui iuris constitutiones aliter ferant.» In the old Code, the maximum length of a local superior's term of office was specified at three years. V. CIC can. 505: « . . . Superiores autem minores locales ne constituantur ad tempus ultra triennium . . . »

15 Can. 624, §2: «Ius proprium aptis normis provideat, ne Superiores, ad tempus definitum constituti, diutius sine intermissione in regiminis officiis versentur.»

individual to carry continually the burden of leadership positions. And harm can also be done to a community that remains for an excessive period of time under the rule of the same superior.

According to the Order's Constitutions, the Prior's term of office is four years.[16] There may, however, be special circumstances which shorten the Prior's term. The most common of these would be the case in which a Prior is appointed in the middle of the Provincial's term as the result of a vacancy of office. In this case, the new local Prior is appointed «pro tempore» until the end of the current Provincial's term.

The local Prior can be appointed for a second term of four years, but not for a third time successively to the same office without the express permission of the Prior General. Such permission is to be granted only in extraordinary cases.[17] There is need for clarification on these last two points. The wording of the Constitutions could create a certain ambiguity regarding the possibility of a Prior's serving in that role for more than two successive terms, provided that the community of which he is Prior is not the same one for more than eight years at one time. The question arises from the meaning of the words «ad idem munus», the same office, of number 314 of the Constitutions. Does this expression refer to the office of Prior in any community, or is it a specific reference to that office in that particular community? Clearly the mind of the legislator is that *munus* be the office of Prior in *any* house. The Constitutions were drawn up under the

---

16 *Constitutiones*, no. 314: «Prior a Priore Provinciali, de consensu sui Consilii, post Capitulum Provinciale Ordinarium nominatur et, nisi rationes speciales et graves aliud suadeant, in suo officio ad quatriennium ordinarie manet . . . »

17 Ibid., « . . . quo exacto, ad idem munus iterum assumi potest, sed non tertio, immediato quatriennio perdurante, nisi in casu aliquo extraordinario et de expressa licentia Prioris Generalis . . . »

old Code, which specifically stated that a Prior (local superior) was allowed two terms of office, but could not assume a third term immediately following in the same religious house.[18] But the Constitutions would not merely have repeated a provision already given in the Code. The limitation which allowed only two terms as Prior in any house was a new idea, and the requirement that a local Prior not be appointed for more than two terms of office was thus written into the Constitutions.

The new Code leaves the specification of such matters up to the particular law of each institute, suggesting that no person be allowed to remain in offices of governance for too long a period without interruption.[19] There is no determination of what these offices might be. Thus, some might interpret that the canon is referring to any and all offices of governance, and even from passing from one level of governance to another. Consequently, one might want to understand the canon as a recommendation against a man's being elected Provincial who has just completed two consecutive terms as a local Prior. On the other hand, and more reasonably, the spirit of the law can be viewed as seeking to avoid the tendency of having too few people control positions of government for too long a period of time.[20] At any rate, the

---

18 V.CIC, can. 505: «... Superiores autem minores locales ne constituantur ad tempus ultra triennium: quo exacto possunt ad idem munus iterum assumi, si constitutiones ita ferant, sed non tertio immediate in eadem religiosa domo.»

19 Can. 624, §2; see footnote 15.

20 J. GALLEN, *Canon Law for Religious* (New York: Alba House, 1983), p. 61, states: «I do not believe the law extends to different levels of government, e.g., the local superior just described could immediately be designated as general or provincial superior with full eligibility...» An example of the opposite opinion is found in DOMINGO J. ANDRÉS, *El Derecho de los Religiosos* (Madrid: Publicaciones Claretianas y Commentarium pro Religiosis, 1983), p. 121: «Aunque no puede dudarse de que los sujetos de referencia expresa sean los superiores, sin embargo, la cláusula 'en los oficios de régimen' amplía el sentido, desbordando la mera superioridad y orientándolo hacia todo oficio de régimen, es decir, a todo oficio que, sin ser propiamente el de superior, se asemeje de alguna

actual legislation of specifics is left up to the particular law of each institute. Consequently, for Augustinians there is no law which prohibits passing from one level of government to another without a time interval between the different offices. And in terms of the office of local Prior, number 314a of the Constitutions clearly indicates that nomination to a third term of office in any community is not allowed without the express permission of the Prior General.[21]

This then leads to the second point of number 314 of the Constitutions which needs a certain clarification. The permission of the Prior General mentioned just above is, according to the Constitutions, to be granted only in extraordinary cases.[22] What are the circumstances that would designate such a case? In this regard, the following information may be useful in that it gives certain insights as to the criteria used by the Holy See in deciding such questions:

> At times various Roman Dicasteries are petitioned to allow a Religious to remain for a fourth term of office in the same religious house as local superior, or as Provincial in the same Province, despite the contrary provisions of the general law and of their particular Constitutions.
>
> Recently an American congregation of religious women petitioned the Sacred Congregation of Religious and Secular Institutes that a sister working in their mission in Latin America be allowed such a fourth term as local superior. The Congregation only asks that the reasons for such an exception be convincing ones. In this case, the plea was based on the fact

---

manera a éste. Por consiguiente, se pretende evitar la rotación y el mariposeo ininterrumpido por todo oficio . . . »

21 See footnote 17.

22 *Constitutiones*, no. 314; see footnote 17.

that only she had an adequate knowledge of the language and customs of the country coupled with the personal qualifications to serve as superior; the other four religious on the mission were lacking one or the other of these attributes. The indult was granted in September, 1980.

An international missionary congregation of religious men petitioned the Sacred Congregation for the Evangelization of Peoples that a priest who had already served 18 years as Provincial of one of their European Provinces, be permitted to serve another three-year term to which he had just been elected. The Congregation, 'while underlining the importance of moving in the direction of a healthy rotation in regard to the matter of governing personnel within the Institute', granted the permission.[23]

From the summary of responses from Roman Dicasteries, two general criteria can be indicated as guidelines in consideration of whether the Prior General should grant permission (or even be requested for permission by a Province) for a local Prior to assume a third consecutive term of office. First of all, the qualifications of the Prior who currently holds the office and who would be renominated should be noteworthy. This refers not only to juridical requirements, but also to questions of a more «existential» type, i.e., in that given context, is this person the best one available for carrying the responsibilities which are attached to the office of local Prior? And secondly, the condition ought to be present that there is no one else qualified to take on the office. As was indicated above, the reasons should be convincing, and each Province should strive to move more and more in the direction «of

---

23 WILLIAM A. SCHUMACHER, ed., *Roman Replies* (Washington, DC: Canon Law Society of America, 1981), p. 36. This is a summation of responses received from various religious Congregations as to indults received from the Holy See.

a healthy rotation in regard to the matter of governing personnel within the Institute.»[24]

5. Requisites

Canon 149 of the new Code gives a general outline of what requirements must be sought in the candidate who is to be nominated to any ecclesiastical office:

> In order to be promoted to an ecclesiastical office, a person must be in the communion of the Church as well as suitable, namely endowed with those qualities which are required for the office in question by universal or particular law or by the law of the foundation.[25]

Very little is said in the Constitutions regarding the qualifications for being appointed Prior. In fact, what little is said was only added in the General Chapter of 1983 as a result of modifications made in the Constitutions due to the promulgation of the new Code. Canon 623, speaking of superiors in general, prescribes that proper law is to determine a suitable time after perpetual or definitive profession for the valid appointment or election of a member to the office of superior.[26] Thus, number 314 of the Constitutions was lengthened, with the addition of the statement that to be appointed Prior or local Superior, the member must be at least three years

---

[24] Ibid.

[25] Can. 149, §1: «Ut ad officium ecclesiasticum quis promoveatur, debet esse in Ecclesiae communione necnon idoneus, scilicet iis qualitatibus praeditus, quae iure universali vel particulari aut lege fundationis ad idem officium requiruntur.»

[26] Can. 623: «Ut sodales ad munus Superioris valide nominentur aut eligantur, requiritur congruum tempus post professionem perpetuam vel definitivam, a iure pro prio vel, si agatur de Superioribus maioribus, a constitutionibus determinandum.»

solemnly professed.[27] The reasoning behind this legislation is fairly apparent. In order to carry the responsibility that accompanies the office of superior, especially with the kinds of demands that are made upon a Prior, a reasonable amount of time in the Order is not only desirable, but mandatory, not to mention that a certain maturity on the part of the individual is essential. Seeing as how one may make his solemn profession at the age of twenty-three,[28] it is conceivable that in certain cases a Brother could be named to the office of Prior at the age of twenty-six. But age in itself is not the main consideration; if it were, there would be a specified age requirement for the office of local Superior as there is for Provincial and Prior General.[29] A superior must have a well-founded and well-integrated understanding of what is involved in being an Augustinian, and of what is expected of an authority within the Augustinian community. This only develops over a period of time lived in the Order, in which one can gradually gain the kind of knowledge, experience and wisdom necessary. Thus, a three year interval between the profession of solemn vows and the granting of eligibility for the office of local Prior or local Superior is a reasonable requirement. On this point, one final comment is important: this requisite that the man named to the office of local Superior be at least three years solemnly professed is «ad

---

27 *Constitutiones,* no. 314: «... Tam Prior quam Superior localis sit saltem tres annos sollemniter professus (cf. can. 623).» Note that the specification is made both for local Prior and for local Superior.

28 *Constitutiones,* no. 231: «Tempus probationis professione sollemni absolvitur. Iuvenes igitur ad illam non admittantur nisi, expleto vicesimo tertio aetatis anno ac toto probationis tempore, idonei inveniantur...»

29 *Constitutiones,* no. 349: «Ut quis Provincialis eligi possit, requiritur ut sit filius Provinciae, vel in ea adscriptus a tribus saltem annis et saltem triginta annos natus ac quinque sollemniter professus et bonae famae testimonio gaudens.» And regarding eligibility for the office of Prior General, no. 423: «... Sit saltem triginta quinque annos natus et sollemniter professus ab octo...»

validitatem». There can be no doubt of this because of the explicit mention of canon 623 in the text of the Constitutions.[30] According to the new Code, «only those laws which expressly state that an act is null or that a person is incapable of acting are to be considered to be invalidating or incapacitating.»[31] Canon 623 expressly states that «in order that members be *validly* appointed or elected to the office of superior, a suitable time is required after perpetual or definitive profession, to be determined by proper law, or if it is a question of major superiors, by the constitutions.»[32] Thus, for the validity of the nomination, the candidate must be solemnly professed for at least three years.

---

30 *Constitutiones*, no. 314; cf. footnote 27.

31 Canon 10: «Irritantes aut inhabilitantes eae tantum leges habendae sunt, quibus actum esse nullum aut inhabilem esse personam expresse statuitur.»

32 Canon 623; see footnote 26. Two distinctions that this canon makes are not applicable in the case of the Augustinian Order. The first is the reference to «perpetual or definitive profession». This distinction refers to those institutes in which only a temporary profession is made and then regularly repeated. Augustinians make their definitive profession with solemn (perpetual) vows, so that no distinction is necessary here. The second distinction made in canon 623 is between proper law and constitutions. The Code states that there can be two separate legislations for the institute, constitutions and a directory. (cf. can. 587.) (These are obviously both apart from the Rule.) The constitutions would include the primary and fundamental law of the institute; some institutes call these the «fundamental code». Included here would be the basic juridical norms of the institute along with the important spiritual principles of the religious life and the particular form of life of that institute. The other legislation is frequently called a «directory», or the statutes. These could contain legislation in greater detail, or concerns that are not part of the everyday life of the members. (cf. GALLEN, *Canon Law for Religious*, pp. 14-17.) Advantages to having two separate bodies of law are several: the possibility of maintaining a more spiritual nature within the constitutions; the fact that to change constitutions generally requires the approval of the Holy See, whereas it could be legislated that the directory of the institute be modified by a general chapter (cf. can. 587, §2). The Augustinians, however; along with few other Orders, enjoy a privilege which exempts them from this requirement. (cf. Ph. Maroto in *Commentarium pro Religiosis* 18[1937]250-255; Larraona, CpR 4[1923]137-139.) And while the Augustinian Order has no such directory on an Order-wide level, each Province is to have its own statutes. Frequently, the Constitutions will make reference to these, indicating that the statutes are to determine the specific requirements in a given matter (cf., for example, *Const.* nos. 113, 117, 118).

There are other requirements proposed indirectly by the Constitutions. The Provincial Counselors are not to be local Priors, unless there is serious reason.[33] Exception to this rule can only be granted by the Prior General with the consent of his council. The Provincial cannot be a local Prior unless it is within a community that is formed exclusively of his staff.[34] The reasoning behind these restrictions is that the accumulation of too many offices of authority in too few people can be detrimental to the life of the community or Province, and furthermore, especially in the case of Provincial, that the requirements of being Provincial would place great limitation upon his time and energies in regards to his responsibilities as local Prior, and vice versa.

There are many other qualifications that are not in and of themselves juridical in nature. These are primarily based upon a capability of the individual to fulfill this particular ministry, as it was described in Chapter One. Obviously, a Provincial must consider all these aspects before choosing any individual to become the local superior or Prior of a community.

6. Conferral of office

Once the Prior has been nominated, the Provincial shall send him a letter, signed and stamped with the seal of the Province, that certifies his having been named as Prior.[35] Upon his taking

---

33 *Constitutiones*, no. 392: «Consiliarii, qui Priores esse non possunt, nisi gravi de causa a Priore Generali de consensu sui Consilii recognoscenda . . . » This is in keeping with can. 152: «Nemini conferantur duo vel plura officia incompatibilia, videlicet quae una simul ab eodem adimpleri nequeunt.»

34 *Constitutiones*, no. 384: «Prior esse potest illius tantum Domus, quae ad residentiam ipsius Curiae unice destinatur, nec ullum habere officium quod eum a regimine Provinciae distrahere aliquo modo potest . . . »

35 *Constitutiones*, no. 366: «Singulis Prioribus aliisque officialibus litterae a Priore Provinciali subscriptae et sigillo Provinciae munitae mittantur, ex quibus eorum legitima electio vel nominatio pateat.»

possession of office, he shall make the profession of faith in the presence of the Prior Provincial or his delegate.[36] This is a new requirement found in the Constitutions, added by the General Chapter of 1983, as one of the required changes to incorporate modifications found in the new Code of Canon Law. The Constitutions already contained a provision mandating that the newly elected Provincial make the profession of faith,[37] but no mention was made of the local Prior. The basic reason for this is found in the change made in the new Code. The Old Code simply stated that superiors in clerical religious institutes were obliged to make the profession of faith.[38] Thus, there was no need to repeat the same obligation in the Constitutions, as it was already provided by the Code. The new Code, on the other hand, mandates that superiors in clerical religious institutes and societies of apostolic life are obliged to make the profession of faith personally in accord with the formula approved by the Apostolic See, and *in accord with the norm of the constitutions*.[39] In other words, with the new Code, the Constitutions of the Order must determine the way in which superiors in the Order are to comply with this obligation to make the profession of faith. Consequently, the clause was added to the

---

36 *Constitutiones*, no. 242: «... Omnes superiores personaliter professionem fidei, secundum formulam a Sede Apostolica probatam, emittere tenentur coram Capitulo electionis vel Superiore qui eos nominavit eorumve delegato (cf. CIC, can. 833, n. 8).»

37 *Constitutiones*, no. 350: «Prior Provincialis electus, ante confirmationem, coram Praeside et Capitularibus professionem Fidei emittat.»

38 V. can. 1406, §1: «Obligatione emittendi professionem fidei, secundum formulam a Sede Apostolica probatam, tenentur: ... 9° – Coram Capitulo vel Superiore qui eos nominavit eorumve delegato, Superiores in religionibus clericalibus.»

39 Can. 833: «Obligatione emittendi personaliter professionem fidei, secundum formulam a Sede Apostolica probatam, tenentur: ... 8° – Superiores in institutis religiosis et societatibus vitae apostolicae clericalibus, ad normam constitutionum.» Both in the old Code and the new, the obligation is placed upon superiors of «clerical» institutes. While the definition of a clerical institute has changed in the new Code, the Augustinian Order is still considered a clerical order. (Refer to pp. 85-88 for further discussion on this question.)

Constitutions that mandates that all superiors are to make the profession of faith, and in the case of local superiors, they are to make it before the Provincial or his delegate.[40]

The Prior, once his term of office begins, is obliged to reside in the house of the community to which he is assigned.[41] He may not be absent except for brief periods of time. Without his presence in the community, the Prior is obviously unable to fulfill the ministry of his office. The Code makes the same requirement, but is more general in that its provision refers to all superiors.[42] It is furthermore left to proper law to determine the reasons and the amount of time for which a superior is allowed to be absent from his house. The obligation is stricter on the local superior, since his direct area of responsibility is in that specific community, whereas major superiors will have need to travel to the various communities that are under their care. Regarding the amount of time for which a local superior may be absent, the only specification made by the Constitutions is that he may be gone only for brief periods of time. Province Statutes could determine with greater detail the requirements that the membership may expect of the local Priors in this regard. Realistically speaking, however, this kind of issue can only be concretized within the context of a specific community, by giving consideration to all the various needs of that particular group of people.

---

40 *Constitutiones*, no. 242; cf. footnote 36.

41 *Constitutiones*, no. 315: «Toto sui officii tempore in propria Domo residere debet, a qua procul commorari ei non licet nisi ad breve tempus . . . »

42 Can. 629: «In sua quisque domo Superiores commorentur, nec ab eadem discedant, nisi ad normam iuris proprii.» The same canon was found verbatim in the 1917 Code (v. can. 508), with the exception of the words «ad normam constitutionum» instead of «ad normam iuris proprii». This change reflects the attitude of the Code Commission regarding the distinction between the constitutions and the «directory» of an institute (see discussion above, footnote 32).

7. Termination of office

Termination of office can take place in one of several ways. The most common is the expiration of the Prior's mandate, which takes place at the time of the Ordinary Provincial Chapter, but removal and transfer are also possibilities, as well as resignation. Consideration of this material is based upon the Constitutions as well as on the applicable section of the Code, canons 184 to 196, «De amissione officii ecclesiastici».

a) Expiration of term of office

The ordinary term of office is four years, and thus at the end of this time, either the Prior must be reappointed, or a new Prior appointed to that community. The situation may develop in which, for a various number of possible reasons, no new Prior is immediately appointed. In that case, the outgoing Prior continues to govern, and there is usually no need for an interim appointment. By virtue of common practice in the Order (for the Constitutions make no specification on this point) the term of office continues until a new Prior is appointed.[43] In addition, «loss of office by lapse of the determined time or by reaching a certain age takes effect only from the moment when it has been communicated in writing by the competent authority.»[44] The outgoing Prior therefore will remain in office until official communication has made it clear to him that his term has expired. The competent authority in this case is the Prior Provincial.

---

43 GALLEN, op. cit., p. 63.

44 Can. 186: «Lapsu temporis praefiniti vel adimpleta aetate, amissio officii effectum habet tantum a momento, quo a competenti auctoritate scripto intimatur.»

In the case in which a Prior was appointed after the start of the Provincial's term, the Prior's term of office does not last four years, but rather until the time of the next ordinary Provincial Chapter.[45] Thus with the election of a new Provincial, or the re-election of the current Provincial, the Prior's mandate must also be renewed if he is to continue in that community as Prior.

b) Resignation

The Order's Constitutions neither explicitly grant nor deny the right of the Prior to resign his office.[46] By canon law therefore, he has this right.[47] Various factors however must be taken into consideration in order that the resignation be valid.

In order to resign, the Prior must have a just and proportionate reason.[48] The Provincial must not accept the resignation if he does not believe it to be justified.[49] Thus, there is an obligation that rests both on the Prior who wishes to resign as well us upon the Provincial to evaluate carefully the reasons which indicate that a Prior ought to resign. Such reasons could be based upon the good

---

45 *Constitutiones,* no. 316: «Officium Prioris vacans exercetur a Subpriore, qui si desit, a Fratre qui primum locum in Communitate tenet, usque dum Superior Maior competens, de consensu sui Consilii, novum Priorem nominet, qui usque ad Capitulum Provinciale Ordinarium Communitatem regat.»

46 In one case, the Constitutions explicitly say that the Prior is to be given the opportunity to resign if he so wishes: in order to avoid being removed from office (cf. *Const.* no. 514). This case shall be discussed in a subsequent section (d. Removal).

47 Can. 187: «Quisquis sui compos potest officio ecclesiastico iusta de causa renuntiare.»

48 Ibid. Note the words «iusta de causa».

49 Can. 189, §2: «Auctoritas renuntiationem iusta et proportionata causa non innixam ne acceptet.» The Constitutions indicate as well that there must be special and serious reasons for the Prior's term of office to be shortened from the usual term of four years; no. 314: «... nisi rationes speciales et graves aliud suadeant, in suo officio ad quatriennium ordinarie manet...» This general statement refers to resignation as well as to removal from office.

of the individual, or the good of the community. The Prior's health may be one such motive for considering resigning from office. There are also such factors as inability to fulfill the responsibilities of the office, as a result, for example, of a lack of time due to other commitments, ministries, activities, etc., in which the individual may be involved. At times, there may be a certain incompatibility between the Prior and the community which he has been asked to serve, thereby requiring that the Prior resign and another be appointed. In this case, however, the Prior, the Provincial and the entire community involved must carefully evaluate the various elements that appear to be causing the difficulty.

A resignation does not take effect until it is accepted by the Provincial with the consent of his Council.[50] Thus, the Prior may not quit his office immediately upon tendering his resignation. If the Provincial has not yet accepted the resignation, it can be withdrawn.[51] But if within three months the Provincial has neither accepted nor refused the resignation, it lacks all effect.[52] For the validity of the resignation, it must be made in writing, or orally in

---

50 Can. 189, §1: «Renuntiatio, ut valeat, sive acceptatione eget sive non, auctoritati fieri debet cui provisio ad officium de quo agitur pertinet . . . » For the provision of office of local Prior, the competent authority is the Provincial with consent of his council (cf. *Const.*, no. 314). Can. 189, §3: «Renuntiatio quae acceptatione indiget, nisi intra tres menses acceptetur, omni vi caret . . . »

51 Can. 189, §4: «Renuntiatio, quamdiu effectum sortita non fuerit, a renuntiante revocari potest . . . »

52 Can. 189, §3 (cf. footnote 50). This is a change from the old Code (v. can. 189, §2). The old Code stated that the resignation was to be accepted within one month. But according to an interpretation of the Commission for the Interpretation of the Code, the resignation could still be accepted after the one month period, as long as it had not been explicitly withdrawn. (cf. Comm. Int. Cod., July 14, 1922, in AAS 14[1922]526-527.) According to the wording of the new Code, the resignation can no longer be accepted after the expiration of a three-month period from the time at which it is tendered, since the canon states that it loses all effect («omni vi caret»).

the presence of two witnesses.⁵³ Any resignation submitted because of grave fear, fraud, substantial error or simony is automatically invalid.⁵⁴

c) Transfer

Certain circumstances may require that a Prior be transferred to a new assignment. The authority competent in making such a decision is once again the Prior Provincial with the consent of his Council.⁵⁵ The reasons must be sufficient for transferring him, and according to the Constitutions, «special and serious».⁵⁶ If the Prior is unwilling, an even more serious cause is required, and the opportunity must be given to the Prior to offer arguments against the transfer.⁵⁷ His office becomes vacant upon his acceptance of a new office, unless the Provincial makes some other provision.⁵⁸

Since transfer generally involves a move from one office to another, the usual cause that necessitates this action would be a vacancy in another position. The Prior of a certain community may be asked to become Prior in a different community,

---

53 Can. 189, §1: «Renuntiatio, ut valeat, sive acceptatione eget sive non, auctoritati fieri debet cui provisio ad officium de quo agitur pertinet, et quidem scripto vel oretenus coram duobus testibus.»

54 Can. 188: «Renuntiatio ex metu gravi, iniuste incusso, dolo vel errore substantiali aut simoniace facta, ipso iure irrita est.»

55 Can. 190, §1: «Translatio ab eo tantum fieri potest, qui ius habet providendi officio quod amittitur et simul officio quod committitur.»

56 *Constitutiones*, no. 314: «Prior . . . nisi rationes speciales et graves aliud suadeant, in suo officio ad quatriennium ordinarie manet . . . »

57 Can. 190, §2: «Si translatio fiat invito officii titulari, gravis requiritur causa et, firmo semper iure rationes contrarias exponendi, servetur modus procedendi iure praescriptus.»

58 Can. 191, §1: «In translatione, prius officium vacat per possessionem alterius officii canonice habitam, nisi aliud iure cautum aut a competenti auctoritate praescriptum fuerit.»

or because of a certain qualification is needed to fulfill a task in some other apostolate. He is therefore transferred, but of course this creates a vacancy for the first community. There is no need to emphasize the fact that good personnel planning is essential to avoid as much as possible the frequent transfers of the men in a community, especially of those who hold positions of authority. While the Augustinians make no vow of stability, a certain amount of continuity is necessary to ensure a stable community life and to provide a solid basis on which the apostolic activity of the community can be founded.

d) Removal

A Prior can be removed from office either by an act of the Provincial with the consent of his council, or by the law itself.[59] The reasons for such an action must be grave, but there need not be a criminal offense on the part of the Prior in order to justify such an action.[60] By virtue of the law itself, one is removed from his office as Prior in the following cases:

1) if he has lost the clerical state;
2) if he has publicly defected from the Catholic faith or from the communion of the Church;
3) if he has attempted marriage even civilly.[61]

Besides these rather grave reasons, a Provincial may, with the consent of his Council, remove a Prior from office for a cause which

---

[59] Can. 624, §3: «Possunt tamen durante munere ab officio amoveri vel in aliud transferri ob causas iure proprio statutas.»

[60] When loss of office is imposed as a penalty for a criminal offense (privation), it is a different juridical figure. (Cf. the following section.)

[61] Can. 194, §1: «Ipso iure ab officio ecclesiastico amovetur: 1.– qui statum clericalem amiserit; 2.– qui a fide catholica aut a communione Ecclesiae publice defecerit; 3.– clericus qui matrimonium etiam civile tantum attentaverit.»

in his judgment he considers to be just.⁶² There are many reasons which might precipitate such a decision, such as advanced age, ineffectiveness on the part of the Prior in his office, or a judgment made due to prudence in order to avoid a particular situation that might cause harm to the individual or the community. Since removal from office could be against the will of the office holder, he should be given the right to defend himself if there is a question of accusation being made against him, or if he wishes to present arguments in favor of his remaining in office. The Prior should also be given the option of resigning in order to avoid his being removed from office.⁶³

e) Privation of office

If a Prior has committed some kind of offense which is so serious that an accusation has been brought against him and for which he is to be tried, the Provincial with the consent of his council may impose as a penalty the privation of his office. This can only be done according to the norms of penal law.⁶⁴

The Constitutions specify the following motives for which a Superior can be deprived of his office:

1) if he lives irreligiously with grave scandal to the community or to the faithful;

---

62 Can. 193, §3: «Ab officio quod, secundum iuris praescripta, alicui confertur ad prudentem discretionem auctoritatis competentis, potest quis iusta ex causa, de iudicio eiusdem auctoritatis, amoveri.»

63 *Constitutiones,* no. 514: «Fratri ab officio suspendendo vel removendo, si ipse maluerit, renuntiandi possibilitas detur.»

64 Can. 196, §1: «Privatio ab officio, in poenam scilicet delicti, ad normam iuris tantummodo fieri potest. §2 – Privatio effectum sortitur secundum praescripta canonum de iure poenali.»

2) if he is gravely abusive toward the community or the Brothers;
3) if he is found gravely negligent in the fulfillment of the duties of his office;
4) if he is habitually absent, without a just cause, from the common exercises with the other Brothers;
5) if he should attempt to prevent the exercise of legitimate authority;
6) if he gravely neglects the administration of goods, or administers them contrary to the laws of the Order, the Province or the Vice-province.[65]

As is the case in the removal of a Prior, when privation is being considered as a penalty, the option should be given him of resigning his office.[66]

8. Vacancy of office

When the office of Prior in a community is vacant, whether due to any of the above reasons (expiration of the term, resignation, transfer, removal, privation) or due to the death of the Prior, the Subprior is to take charge, or in the case where there is no Subprior, the Brother who is oldest in profession is to assume the

---

[65] *Constitutiones*, no. 513: «Superiores aliique officiales, habita ratione muneris seu condicionis, officio privari possunt his de causis:
 a) si irreligiose vivant cum gravi scandalo Communitatis vel fidelium;
 b) si graviter, contumeliosi contra Communitatem vel Fratres existant;
 c) si graviter negligentes inveniantur in obligationibus proprii officii implendis;
 d) si actibus communibus cum ceteris Fratribus sine iusta causa habitualiter non intersint;
 e) si exercitium legitimae auctoritatis impedire temptaverint;
 f) si administrationem bonorum graviter neglexerint vel iuxta leges Ordinis, Provinciae vel Viceprovinciae ea non administraverint.»
[66] *Constitutiones*, no. 514; cf. footnote 63.

duties of the Prior.⁶⁷ He will continue to exercise the authority of the Superior until the Major Superior with the consent of his council appoints a new Prior. Since no provision has been made by the Constitutions, the new appointment must be made within the time limit set by canon law: i.e. within three months from the time notice is received.⁶⁸

---

67 *Constitutiones*, no. 316: «Officium Prioris vacans exercetur a Subpriore, qui si desit, a Fratre qui primum locum in Communitate tenet, usque dum Superior Maior competens, de consensu sui Consilii, novum Priorem nominet...» Regarding precedence in the community, cf. *Const.* no. 121b: «Cum autem, quadam de causa, praecedentia servanda sit, Fratres ordinem professionis simplicis vel, inter eodem die professos, ordinem aetatis servent; eosque subsequentur novitii et probandi.»

68 Can. 158, §1: «Praesentatio ad officium ecclesiasticum ab eo, cui ius praesentandi competit, fieri debet auctoritati cuius est ad officium de quo agitur institutionem dare, et quidem, nisi aliud legitime cautum sit, intra tres menses ad habita vacationis officii notitia.»

CHAPTER FOUR

THE MUNUS DOCENDI

The office of teaching which is part of the religious authority given to superiors provides a very important service to the local community. *Mutuae relationes*, as already seen, expresses this aspect of the Prior's responsibility in terms of the superior's having the authority of a *magister spiritus*,[1] a teacher of the spirit, in direct relation to the gospel values and witness proper to the particular institute. Superiors must therefore provide a true spiritual direction for their individual community, discharging their responsibility

---

1 While MR, no. 13a uses this expression, reference to the local Prior as *magister* is made here with a certain concept in mind. The leadership given cannot be that of a teacher in a classroom. It is, perhaps, much closer to what Augustine considered the role of the *magister*. He elaborates his theory of education in *De magistro*, in a form of a discussion between himself and his son, Adeodatus. A teacher does not cause the student to think or to recognize the truth. A teacher can only stimulate the student to use his own talents, by use of illustrations and arguments. If the student is to see the truth for what it is, he needs an internal Teacher who shows truth directly to the minds of his students: the Word of God alone enables the person to recognize the truth. Aug: «Nunc enim ne plus eis quam oportet tribueremus, admonui te, ut iam non crederemus tantum, sed etiam intellegere inciperemus quam vere scriptum sit auctoritate divina, ne nobis quemquam magistrum dicamus in terris, quod omnium magister in caelis sit (Mt. 23:8-10) . . . » Ad. «Ego vero didici admonitione verborum tuorum, nihil aliud verbis quam admoneri hominem ut discat, et perparum esse quod per locutionem aliquanta cogitatio loquentis apparet: utrum autem vera dicantur, eum docere solum, qui se intus habitare, cum foris loqueretur, admonuit . . . » *(De magistro*, 14,46; PL 32,1220). See also, G. CORCORAN, *A Guide to the Confessions of St Augustine* (Dublin: Carmelite Centre of Spirituality, 1981), p. 13.

in concordance with the authentic magisterium of the hierarchy, fully aware of the important mandate which they have received in the area of the evangelical plan established by the founder.[2]

The authority which the local Prior exercises is not the same as that which pertains to the pope or to the college of bishops,[3] but it is analogous to it, and there is thus a particular importance to this educational aspect of leadership which a Prior is asked to offer his community. Over and above a direct ministry of the Word, a Prior's exercise of this teaching authority must be conveyed in the normal events of the community's life, by example as much as in word. Joseph Moingt, in speaking of the «period of origins» of the teaching ministry of the Church, describes the role that was played by local community leaders, which was somewhat different from the Apostles' mission of preaching. He writes:

> The ministry of the spoken word exercised in communities goes beyond the strict limits of a teaching function. It includes a more relational and existential character; its goal is rather spiritual and practical. It is addressed to specific individuals and draws its inspiration from what is taking place in communities. It informs, reprimands, advises, and looks to the common good, to shared life experiences, and to the concrete realization of Christian life and action . . .[4]

This description in many ways applies quite well to the kind of teaching ministry which a Prior is asked to fulfill in a local

---

2 MR, 13a. See also p. 60-61.

3 The pope and the college of bishops possess «infallible teaching authority» in certain circumstances (see can. 749, §§1,2) and the bishops are «authentic teachers of the faith» (can. 753).

4 J. MOINGT, «Authority and Ministry» in AA.VV., *Authority in the Church and the Schillebeeckx Case* (New York: Crossroad Publishing Co., 1982), p. 205.

community. It must be developed within the concrete circumstances of the particular community.

At the outset, a word must be said about a very important tool that will help the Prior in this dimension of his ministry. Profound theological reflection on the Prior's part is a virtual «must», if the Prior's leadership is to be effective and meaningful in being a *magister spiritus* within the community. He must consider his own theological position, and be aware of the talents he has and does not have. «Any miscalculation would result in taking a wrong turn in government; while the knowledge of the truth will always have a liberating effect on him and his community, and will help them all to use the available sources fully.»[5] Furthermore, by reflecting in this manner, the superior will find a greater integration of the various elements that come together to form the content of his teaching ministry: the Word of God, the history and traditions of the Order, the needs of his particular community. Through this ministry, the Prior aids the individuals and the entire community to arrive at a greater integration of the witness value of religious life, the ecclesial dimension of the community's life, and their apostolic activity. Obviously, a serious commitment on the part of the Prior to continue to read, study, reflect and pray so that he might be an aid to such integration is indispensable for the fruitful effectiveness of his ministry.

1. The Community as an educational environment

«The intention of the founders and their determination concerning the nature, purpose, spirit and character of the institute which

---

[5] L. ÖRSY, op. cit., p. 103.

have been ratified by competent ecclesiastical authority as well as its wholesome traditions, all of which constitute the patrimony of the institute itself, are to be observed faithfully by all.»[6]

It is this patrimony which forms the fundamental content of the Prior's teaching ministry in the community. That he therefore be thoroughly familiar with these aspects of the Order is essential. The local Prior must be a living witness to the very nature of the Order, offering to the community inspiration to seek out a more radical adherence to those values which are fundamental in the Order. He must know the Constitutions, especially those numbers which deal with the nature and purpose of the Order.[7] Frequent reflection on the Constitutions, the Rule, and other sources of Augustinian spirituality would also be of great importance to him, as well as knowledge of the history of the Order and at least a general background in the thought of St. Augustine.

As a Prior seeks to enhance the Augustinian dimension of the community, there are two specific and essential aspects which must be given consideration. For the Order has as a founder, not an individual, but two great sources out of which the foundation was established: St. Augustine and the Church. In a visit by Pope John Paul II to the Augustinians on May 7, 1982, his address in the chapel of the International College emphasized the very special circumstances which combined to create the Order as it exists today, and which give the Order those characteristics which provide its specific Augustinian identity:

---

6 Can. 578: «Fundatorum mens atque proposita a competenti auctoritate ecclesiastica sanctia circa naturam, finem, spiritum et indolem instituti, necnon eius sanae traditiones, quae omnia patrimonium eiusdem instituti constituunt, ab omnibus fideliter servanda sunt.»

7 *Constitutiones*, nn. 7-17.

Having been called to govern the Church in this period of history, I cannot forget the special origin of your Order. Indeed, it was born in the very heart of the middle ages through the initiative of my predecessors Innocent IV and Alexander IV, and for this reason it is different from other religious institutes, taking a characteristic shape amid the vast range of the different canonical forms and structures for the profession of the evangelical counsels. Your Order, while relating to the letter and the spirit of the Augustinian *Rule* and bearing the lofty and noble title which Augustine's very name gives it, has holy Mother Church for the foundress of its juridic reality.

Augustine and the Church, then. Two great names, my dear brothers, which combine to define your specific characteristics as religious. The heritage of the former and the very reality of the latter (of which, needless to say, Augustine is an unsurpassed teacher because of the depth of his ecclesial insights) urge you to live in a very close and exemplary communion of life, to practice and express this life in ways that are always authentic, and never to betray what is rightly called the «Augustinian charism» of a community life unified through love.

Act in such a way that what the Church is on a general plane (as your father Augustine reminds and teaches you) may become true for each of your communities. Know how to promote in them such a cohesive relationship that the many who live there will be bound together through love and have «one mind and heart intent upon God.»[8] Then you will be able to understand perfectly the words of the Psalm already cited: «How good and how pleasant it is when the brothers live in unity.»[9]

---

8 *Regula*, c. 1.
9 Psalm 132:1.

At the same time that I repeat such meaningful and authoritative reminders, I encourage you fraternally to remain faithful to the community life which is born and rooted in love, accepting the necessary sacrifices and respecting the intrinsic demands of such a life.

Understand well that this life does not imply in any way a closing in on oneself to the exclusion of others. Much less, would I say, could it mean this for you, sons of St. Augustine. Yours is and must be an apostolic community, that is, open and dynamic, intent upon God, as I have already reminded you, but for this very reason reaching out also towards others . . .[10]

These words of the Holy Father provide a concise summation of the essential aspects that form the «intention of the founders and their determination»[11] in the Augustinian Order. In exercising his ministry of *magister* in the community, the Prior must seek to give direction to the community using these characteristics as the foundation of his teaching. In this way, he will be able to create within the community an atmosphere of continual learning so that each member can develop the specifically Augustinian attributes of his vocation. The context in which this education develops will take on a variety of forms: study and discussion of the fundamental legislation of the Order (the Rule and Constitutions[12]) as well as of other documents published or promulgated by the Order and

---

10 JOHN PAUL II, «Discorso all'Ordine Agostiniano» in *Insegnamenti di Giovanni Paolo II,* Vol. 5 (Vatican: Ed. Tipografia Poliglotta Vaticana, 1983) pp. 1438-1441. English translation from «John Paul II Visits the Augustinians» (Rome: Curia Generalizia Agostiniana, 1982) pp. 22-23.

11 Can. 578; see footnote 6.

12 *Constitutiones,* no. 522: « . . . Omnes igitur nos principia, exhortationes, et normas Regulae et Constitutionum frequenter meditari et in nos conferre oportet. Statuta Provincialia sive Capitulum Locale provideant, ut Regula et Constitutiones publice legantur vel in communi refectione vel in Capitulo renovationis vel in exercitiis spiritualibus vel alio opportuno tempore . . . »

the Church; preaching; workshops, conferences, study programs, etc., that make up part of a program of continuing formation. What is important is that the Prior recognize his role in creating the atmosphere in which the Augustinian education can flourish, and that members of the community be given opportunity and encouragement to deepen their appreciation for and knowledge of what it means to live the Augustinian religious life.

Finally, the Constitutions give particular emphasis to this aspect of the community's life in requiring that there be made available the resources for the continual study which should be done by all the community members:

> In every house there should be a library which contains at least those literary means and aids that the Brothers need for the continual updating of their learning and teaching to meet the needs of their own spiritual life, and of their duties and apostolate ...[13]

In the following sections of this chapter, certain specific aspects of the Prior's role in implementing his responsibility as magister will be presented.

2. The Prior's role in formation

Of greatest concern to all members of the Order, formation, whether in the initial stages or that continuing education of members who are already fully incorporated in the Order, must be given great importance among the various ministries of the

---

13 *Constitutiones*, no. 147: «In omnibus Domibus habeatur bibliotheca quae saltem subsidia litteraria et instrumenta contineat, quibus Fratres indigent ut eruditionem suam atque doctrinam exigentiis propriae vitae spiritualis, sui muneris atque apostolatus continuo accommodent...»

Order.[14] Superiors have a special responsibility to develop, coordinate and direct programs of formation on all levels, keeping in mind the personal development of the individual, the good of the Order, and the Order's service to the Church. While the term «formation» generally refers to that period of study, personal development, vocational discernment and apostolic training that comes before solemn profession and in the case of clerical candidates, ordination to the priesthood, in recent years great importance has been placed as well on the concept of «on-going formation», whereby all members of the Order are given the opportunity to devote time to any number of kinds of study, spiritual renewal programs, etc. While primary responsibility for either of these stages does not necessarily rest upon the local Prior, because of his role in the community, he does have a specific duty to aid in the various dimensions of the work of formation, whether in houses which are specifically designated as houses of formation, or in other communities where any of the Brothers might benefit from participation in some form of program for ongoing formation.

a) In houses of formation

In those communities designated by the proper authorities as houses of formation,[15] the Constitutions recognize that it is the work of the whole community to aid in the process of formation. However, «special responsibility is committed to Major Superiors,

---

14 *Constitutiones*, no. 204: «Nobis igitur omnibus, praesertim quibus iuvenum Fratrum cura committitur, momentum institutionis cordi esse debet...» See also *Const.* nn. 151, 159, 188; chapter 9, nn. 200-239, is entirely devoted to the theme of formation of members of the Order.

15 The Constitutions specify that the house or houses of novitiate are to be designated by the Prior General with the consent of his Council (no. 229). All other houses of formation would be established in accordance with Provincial Statutes or by decision of the Major Superior and his Council.

to local Superiors, and to [the] Director [of formation] or the Formation Team, with due regard for the principle of subsidiarity and for the general laws of the Church and the Order.»[16]

Regarding the relationship between the Director of Formation and the local Prior, as well as between the Formation Team (if one has been established) and the rest of the community, the Province Statutes are to make any appropriate or necessary determinations. The Prior and the Director or Formation Team should work together in the task of formation «with tranquility and fraternal understanding, so that they, along with the other Brothers of the Community and the young men, may form a united Augustinian family which corresponds to the prayer of the Lord: 'That they may be one',[17] and which offers encouragement to the young men in their vocation.»[18]

The Constitutions throughout this chapter on formation draw frequently from the Vatican Council Decree on the training of priests, *Optatam totius*, as a principal source. While this decree is primarily directed toward the formation of priests in diocesan seminaries, it is also to be taken into account by religious superiors in the formation of members who will be ordained to

---

[16] *Constitutiones*, no. 237: «Quamvis iuvenum efformatio ad totam pertineat Communitatem, specialis tamen institutionis cura committitur Superioribus Maioribus, Superioribus Localibus et eorum Magistro vel formationis Coetui, servato principio subsidiaritatis et iuxta leges generales Ecclesiae et Ordinis...»

[17] John 17:11.

[18] *Constitutiones*, no. 238: «Statuta Provincialia in unaquaque Provincia relationes definient quae dari debent inter Magistrum vel Coetum Formationis et Priorem aliosque Fratres Communitatis. Prior et Magister vel Coetus Formationis aequo animo et fraterna comprehensione in hunc laborem enixe incumbant, ut inter semetipsos aliosque Fratres Communitatis simul cum iuvenibus eam Familiam augustinianam constituant quae Domini orationi 'ut sint unum' (Io. 17,11) respondeat et iuvenibus propriae vocationis gaudium nutriat.» (cf. OT, no. 5).

the priesthood.[19] One of the principles insisted upon in *Optatam totius* is that superiors of seminaries (and, consequently, religious houses of formation) must be chosen from among the best men available, because of the importance of the work which they are asked to perform. Already, Pope Pius XI, in his encyclical letter *Ad catholici sacerdotii*, had stated:

> In the first place let careful choice be made of superiors and professors. Give these sacred colleges priests of the greatest virtue, and do not hesitate to withdraw them from tasks which seem indeed to be of greater importance, but which cannot be compared with this supremely important matter, the place of which nothing else can supply.[20]

While this principle applies even more to the choosing of the Director of Formation, and members of a formation team, it is evident and extremely important that those men who are chosen to be Priors in houses of formation be well-qualified for such a position. *Optatam totius* repeats this principle, and then goes on to make two additional considerations regarding superiors of formation houses. They should receive special training and have suitable pastoral experience, and secondly, they «should be keenly aware of the extent to which their mental outlook and conduct affects

---

19 The opening paragraph of the Decree states: «Quae sacerdotalis conformatio ob ipsam catholici sacerdotii unitatem, omnibus sacerdotibus utriusque cleri et cuiusvis ritus necessaria est; ideoque haec praescripta, quae clerum diocesanum directe respiciunt, congrua congruis referenda, omnibus accommodanda sunt.» The words «utriusque cleri» refer to the secular and the «regular» clergy, so that training of religious for the priesthood is directly intended. (OT, Prooemium).

20 PIUS XI, Litt. Encycl. *Ad catholici sacerdotii*, December 20, 1935, AAS 28(1936)5-53. «Diligens imprimis esto moderatorum magistrorumque delectus atque illius, peculiari modo, cui gravissimum concredatur officium sacerdotalis animorum conformationis. Sacris eiusmodi conlegiis sacerdotes tribuite maxima virtute ornatos; neque gravemini eos a muneribus abstrahere, specie quidem maioris ponderis, quae tamen cum hac capitali re, cuius partes nulla alia susceperit, comparari nequeunt» (p. 37).

the formation of their students.»[21] No one should underestimate the value of the presence of a well-prepared superior in a house of formation, nor the damage that can be done by a Prior who, even though he may have good intentions, is incapable of carrying out the responsibilities that are entrusted to him as superior of a formation community.

The Constitutions leave to the Provincial Statutes the determination of the relationship between the Director of Formation and the local Prior,[22] since the context in which formation programs are placed varies greatly from province to province. There are those communities which are established with the single purpose of being houses of formation, while in other cases the Director of Formation and students form just a small part of the community. Thus, the relationship between the Prior and the Director, the extent to which the Prior might be directly involved in the formation process, and even the relationship between the formation program and the rest of the community will have to be determined by each Province depending on the given situation, always keeping in mind the principle of subsidiarity.

In communities which serve as houses of formation, the judgment of the House Chapter is requested before approval of a candidate for entrance to the novitiate, as well as for advancement to the various stages of formation in the Order.[23] If the Provincial

---

21 OT, no. 5: «Cum alumnorum institutio et a sapientibus legibus et maxime quidem ab idoneis educatoribus pendeat, Seminariorum moderatores et magistri ex optimis viris seligantur atque solida doctrina, congrua experientia pastorali et peculiari institutione spirituali et paedagogica diligenter praeparentur... Moderatores vero et magistri persentiant quantopere a suipsorum cogitandi agendique ratione pendeat alumnorum formationis exitus ...»

22 *Constitutiones*, no. 238 (See footnote, no. 18).

23 *Constitutiones*, no. 227: «Admissio candidatorum ad tempus probationis, ad Novitiatum et ad professionem tum annualem tum sollemnem ad Superiorem Maiorem pertinet de consensu sui Consilii, habita ratione suffragii Capituli Localis,

Statutes so determine, a secret canvassing of the members of the community who do not yet have active voice may also be done.[24] The Prior, as the one who convenes and directs the House Chapter, should keep in mind his responsibility in giving these issues their due importance. Depending upon what is stipulated in the Province Statutes, the Prior may also have the responsibility for the «secret canvassing» which can be made among the members of the community who do not have active voice in the Chapter.

b) Ongoing formation

Although the period of initial formation concludes with the profession of solemn vows, or for those Brothers who are clerical candidates, with the completion of their theological program,[25] Augustinians are expected to continue their personal formation for their own benefit as well as for the good of the apostolate and the community.

> Throughout their entire life religious are to continue carefully their own spiritual, doctrinal, and practical formation, and

---

ubi candidati degunt, et praesertim, Coetus Formationis, si iuxta Statuta Provincialia adest . . .» This topic will be given further consideration in Chapter Six, in the section dealing with the House Chapter.

24 *Constitutiones*, no. 227: « . . . Suffragio Capituli et Coetus Formationis praecedere potest, iuxta Statuta Provincialia, exploratio secreta, omnino consultiva, Fratrum qui in eadem Domo commorantur et vocem activam nondum habent.» The English translation of this last sentence omits «iuxta Statuta Provincialia», according to the Province Statutes; it is an omission which is significant. A Province may decide that such a canvassing should not be done; or that it must be done, specifying a particular method or a particular person (the Director of Formation or the Prior, for example) responsible for gathering the opinions of those concerned.

25 *Constitutiones*, no. 231: «Tempus probationis professione sollemni absolvitur . . .» No. 232: «Formatio autem illorum qui ad sacerdotium contendunt amplectitur etiam aspectus specifice sacerdotales et, quamvis praecedat professio sollemnis, protrahitur usque ad absolutum curriculum theologicum . . .»

superiors are to provide them with the resources and time to do this.[26]

The source of this canon is found in *Perfectae caritatis*.[27] In addition, *Mutuae relationes* dedicates an entire chapter to the topic of formation, dealing with the theme in a broad enough way to include both initial and ongoing formation. Here again, religious superiors are given the task of directing and encouraging the participation of religious in programs which will be of benefit to the individual in the perseverance in his vocation, for the institute and for the service of the needs of the Church.[28] The document goes on to give certain criteria for the evaluation of studies that might be chosen as part of a continuing education/formation program:

> The choice of these studies should be prompted not by a misdirected desire for self-fulfillment with a view to achieving personal ends, but with the sole intention of meeting the apostolic commitments of the religious family itself, in the context of the needs of the Church.[29]

---

[26] Can. 661: «Per totam vitam religiosi formationem suam spiritualem, doctrinalem et practicam sedulo prosequantur; Superiores autem eis adiumenta et tempus ad hoc procurent.»

[27] PC, no. 18c: «Per totam autem vitam sodales intendant hanc culturam spiritualem, doctrinalem et technicam sedulo perficere, et Superiores, pro viribus, opportunitatem, adiumenta et tempus ad hoc eis procurent.»

[28] MR, no. 26: «Superiores Religiosi omni studio curent, ut suos confratres et consorores fideliter perseverent in propria vocatione. Congruas quoque foveant accommodationes culturalibus, socialibus et oeconomicis condicionibus iuxta temporum exigentias, providentes tamen, ne ullo modo ad mores religiosae consecrationi contrarios deferantur. Culturales autem accommodationes et confratrum studia alicuius specializationis versentur in materiis proprie coniunctis cum specifica Instituti vocatione, eademque praefiniantur non quasi quaedam false intellectae sui ipsius expressiones, ita ut fines personales obtineantur, sed ut vere ad exigentias apostolicorum propositorum ipsius Religiosae Familiae respondere valeant in harmonia cum Ecclesiae necessitatibus.»

[29] Ibid.

> In promoting ongoing formation of religious, it is important to insist on the witness of poverty and the service of the most deprived. Care should also be taken that, through a renewed spirit of obedience and chastity, communities may be clear signs of fraternal love and unity.[30]
>
> In Institutes of the active life, where the apostolate constitutes an essential element of their religious life, the apostolate must be duly emphasized in both initial and ongoing formation.[31]

While the local Prior will not usually be the one to organize programs of ongoing formation, he will be called upon to aid in the choice of various options that might be available; such a decision should be based upon, in addition to the particular needs of the individual concerned, certain objective criteria such as the guidelines given in *Mutuae relationes*. He may, furthermore, have to encourage some Brothers to consider participation in a program of theological or pastoral updating, in order to aid that member in the fulfillment of his pastoral work. While a decision asking a somewhat reluctant religious to participate in a program of ongoing formation would usually come from the provincial level, it is the local Prior who is closest to the individual and who therefore may have to initiate such a proposal.

Apart from structured programs of continuing education or ongoing formation, there are several other resources which the Prior should utilize in facilitating the «spiritual, doctrinal and

---

[30] MR, no. 27: «Dum Religiosorum et Religiosarum continua formatio promovetur, insistendum est in renovando testimonio paupertatis et servitii erga indigentiores; atque prospiciendum quoque est, ut in renovata oboedientia et castitate Communitates clarum fiant signum amoris fraternitatis atque unitatis.»

[31] Ibid.: «In Institutis vitae activae, in quibus tamquam elementum essentiale vitae religiosae apostolatus exstat (cf. PC 8; AG 25), in ipsa evolvenda formatione, sive initiali sive continua, idem apostolatus in congruam lucem proferatur.»

practical formation»[32] of the community members. Obviously, in terms of Augustinian spirituality the Rule and Constitutions (especially those sections dealing with the spirituality of the Order) should be read regularly; the Prior or House Chapter could decide when and in what context this would best be done. There are, furthermore, the documents published by the Holy See and by the bishops' conferences. In this regard, the Prior has a responsibility to make the documents of the Apostolic See known and available to the community:

> The moderators of every institute are to promote knowledge of the documents of the Holy See which affect members entrusted to them and be concerned about their observance of them.[33]

Another resource that might be all too often overlooked can frequently be found among the members of the community itself. Brothers who have skills in a particular area that could be of benefit to the community should be encouraged to «share with others all the fruits of their intellectual labor.»[34] A Prior

---

32 Can. 661 (See footnote no. 26).

33 Can. 592, §2: «Cuiuslibet instituti Moderatores promoveant notitiam documentorum Sanctae Sedis, quae sodales sibi concreditos respiciunt, eorumque observantiam curent.» Compare this canon to Canon 32 of the *Schema Canonum de Institutis Vitae Consecratae per Professionem Consilium Evangelicorum* (1977). As in the new Code, the canon came under the section covering matters common to all Institutes of consecrated life. In the 1977 Schema, all references to «superiors» were made using the word «moderator», whereas in the 1980 Schema and in the new Code, the word «superior» was once again used. «Moderator» is used only in reference to the «supremus Moderator», as in can. 592, §1. On the other hand, where reference is made to all superiors, such as in can. 596, the word «superior» is used. Thus, the use of moderator here in 592, §2 could lead one to conclude that it refers only to the supreme moderator of an institute, whereas by the context of the canon, and in light of its development (as in the Schema of 1977), it is evident that the canon refers to superiors at any level. The same is true in light of MR, no. 29.

34 *Constitutiones*, no. 154: «Curent Superiores vitam in Domo, Provincia vel Ordine ita regere, ut scientia peritorum ad bonum commune sponte verti possit et ut Fratres omnes laboris intellectualis fructus libenter cum aliis communicent.»

should, in addition, make known to the community the various workshops, conferences, etc., that are being offered in the diocese, or elsewhere, so that people who are interested will be able to participate and profit from the many resources that are available. It may also be advantageous to invite experts in a given field to come to speak to the community about subjects that could benefit the group as a whole. All of these resources will contribute to an environment which fosters the ongoing formation that is vital in the life of members of the consecrated life.

3. Preaching the Word of God

«Superiors are to nourish the members of their community with the food of the Word of God.»[35] While reference to the office of preaching the Gospel in the Constitutions is primarily reserved to those «external» apostolic activities in which priests and deacons are involved,[36] the phrase of canon 619 quoted above makes it clear that Priors have a responsibility to provide their community with opportunities to reflect upon, to be nourished by, the Word of God. Although this can be done in many different ways, the Prior's role as teacher, magister, in the community should include the dimension of preaching, of offering his own reflections on the Scriptures, to the members of his community. Further support for this understanding of the Prior's role is offered by canon 757: « . . . those entrusted with the care of souls are especially bound [to the ministry of the divine Word] as regards the people entrusted

---

35 Canon 619: « . . . [Superiores] igitur nutriant sodales frequenti verbi Dei pabulo . . . » For the entire text of the canon, see chapter one, footnote 34, pp. 22-23.

36 Cf. for example, *Constitutiones*, nn. 166, 167, 218.

to them.»³⁷ Since it is the Word of God which first brings people together into the Christian family,³⁸ it is fitting and even necessary that a principal source of the unity in Augustinian life be found in a profound and frequent listening to the Word of God and to preaching which aids the members of the community to be strengthened in their vocation and in their apostolic work. Obviously it is not only the Prior who can contribute in such a manner. Other members of the community as well as guest-homilists can certainly be encouraged to aid the community in an ever-deepening appreciation of the nourishment that is offered by the Scriptures.

Another aspect related to the question of preaching has to do with the «faculties» to preach. The legislation in this regard has been considerably simplified in the new Code. Instead of a rather complicated regulation regarding the necessary faculties to preach as found in the Old Code,³⁹ there is a much more straightforward approach in the new Code to this aspect of the Church's teaching function.

The fundamental presupposition of the new Code is the exact opposite of that of the old:

---

37 Can. 757: «Presbyterorum, qui quidem episcoporum cooperatores sunt, proprium est Evangelium Dei annuntiare; praesertim hoc officio tenentur, quoad populum sibi commissum, parochi aliique quibus cura animarum concreditur . . . » For a thorough treatment of the Prior's role in the care of souls, see Chapter 5.

38 Cf. can. 762: «Cum Dei populus primum coadunetur verbo Dei vivi . . . »

39 In the old Code, this legislation was found in cann. 1337-1348. The fundamental rule was found in can. 1328: «Nemini ministerium praedicationis licet exercere, nisi a legitimo Superiore missionem receperit, facultate peculiariter data, vel officio collato, cui ex sacris canonibus praedicandi munus inhaereat.» In most cases, the local ordinary granted the faculties (v. can. 1337), and in the case of exempt religious, it was the competent religious superior who would grant the authority (v. can. 1338, §1). If, however, there were other factors involved (preaching to the people, to cloistered nuns, etc.), permission was to be received both from the local ordinary and from the competent religious superior (cf. v. can. 1338, §§2,3). For the Augustinian Order, a local Superior was competent to grant the faculties for his community (cf. *Constitutiones* [1926] nn. 1093, 1097).

With due regard for the prescription of can. 765, presbyters and deacons possess the faculty to preach everywhere, to be exercised with at least the presumed consent of the rector of the church, unless that faculty has been restricted or taken away by the competent ordinary or unless express permission is required by particular law.[40]

There is, thus, much less relevance to the fact that a local Superior would have the authority to grant faculties for preaching to members of his community. However, the restriction placed by the above canon on the general recognition of preaching faculties for all priests and deacons is of importance. Canon 765 states:

> Preaching to religious in their churches or oratories requires the permission of the superior who is competent in accord with the norm of the constitutions.[41]

Although the Order's Constitutions do not specify the competent superior in matters of preaching faculties, regarding the granting or denying of such permission in the local community, the Prior is certainly competent. Such a conclusion can be based upon the following factors: 1) the local Prior enjoys the ordinary power of governance within the community;[42] 2) he is charged with the care of the brothers entrusted to him,[43] in a similar way as

---

40 Can. 764: «Salvo praescripto can. 765, facultate ubique praedicandi, de consensu saltem praesumpto rectoris ecclesiae exercenda, gaudent presbyteri et diaconi, nisi ab Ordinario competenti eadem facultas restricta fuerit aut sublata, aut lege particulari licentia expressa requiratur.»

41 Can. 765: «Ad praedicandum religiosis in eorum ecclesiis vel oratoriis licentia requiritur Superioris ad normam constitutionum competentis.»

42 Can. 596, §2: «In institutis autem religiosis clericalibus iuris pontificii pollent insuper potestate ecclesiastica regiminis pro foro tam externo quam interno.» Refer to the discussion on this point, pp. 51 ss.

43 Cf. cann. 618-619. See also the discussion on the care of souls, chapter five, pp. 114-117.

are pastors and rectors of churches, who are responsible for the preaching done within the context of their pastoral responsibility;[44] 4) since the Constitutions do not specify any limitation on who the competent superior is in granting the permission indicated in canon 765, the local Prior as a legitimate superior is competent to grant or deny the authorization.[45]

4. In the apostolate

While the Prior's ministry is frequently centered primarily around the «internal» workings of a community, his office is also connected in some way to the apostolic activity of the community. Given the fact that the Order is by nature apostolic,[46] there is no way that a total separation can be made between the life of the community and the ministerial work which the members of the community perform. Even if the Prior himself has no direct involvement in the apostolic work of some of the community members, the nature of his ministry is such that he must in some way aid these members in their faithful and dedicated fulfillment of the mission to preach

---

44 Can. 757: «Presbyterorum, qui quidem Episcoporum cooperatores sunt, proprium est Evangelium Dei annuntiare; praesertim hoc officio tenentur, quoad populum sibi commissum, parochi aliique quibus cura animarum concreditur . . . » While there are obviously many differences between the ministry of a pastor in a parish and that of the Prior in the community, the very reason for the prescription of canon 765 is to provide the superior with the authority to watch over the ministry of the Word which is carried out in the given community.

45 Such interpretation is based upon the principles established in canons 17-19. In this particular case, reference is made to parallel situations in the law (between the pastor and the Prior, due to the common ministry of the «care of souls»), as well as to the purpose and circumstances of the law. The former Constitutions (1926) also gave the authority of determining preaching faculties in certain cases to the local Prior. Cf. nn. 1093ss.

46 *Constitutiones*, no. 10: «Religio enim nostra est fraternitatis apostolicae seu Communitas Fratrum, quae cum populo Dei vivit, praebens exemplum, testimonium nempe caritatis et paupertatis evangelicae et sanam doctrinam.»

the Word. In the eighth chapter of the Constitutions, «Apostolic Activity», emphasis is placed on this point:

> Superiors should willingly encourage the zeal of all the Brethren, accept their initiatives with understanding, direct them in such a way as to permit as much true freedom as may be judged necessary for fulfilling their apostolic work, and offer good example by their own devotion to work.[47]

At the same time, however, a Prior must be cautious not to interfere in areas of responsibility which have been entrusted to other members of the community. One of the most usual examples where there exists a fairly clear separation in responsibilities would be that of the parish apostolate. In addition to the Prior of the community, there is frequently a different member of the house who is named as Pastor. Here again, the Constitutions make a specific recommendation:

> Provincial Statutes should lay down norms whereby common life and the offices of Prior and Pastor are so harmonized with the demands of pastoral care that they mutually complement one another.[48]

Such harmonization will be a great aid to both the Prior and the Pastor, and it will, furthermore, contribute significantly to the life of the community and to the Brothers' effective and fruitful ministry in the apostolate.

---

[47] *Constitutiones*, no. 161, a: «Superiores libenter foveant omnium Fratrum zelum eorumque incepta benevole accipiant et ita moderentur, ut veram eis, quantum oportet, libertatem tribuant in opere apostolico exsequendo; ipsi autem suo impenso labore bonum exemplum praebeant.»

[48] *Constitutiones*, no. 177: «Statuta provincialia normas ferant quibus vita communis et officium Prioris et Parochi cum exigentiis curae pastoralis ita harmonice ordinentur ut sese mutuo compleant.»

There are other contexts, however, where the Prior may have a more direct role in the direction or organization of the community's apostolic activity. For example, in many communities where there is a church available for public worship, the Prior is at the same time Rector of the Church. In these cases, the Code makes several provisions which regard this aspect of the superior's ministry as teacher of the Word of God. Regarding preaching at Mass, canon 767 places the following responsibilities on the Rector of a church:

> Whenever a congregation is present a homily is to be given at all Sunday Masses and at Masses celebrated on holy days of obligation; it cannot be omitted without a serious reason.
>
> If a sufficient number of people are present it is strongly recommended that a homily also be given at Masses celebrated during the week, especially during Advent or Lent or on the occasion of some feast day or time of mourning.
>
> It is the duty of the pastor or the rector of a church to see to it that these prescriptions are conscientiously observed.[49]

And, while keeping in mind the principle of subsidiarity,[50] the Prior also has a responsibility to supervise the proper catechetical training which is given in the community's apostolic work:

---

49 Can. 767, §2: «In omnibus Missis diebus dominicis et festis de praecepto, quae concursu populi celebrantur, homilia habenda est nec omitti potest nisi gravi de c ausa.». §3: «Valde commendatur ut, si sufficiens detur populi concursus, homilia habeatur etiam in Missis quae infra hebdomadam, praesertim tempore adventus et quadragesimae aut occasione alicuius festi vel luctuosi eventus celebrentur.» §4: «Parochi aut ecclesiae rectoris est curare ut haec praescripta religiose serventur.»

50 Simply put, the principle of subsidiarity states that decisions should be made at the lowest appropriate level. The word «appropriate» here is obviously very important, for there are certain decisions which by their very nature must be made by superiors, or major superiors, and others which ought be left to the individual involved in the given situation.

Superiors of religious institutes and of societies of apostolic life are to see to it that catechetical formation is diligently imparted in their churches, schools and in other works entrusted to them in any manner.[51]

5. Lay fraternities

Among the various groups which make up the entire Augustinian family,[52] there are associations of laity who, while living a secular life, wish to follow more closely the Augustinian spirit of Christian living.

> Accordingly, a formation imbued with the Augustinian spirit should be given to the members of these Fraternities, along with a solid doctrinal instruction, which is to be continually perfected. This instruction should be theological, ethical, and social, in keeping with differences of age, state of life and natural talents, and should be imparted by selected Brothers.[53]

There are also societies of groups of the faithful, who, «imbued with the love of St. Augustine and desirous of imitating him, have

---

51 Can. 778: «Curent Superiores religiosi et societatum vitae apostolicae ut in suis ecclesiis, scholis aliisve operibus sibi quoquo modo concreditis, catechetica institutio sedulo impertiatur.»

52 Cf. Chpt. 3 of the Constitutions, entitled, *«The Extent of the Entire Augustinian Family»*. In addition to the men who make solemn vows, there are sisters of contemplative life, religious congregations and lay fraternities, and the lay societies.

53 *Constitutiones*, no. 48: «... Proinde harum Fraternitatum sodales imbui debent formatione spiritu augustiniano perfusa, quae solida institutione doctrinali, et quidem theologica, ethica atque sociali, pro eorum aetate, condicione et ingenio, Fratribus opportune selectis semper perficienda est...»

gathered together in St. Augustine Societies without the duties and obligations of the other branches of the Order.»[54]

Depending upon the statutes of these groups, and upon the way in which they are structured, it may frequently be the case that these groups are particularly associated to a specific local community of the Order. Especially in these cases, the local Prior should seek to insure that these groups receive the spiritual formation which is rightfully owed them by the Order. The Code places this responsibility upon the whole Order,[55] but it is only logical that, unless other specific provisions are made, the local Prior take it upon himself to see to it that these groups of the Augustinian family are given the opportunity to deepen the spirit of following St. Augustine in their Christian lives.

---

54 *Constitutiones*, no. 49: «Quarta tandem Ordinis pars iis fidelibus efformatur qui S.P. Augustini amore flagrantes eumque imitari cupientes sine officiis et obligationibus aliarum partium Ordinis, in Societates Sancti Augustini coaluerunt.»

55 Can. 677, §2: «Instituta autem, si quas habeant associationes christifidelium sibi coniunctas, speciali cura adiuvent, ut genuino spiritu suae familiae imbuantur.»

CHAPTER FIVE

THE MUNUS SANCTIFICANDI

The office of Prior is one of service, and one of the most important things that he can offer to his community is living witness to the call of holiness. The juridical dimension of a superior's authority must never become predominant over the spiritual role which he is asked to fulfill. Nor must temporal administration be the primary concern of a Prior. The parallel of his role to that of Christ in the Church includes the office of sanctifying those people to whom he is called to serve. The superior, called to minister not only to the community as a whole, but also to the individual religious, becomes an instrument, a «sacrament», of the mysteries of God's love to the community. Thus, the words of St. Paul could well be those of any religious superior: «Men should regard us as servants of Christ and administrators of the mysteries of God.»[1]

Mutuae relationes expresses the particular aspects which pertain to this dimension of the Superior's authority: the Superior has a special responsibility to work for the perfection of the life of charity according to the particular nature of the given institute.[2]

---

1 1 Cor. 4:1. Cf. E. GAMBARI, *Consacrati e inviati* (Milano: Ed. Ancora, 1979), p. 549.

2 MR 13, b: «Quoad munus sanctificandi: Superiores peculiarem competentiam atque mandatum habent perficiendi, distinctis tamen muneribus, in iis quae ad incrementum vitae caritatis secundum Instituti propositum spectant...»

CHAPTER FIVE

In order better to analyze the particular responsibilities which are entrusted to the local Prior, this chapter will first give consideration to the special duty which the Prior has regarding spiritual care for the members of the community. Subsequently, some specific questions related to the prayer life of the community, celebration of the Eucharist and administration of the other sacraments will be presented.

1. The «Cura animarum»

Perfectae caritatis, the Second Vatican Council's decree on the renewal of religious life, in discussing the role of the superior states: «For his part, as one who will render an account for the souls entrusted to him,[3] each superior should himself be docile to God's will in the exercise of his office . . . »[4] As already mentioned in Chapter One,[5] this paragraph of *Perfectae caritatis* has been utilized as the principal source of canon 618 of the new Code. There was, however, an omission of the words «rationem pro animabus sibi commissis reddituri». Nevertheless, the following canon does speak of "the members entrusted to the superior."[6] This concept of having responsibility for the spiritual wellbeing of the members of the community can be paralleled to, and probably made equivalent to the concept of the *cura animarum*, the care of

---

3 Cf. Hebrews 13:17.

4 PC, no. 14c: «Superiores vero, rationem pro animabus sibi commissis reddituri, voluntati Dei in munere explendo dociles . . . »

5 See pp. 14-15. Canon 618 reads: «Superiores in spiritu servitii suam potestatem a Deo per ministerium Ecclesiae receptam exerceant. Voluntati igitur Dei in munere explendo dociles, ipsi subditos regant uti filios Dei, ac promoventes cum reverentia personae humanae illorum voluntariam oboedientiam, libenter eos audiant necnon eorum conspirationem in bonum instituti et Ecclesiae foveant, firma tamen ipsorum auctoritate decernendi et praecipiendi quae agenda sunt.»

6 Can. 619: «Superiores suo officio sedulo incumbant et una cum sodalibus sibi commissis studeant aedificare fraternam in Christo communitatem . . . »

souls. Such a conclusion is based upon several factors. Although the expression is not found in the current Constitutions, and it is found only once in the entire section of the new Code that deals with religious institutes, and there in a context of works of the apostolate,[7] there is an explicit reference made to the *cura animarum* in one of the sources used in writing the Constitutions. The Constitutions affirm «that the Superior is a Brother whose duty it is to govern as sons of God the Brethren whose care is entrusted to him by the Order.»[8] This statement is then footnoted, making reference to the earliest known Constitutions of the Order, in which it is expressly stated that the Prior has been entrusted with the *cura animarum* of his subjects.[9] The 1926 Constitutions likewise give explicit recognition to this aspect of the Prior's ministry.[10] These factors, coupled with a careful reading of the Code, especially of canons 618 and 619, support the conclusion that the Prior is indeed entrusted with a certain responsibility for the spiritual well-being of the members of his community. The juridical concept of the *cura animarum* is itself worthy of a thorough study, something which cannot be done here.[11] There are, nevertheless, a couple of important aspects of the Prior's ministry which can be studied

---

7 Cf. can. 678, §1: «Religiosi subsunt potestati Episcoporum, quos devoto obsequio ac reverentia prosequi tenentur, in iis quae curam animarum, exercitium publicum cultus divini et alia apostolatus opera respiciunt.» The second and third paragraphs of this canon also speak of works of the apostolate.

8 *Constitutiones*, no. 14: «Superior proinde Frater est ad quem pertinet Fratres, quorum cura ei ab Ordine est commissa, qua filios Dei regere, eiusque administratio Capitulo submittitur ad vitam communitariam efficaciorem reddendam . . . »

9 *Constitutiones* (1290), c. 31, no. 231: «Prior quoque cura animarum subditorum suorum ab Ordine est commissa et pro quibus Deo debet reddere rationem, inter cetera, suos subditos ad humilitatem, obedientiam, paupertatem et castitatem integram servendam frequenter hortetur et moneat.»

10 Cf., for example, *Constitutiones* (1926), no. 646.

11 The expression is found in the Code numerous times: cf. cann. 150,151,463, §1,8°;678, §1; 738, §2;757;771, §2;922;986, §1; 1003, §2. See also, C. FORCHIA, *La cura d'anime come istituto giuridico* (Roma: Pont. Univ. Gregoriana, 1956).

through a consideration of this concept, and which highlight the rather serious responsibility taken on by a Prior. To begin, it is essential to avoid any misunderstanding of the terminology used. It would be a mistake to attribute to the use of the word *anima* a dualistic interpretation which divides the soul from the body. In the adaptation of the terminology found in the Constitutions, eliminating the expression *cura animarum*, but retaining the same concept, it is conceivable that it is this very understanding which led to the change. The *cura animarum* is a concern for the salvation of the human person.[12] The Prior receives, is entrusted with, the care of those men who are members of that particular community. But in speaking of *cura animarum* an extremely important reality is being stressed which could otherwise be forgotten. The Prior is not primarily concerned with the material necessities of the house and those who live there. (This is primarily the duty of the treasurer.[13]) The Prior's responsibility has a spiritual dimension, or better, has its foundation within the context of caring for the quality of the religious life of the Augustinians living in that community. Superiors have the care of the Brothers, «especially in spiritual matters».[14] Thus, questions of the personal holiness of the Brothers, of the recognition and respect for each man's dignity and worth, of effectiveness in the apostolate all carry with them aspects which demand the interest and concern of the Prior.

---

12 The same kind of understanding, and avoidance of a tendency towards dualism, can be found in, for example, changes made in the liturgy. The prayer which the priest says before receiving communion: in the old Missale Romanum, «Corpus Domini Nostri Jesu Christi custodiat *animam meam* in vitam aeternam», whereas in the reformed Vatican II liturgy: «Corpus Christi custodiat *me* in vitam aeternam.»

13 *Constitutiones*, no. 321: «Oeconomus: Ipsius est bonorum Domus accurata administratio, iuxta normas nn. 486-499, sub moderamine Prioris . . . »

14 *Constitutiones*, no. 504: «Superiores vero, quibus Fratrum singularis cura, praesertim spiritualis, committitur quique tamquam filios ac Fratres eos diligere debent . . . »

There is, too, another dimension to this aspect of the Prior's role. *Perfectae caritatis*, as well as the Constitutions, make the affirmation that the Prior is a trustee, one who cares for something in the name of the other. In this respect, the Prior represents the Order, for it is the Order that gives him his charge as superior of the community.[15] And still much more fundamental, the Prior is acting in the place of Christ. Thus, his is a responsibility not to be at all underestimated. An important principle, from a juridical point of view as well as from the spiritual, is not at all out of place in a discussion of the Prior's duty: *suprema lex salus animarum*.[16]

The Prior fulfills his office of sanctifying in a variety of ways within the community, as well as in his involvement in the apostolic work of the community. His concern for the prayer life of the community and for the celebration of the sacraments would be the principal areas in which he exercises the sanctifying office. The Constitutions thoroughly outline and emphasize the importance of sacramental worship, as well as of common and individual prayer. It is not necessary to repeat here all of what is found in Chapter five of the Constitutions, «Life with God».[17] There are, however, some particular numbers which refer directly to the Prior, and which must be considered as they refer directly to his responsibility within the community. And too, a section will be included at the end of this chapter, which deals with the care of the sick, both in terms of temporal and spiritual needs.

---

15 *Constitutiones*, no. 14; cf. footnote 8. p. 115.

16 This is included as well in the last canon of the new Code, can. 1752: «... et prae oculis habita salute animarum, quae in Ecclesia suprema semper lex esse debet.»

17 *Constitutiones, Caput V, «De conversatione cum Deo»*.

2. Prayer life of the community

«Since by reason of our religious profession we are dedicated to the service and honor of God under a new title, it is fitting that our lives be related to His worship in a special manner. Our religious profession calls us, therefore, to a special responsibility for prayer and celebration of the liturgy of the Church.»[18] Pope Paul VI spoke of religious as being called «specialists in prayer».[19] Today, too, there are many people who are searching for guidance in developing their own prayer life. Frequently they come looking for spiritual direction and help in developing this aspect of their faith. Thus, the importance of individual and common prayer on the part of Augustinians (and all religious) is paramount.

Once again, the Prior is called upon to be a model to those whom he serves as well as an aid in fostering this aspect of the life of the community.[20] The vitality of the community's life together will often times hinge on this very aspect. While each Prior will have his own individual style of leadership, and will, therefore, have to develop the particular way in which he can best carry out this task, there can be no doubt as to the expectations which are placed on the local Prior in this regard. By committing himself and the whole community to developing life with Christ through prayer, one more easily arrives at a fruitful and authentic love and service of one's neighbor.[21]

---

18 *Constitutiones*, no. 82: «Quia vi professionis religiosae Dei servitio et honori mancipamur novo titulo, congruum est ut vita nostra ad Eius cultum speciali modo referatur. Ideo professio nostra religiosa peculiarem in nobis obligationem gignit orationi instandi et Ecclesiae sacram liturgiam celebrandi.»

19 PP. PAUL VI, Discourse, October 28, 1966: AAS 58 (1966)1155-1162.

20 Cf. *Constitutiones*, no. 311: «Sua erga Dei voluntatem oboedientia atque fidelitate, gregis sibi commissi forma factus ex animo (cf. 1 Petr. 5,3) ... » See also can. 619.

21 PC, no. 6: «Ita in mensa divinae Legis et sacri altaris refecti Christi membra fraterne ament, pastores spiritu filiali revereantur atque diligant; magis magisque vivant et sentiant cum Ecclesia eiusque missioni totaliter se devoveant.»

Besides the celebration of the Eucharist, the principal moments of the community's prayer life as presented in the Constitutions are the Liturgy of the Hours, days of recollection, and the annual retreat. In addition, the Constitutions emphasize the importance of the formation and development of the individual's spiritual life.

a) Liturgy of the Hours

«Because of our particular relationship to the example of the early Christian community,[22] Augustinians are called in a special way to common prayer. In this type of prayer we give expression to the very essence of the Church as community . . . »[23] The Liturgy of the Hours is the primary way in which the Order exercises this aspect of its prayer life. The Prayer of the Church, the way in which the Church responds to the exhortation of Christ to «pray without ceasing,»[24] is an expression of the unity of the entire Church.

Although a certain moment of attention ought to be given to the obligation to pray the Liturgy of the Hours, very little will be said here so as not to distract too greatly from the central theme of the Prior's role in guiding the prayer life of the community.[25] Nevertheless, since the Prior is entrusted in a special way with animating the prayer life of the community, the following paragraphs of the Constitutions are included here:

---

[22] Cf. Acts 4:32; *Regula*, c. 1.

[23] *Constitutiones*, no. 95: «Quia exemplum primaevae Communitatis christianae modo singulari ad vitam nostram attinet, Augustinenses titulo speciali ad orationem communitariam vocamur. Hac oratione intimam essentiam Ecclesiae exprimimus, quae Communitas est . . . »

[24] Cf. Luke 18:1; *Inst. gen. de Liturgia Horarum*, nn. 9-10.

[25] For a clearer understanding of the Church's teaching as regards the Liturgy of the Hours, the following should be consulted: *Institutio generalis de Liturgia Horarum*, S. Cong. pro Culto Divino, February 2, 1971: Prot. no. 165/71. It is found in English translation in Vol. 1 of the *Liturgy of the Hours* (New York: Catholic Book Publishing Co., 1975). See especially nos. 29, 37, 40. Also can. 663.

> Because the Liturgy of the Hours is not only a source of piety and nourishment for personal prayer, but also offers no small aid to strengthening and demonstrating unity and harmony, it is to be considered the common prayer of all the Brothers . . . [26]
>
> In every community where the full Office is not recited, due importance is to be given to morning and evening prayer. For such communities, the Prior General, with the consent of his Council, is to issue general norms, whose application to particular cases is committed to the Prior Provincial or Viceprovincial.[27]

The Prior General published these norms as required by the Constitutions, and in these major emphasis was placed on the importance of daily community prayer, on the desire that at least morning and evening prayer be celebrated in common, and upon the responsibility of the Provincial or Viceprovincial in seeking to implement these norms.[28]

The Prior too should concern himself with the implementation of these guidelines, and he should inspire within the community the realization that, by praying the Liturgy of the Hours, the community is participating in the whole Church's praying together, and it is contributing to a sign and a cause of the building of unity.

---

26 *Constitutiones*, no. 96: «Liturgia Horarum, quia non solum fons est pietatis et nutrimentum orationis personalis, sed et magnum subsidium praebet ad unitatem et concordiam firmandam atque exhibendam, habenda est velut communis omnium Fratrum oratio . . . »

27 *Constitutiones*, no. 97: «In omnibus Communitatibus, ubi integrum Officium non recitatur, debitum momentum tribuatur Horis matutinis et vespertinis. Attamen Prior Generalis, de consensu sui Consilii, normas generales pro his Communitatibus edat, earum applicationem ad casus particulares Priori Provinciali vel Viceprovinciali committendo.» See Letter of the SCRSI May 15, 1978, Prot. no. A 72-1/78, published in *Acta OSA* 23(1978)24-25.

28 These norms were published in *Acta OSA* 23(1978)82-83.

Two other factors must be mentioned regarding the Prior's role and the Liturgy of the Hours. The Prior has, as found in the Constitutions and by virtue of a privilege, the right to dispense from the obligation of the Office.[29] Secondly, and well worth consideration, the Prior with the community should evaluate the possibility of inviting people from outside the community into the common celebration of the Liturgy of the Hours.[30] This would be one concrete way for the community to give witness of its life in the Church, and would provide the opportunity for others to participate more fully in the prayer which is so important in the universal Church.

b) Devotional practices and retreat

Besides the Liturgy of the Hours, the Constitutions recommend other practices which are intended to be an aid in the development of personal and communal holiness. Once again, the Prior has a particular responsibility in the implementing of these norms:

> Priors on their part should take care that everyone has sufficient time to cultivate an interior life through spiritual exercises. Otherwise there is danger that because of the crushing labors

---

[29] *Constitutiones*, no. 98: «In casibus singularibus iustaque de causa, Superiores Maiores possunt fratres ab obligatione officium recitandi, etiam in communi, ex toto vel ex parte dispensare vel id commutare; Superiores vero Locales tantum dispensare.» Regarding the privilege, see T. SCHAEFER, *De Religiosis ad normam Codicis Iuris Canonici*, 3rd ed. (Rome: SALER, 1940), no. 371.

[30] *Constitutiones*, no. 96: «... Ordinarie in ecclesia vel in oratorio, iuxta leges ecclesiasticas, recitari debet, quo efficacius orationis et unitatis testimonium Populo Dei reddamus. Expedit insuper fideles invitare ut nobiscum hanc orationem participent.» See also SC, nos. 84, 85, 100.

of life the delight in acquiring and contemplating divine truth may be taken away.[31]

Various elements are suggested to the community for the development of its prayer life, and among these are daily prayer for the benefactors of the Order,[32] veneration of Mary the Mother of God,[33] a half hour of meditation daily,[34] the reading and study of Sacred Scripture,[35] and, «other forms of prayer in common, such as that known as shared prayer, are also recommended.»[36]

---

31 *Constitutiones*, no. 105: «... Provideant autem Priores ut omnes, ad vitam interiorem pietatis exercitiis colendam, sufficiens tempus habeant, ne, laboribus vitae tam opprimentibus, delectatio percipiendae atque intuendae veritatis subtrahatur.» The English translation has used the expression «spiritual exercises», which carries with it a connotation of the Ignatian style retreat. That is not, however, the meaning intended. It is rather an expression which includes various forms of spiritual practices as aids in strengthening the spiritual life.

32 *Constitutiones*, no. 106: «Cotidie, hora magis opportuna, oratio communis fiat pro toto Ordine et pro nostris benefactoribus vel formula in Rituali praescripta vel in Missa vel in Liturgia Horarum.»

33 *Constitutiones*, no. 107: «Matrem Dei filiali amore honorare debemus iuxta Ecclesiae praxim et Ordinis traditionem, qui Beatam Virginem patronam habet antiquitus renuntiatam ...»

34 *Constitutiones*, no. 101: «Omnes igitur orationi mentali ita assueti esse debemus, ut cotidie saltem dimidiam horam eidem dedicemus ...»

35 *Constitutiones*, no. 102: «Praeterea, cum ad hanc orationem mentalem maxime conferat Sacrarum Scripturarum lectio et studium, et eminentem Iesu Christi scientiam addiscamus, omnes Fratres invitantur et admonentur ut cotidie piae Sacrae Scripturae lectioni per congruum tempus vacent.» Also, canon 663, §3: «Lectioni sacrae Scripturae et orationi mentali vacent ...»

36 *Constitutiones*, no. 101: «... Commendantur etiam formae orationis in communi, v. gr. oratio sic dicta participata.» This sentence was added to the Constitutions at the General Chapter of 1977, and confirmed by the General Chapter of 1983. It makes reference in a footnote to the document promulgated by the Intermediate Chapter of 1974, familiarly known as the Dublin Document. Number 67 reads: «The Augustinian community is something like a small Church, a group of persons who live their faith. For them, prayer is not just an act of piety, it is a style of life. Dialogue with God is the summit of dialogue with our brothers; with them and through them we come to encounter with the Lord. For the maturation of this shared faith, we have to experience not just the usual prayer in common, but a shared or community prayer, in which our brothers' personal experiences of union with God become our own. We need also to

Occasional days of recollection have their value as well for community life, and are therefore mandated by the Constitutions.[37] These are to be celebrated according to norms established by the Province Statutes, at least several times a year. The format for these days is to be decided by the community itself. Thus, the Prior together with the entire community, or with the Council or the Director of Liturgy[38] (all obviously depending upon the size of the community) should plan these days in accordance with the periods of the liturgical calendar,[39] keeping in mind the needs of the given group. One suggestion that the Constitutions make is that on these days of recollection, or even more frequently, the Prior lead the community in a «Chapter of Renewal».[40]

> The Prior should take the opportunity to foster the religious and apostolic life of the Brothers by words of encouragement. Then, those matters which seem necessary and useful for enhancing the spirit of the community and for correcting defects and faults against the common good should be proposed

---

extend this prayer experience to the People of God who, though they don't belong to our community, share with us the same spirit of Christ's love.» (Published in English in *Acta OSA* 19[1974]235).

37 *Constitutiones*, no. 108: «Quia vita nostra spiritualis, sicut vita corporalis, opportunis remediis reparari debet, pluries in anno, iuxta Statuta Provincialia, dies secessus seu recollectionis spiritualis in unaquaque Communitate temporibus liturgicis sollemnioribus designentur . . . »

38 The Constitutions suggest that in larger communities a member who is qualified in theological and liturgical matters be given the duty of directing liturgical activity (no. 86).

39 *Constitutiones*, no. 108. (See footnote no. 37.)

40 *Constitutiones*, no. 109: «Occasione diei recollectionis, vel etiam frequentius, iuxta Statuta Provincialia, enixe commendatur Capitulum renovationis, in quo Prior occasionem accipiat ad vitam religiosam et apostolicam Fratrum verbis exhortationis nutriendam. Deinde quae necessaria et utilia videntur ad spiritum Communitatis augendum et ad defectus et transgressiones boni communis emendanda, discussioni Fratrum proponantur ut sub moderamine Prioris, in fraterno ac responsabili dialogo, difficultates solvantur et vita communis melius custodiatur.»

for discussion among the Brothers, so that under the direction of the Prior through fraternal and responsible dialogue difficulties may be resolved and community life be better safeguarded.[41]

In order for the Prior to fulfill effectively the expectations placed upon him by the Constitutions, he must take a good amount of time to consider carefully and to reflect upon these aspects of the community life which he intends to propose to the community in the context of a Chapter of Renewal. Such a structure can prove to be as much a hindrance as it can an aid, all depending upon the way in which the Chapter is led. In certain circumstances, the Prior may wish to consult with other members of the community (his Council, for example) about the matters which he is thinking of presenting, thereby aiding his own reflection and increasing the possibility that the meeting will be effective. The Chapter can thus become a helpful means for enriching the life of the community.

Once a year each member of the Order is to make a retreat of at least five days.[42] The retreat may be individual, or for the

---

41 Ibid. The Document of the 1974 Intermediate General Chapter also made reference to the Chapter of Renewal. In no. 79, it states: «Experience shows that an atmosphere of deep fraternal relationship makes it possible for the community to maintain a constant self-evaluation and an attitude of listening to God. The Chapter of Renewal could serve very well for this purpose. The community will then be better able also to avoid stagnation and to remain adaptable in the face of changing needs of our time.» The Chapter of Renewal is in effect an adaptation of what was once referred to as the Chapter of Faults, found already in the Order's earliest legislation (see the Ratisbon Constitutions, chapters 3 and 4). Each person would, before the Prior and in the presence of the community, confess his failings in a prescribed manner, and the Prior would assign some penance. If a person did not accuse himself of some fault of which he was guilty, another could stan up and accuse him. This obviously is not what is intended in the current Constitutions by «Chapter of Renewal». There is, nevertheless, great value to be found in the community's honest self-evaluation so that productive growth can result.

42 *Constitutiones*, no. 108: «... quotannis quinque saltem dies exercitiorum spiritualium habeantur, in quibus expedit ut doctrina spiritualis S. P. Augustini recolatur

whole community, or organized in some other fashion. Such determination is not made in the Constitutions, and therefore it would depend upon the Provincial, or the individual Priors with their communities to decide upon the way in which the annual retreat is to be made. It is recommended that these retreats include spiritual teaching of St. Augustine, and also that the Brothers renew their vows «so that the spirit of our following of Christ may be renewed and increased.»[43]

3. The Eucharist

«The Eucharistic mystery is the very center of the sacred liturgy and truly of the entire Christian life.»[44] The new Code, drawing on various sources,[45] states the following:

> The Eucharistic Sacrifice ... is the summit and the source of all Christian worship and life; it signifies and effects the unity of the people of God and achieves the building up of the Body of Christ.[46]

---

et renovatio votorum fiat, qua spiritus sequelae Christi restauretur et augeatur.» The same obligation is stated in the code, can. 663, §5, but no specification is made as to the length of time.

43 Ibid. This renewal of vows could refer both to those Brothers who are still in temporary vows, as well as to the solemnly professed members who may make, according to the Ritual of the Order, a renewal of their vows.

44 Instruction of the S. Congregation of Rites, *Eucharisticum mysterium,* May 25, 1967 (AAS 59[1967]539-573), no. 1: «Eucharisticum mysterium sacrae Liturgiae, immo totius christianae vitae, est vere centrum.» This passage is also quoted in the Constitutions, no. 87. In the same Instruction, no. 3: «Quare ipsum Sacrificium eucharisticum totius cultus Ecclesiae totiusque vitae christianae fons et culmen est.» See also LG, no. 11; SC, no. 41; PO, nn. 2, 5, 6; UR, no. 15.

45 While an official listing of the *fontes* has not yet been published, the numbers cited in the footnote above have clearly contributed to canon 897 (below).

46 Can. 897: « ... Sacrificium eucharisticum ... totius cultus et vitae christianae est culmen et fons, quo significatur et efficitur unitas populi Dei et corporis Christi aedificatio perficitur ... »

And in another place further emphasis is placed on the importance of the Eucharist in building Christian community: «No Christian community can be built up unless it has its basis and center in the celebration of the most Holy Eucharist.»⁴⁷ While not going into an excursus on the theology of the Eucharist, it seems that its fundamental place in the life of any community which calls itself Christian is well-established. Just as St. Augustine found the basis for his monastic ideal in the primitive community presented in the Acts of the Apostles, so too *Perfectae caritatis* calls this model to mind in the importance of Eucharist as part of the life of a religious community.⁴⁸ The Constitutions likewise affirm the necessity of the Eucharist as the creative force of real Christian community.⁴⁹ This significance of the Eucharist as center of a religious community is likewise emphasized in the Code, in its insistence that every religious house have «at least an oratory in which the Eucharist is celebrated and reserved so that it is truly the center of the community.»⁵⁰

---

47 PO, no. 6e: «Nulla tamen communitas christiana aedificatur nisi radicem cardinemque habeat in Sanctissimae Eucharistiae celebratione ... »

48 The primitive community described in Acts 4:32 ff. was used many times by Augustine. (See Chapter one, pp. 24-25). PC, no. 15: «Vita in communi agenda, ad exemplum primaevae Ecclesiae in qua multitudo credentium erat cor unum et anima una (cf. Act. 4,32), evangelica doctrina, Sacra Liturgia et praesertim Eucharistia refecta, in oratione et communione eiusdem spiritus perseveret ... »

49 See *Constitutiones*, nn. 87-91. No. 91: «Cum vero nulla Communitas christiana aedificari possit nisi radicem cardinemque habeat in Eucharistiae celebratione et participatione, grato animo hoc sacrificium laudis digne et devote cotidie Deo offerre studeamus, ut nobismetipsis Ordini et Ecclesiae uberrimi fructus ex eo proveniant.»

50 Can. 608: « ... singulae domus habeant saltem oratorium, in quo Eucharistia celebretur et asservetur ut vere sit centrum communitatis.»

a) Community celebration

Regarding the frequency of celebrating the Eucharist as a community, there must be several considerations made. Generally speaking, the Church recommends daily participation in the Eucharistic celebration for religious.[51] Depending upon the make-up of the community, the Prior should see to it that this value is stressed and that members have the opportunity for daily participation in the Eucharist.[52] Obviously, the type of apostolate in which the Brothers are involved will have some bearing on the realization of this ideal. Where all or many of the community members are priests, with obligations to say Mass in, for example, a parish situation, the expectation that they participate in an additional Mass could be unreasonable.[53] On the other hand, larger communities in which many of the members have no such obligations, formation

---

51 Can. 663, §2: «Sodales cotidie pro viribus Sacrificium eucharisticum participent, sanctissimum Corpus Christi recipiant et ipsum Dominum in Sacramento praesentem adorent.»

52 *Constitutiones,* no. 89: «Quapropter in Domibus nostris Missa Communitatis valde commendatur...»

53 Although bination is ordinarily not allowed (cf. can. 905, §1), the community Mass is an exception provided for by law. Cf. Declaratio «In celebratione Missae», S. Congregation of Divine Worship, August 7, 1972 (AAS 64[1972]561-563), no. 1: «Capitulares atque sodales communitatum cuiusvis instituti perfectionis, qui officio in bonum pastorale fidelium celebrandi tenentur, Missam quoque conventualem vel 'communitatis' (cf. Institutio generalis Missalis romani, no. 76) eodem die concelebrare possunt.» The declaration goes on to emphasize the importance of community celebrations of the Eucharist: «Magni enim aestimanda est concelebratio eucharistica in communitatibus. Concelebratio fraterna presbyterorum inter se (cf. LG, no. 28, PO, no. 8) atque totius communitatis vincula significat et firmat, quia in huiusmodi sacrificii celebratione, quam omnes conscie, actuose atque modo uniuscuiusque proprio participant, clarius apparet actio totius communitatis atque praecipua habetur manifestatio Ecclesiae in unitate sacrificii et sacerdotii, in unica gratiarum actione circa unum altare» (cf. *Ecclesiae semper,* March 7, 1965; *Eucharisticum mysterium,* May 25, 1967, no. 47). The last quotation is also cited in the Constitutions, in no. 90: «This way of celebrating the sacrifice with everyone taking part consciously, actively, and in the way proper to him, sets the action of the community more clearly in relief and is a very special manifestation of the Church.»

communities, and communities where there are non-ordained Brothers could be expected to have a scheduled daily community Eucharist. In those cases where it is not possible to celebrate daily as a community, the Prior and community should choose specific occasions (such as a weekly evening specially reserved for this purpose, or the periodic days of recollection) during which the entire community can gather and celebrate the Eucharist. The Constitutions mandate that Provincial Statutes are to make determination in this regard.[54]

b) Mass intentions

Regarding the application of Mass intentions, the Constitutions place an obligation upon the Prior:

> Let him humbly pray for the Brothers entrusted to him and apply the holy sacrifice of the Mass for them at least on the feast of Christmas, the Annunciation, Easter and St. Augustine.[55]

In cases where the Prior is not a priest, an ordained member of the com munity is to be chosen to fulfill this obligation.[56]

---

54 *Constitutiones*, no. 89: «Quapropter in Domibus nostris Missa Communitatis valde commendatur. Singulae Provinciae normas determinent, quibus reapse celebrari possit et ut ei omnes Fratres, suo quisque modo, intersint...»

55 *Constitutiones*, no. 312: «In officio adimplendo, potius quam in suis viribus et ingenio spem in Deo reponat, pro Fratribus sibi commissis humiliter oret et Missae sacrificium saltem in Nativitate Domini, in Annuntiatione Domini, in Paschate necnon in sollemnitate S. P. Augustini pro eis applicet.»

56 In 1977, the General Chapter made the following proposal to change the Constitutions: «no. 12 – Fraternitas ergo in Ordine singulariter manifestari debet in aequalitate omnium Fratrum, nullo privilegio vel titulo honorifico admisso. Omnes elegibiles sunt ad omnia officia...» Then, in no. 243, the provision was added that «if the superior is not a priest, the competent Chapter is to choose one of the priests of the community to carry out those things that pertain by law to a priest Superior.» Responding to this change, the SCRSI (see letter, cited above [footnote 27]) stated: «S. Congregatio pro Religiosis et Institutis saecularibus non censet vigentibus normis, v.g.

While there is no explicit legislation on the issue, it seems that, by reason of analogy, the rules regarding the pastor's obligation to offer the *Missa pro populo* would be applicable here, specifically the provision made in the case that the Mass cannot be offered:

> If he is legitimately prevented from this celebration, he is to apply Mass on these same days through another priest or he himself is to apply it on other days.[57]

All other Mass obligations are to be taken care of by the Sacristan of the community.[58]

4. The Sacrament of Penance

Discussion of the Prior's role in regards to the sacrament of penance must begin with a very important principle, expressed in canon 630, §1:

---

decreto 'Clericalia instituta' die 27 novembris 1969 derogandum esse antequam novus codex iuris canonici de hac re aliquid patefaciat. Insuper, si petitio admitteretur uti sonat idem esset ac praesentem naturam Ordinis mutare eumque Institutis laicalibus annumerare cum omnibus suis consectariis.» The Constitutions (no. 12) were therefore altered, to read: «Omnes eligibiles sunt ad omnia officia, nisi ius commune obstet.» For those cases in which a Provincial with the consent of his Council, and after consulting with the community in question, wishes to nominate a non-ordained Brother as Prior, a dispensation must be requested from the Congregation. The most recent case was from the Chicago Province, and the dispensation was granted. See Rescript dated November 28, 1983, Prot. no. 9555/83. Thus, although the Constitutions no longer include the provision regarding the nomination of an ordained Brother to fulfill those duties which pertain to a priest superior, it can be presumed that such is to be the case in those situations where a non-ordained Brother is made Prior.

[57] Can. 534, §1: «... qui vero ab hac celebratione legitime impediatur, iisdem diebus per alium aut aliis diebus per se ipse applicet.»

[58] *Constitutiones*, no. 320: «Sacrista: Sacristae praeficiatur Frater cuius est ecclesiae cultus et rerum ad eam pertinentium maximam habere curam et eius ordinariae administrationi providere. Ipsius est etiam cura Missarum, quarum onera nomine Communitatis accipit ac eleemosynas Domus deposito tradit...»

Superiors are to recognize the due freedom of their members concerning the sacrament of penance and the direction of conscience, with due regard however for the discipline of the institute.[59]

Several factors are important here: the liberty of the individual member to decide himself about his celebration of the sacrament (i.e., frequency, the confessor); the integrity and inviolability of the individual conscience, in which the Prior cannot interfere; the discipline of the Augustinian Order regarding the sacrament of penance. Already in the first chapter of this study, emphasis has been made upon the attitude of respect that the Prior must have toward the members of his community, recognizing the dignity and maturity of each person.[60] An important part of this recognition is seen in his respect for the Brothers' freedom in a matter as personal as the sacrament of penance.

While members are encouraged to speak freely to their superiors, even about matters of conscience, superiors are forbidden to lead their subjects in any way to make a manifestation of conscience.[61] If a member decides to reveal to his Prior something that is a matter of conscience, he must do so of his own free will. The Prior must never try to persuade or coax an individual to

---

59 Can. 630, §1: «Superiores sodalibus debitam agnoscant libertatem circa paenitentiae sacramentum et conscientiae moderamen, salva tamen instituti disciplina.» The source for this canon can be found in *Perfectae caritatis,* no. 14c: «Subditos regant qua filios Dei et cum respectu personae humanae, illorum voluntarium subiectionem promoventes. Ideoque speciatim debitam eis libertatem relinquant quoad poenitentiae sacramentum et conscientiae moderamen.»

60 See chapter one, p. 16. Note that the phrase from PC, no. 14c cited above is also used as the source for that of canon 618: «... ipsi subditos regant uti filios Dei, ac promoventes cum reverentia personae humanae illorum voluntariam oboedientiam...»

61 Can. 630, §5: «Sodales cum fiducia Superiores adeant, quibus animum suum libere ac sponte aperire possunt. Vetantur autem Superiores eos quoquo modo inducere ad conscientiae manifestationem sibi peragendam.»

tell him something, even if he thinks it is in the better interest of the individual or community. (Actions which are external and knowable to others are not matters of conscience, and therefore a Prior can ask an individual about such things.) If an individual makes a voluntary manifestation of conscience, the superior is forbidden to reveal such information without the express permission of the Brother. «A manifestation constitutes an official and quasi-sacramental secret and excludes all revelation, without the express consent of the one making the manifestation.»[62]

Regarding the frequency with which the sacrament of penance is celebrated, here too freedom is left to the individual. In the old Code, the religious was to go to confession at least once a week, and it was the responsibility of the superior to see that such practice was carried out.[63] Moreover, the Order's Constitutions (1926) were even more demanding in their expectation upon the Prior in this matter: men who did not go to the sacrament at least once a week were to be punished publicly by the superior.[64]

Much different, then, is the new Code which recommends «frequent» confession, but with no exact specification of a time span between one celebration of the sacrament and the next.[65] And too, the responsibility is placed upon the individual Brother, and not primarily on the superior, to regulate this important aspect of the spiritual life. The same change in attitude is found in the new

---

[62] J. GALLEN, *Canon Law for Religious* (New York: Alba House, 1983), p. 88.

[63] CIC (1917) can. 595, §1, no. 3: «Curent Superiores ut omnes religiosi: . . . ad poenitentiae sacramentum semel saltem in hebdomada accedant.»

[64] *Constitutiones* (1926), no. 125: «Omnes Fratres, cuiusque gradus et conditionis sint, semel saltem in hebdomada ad Poenitentiae sacramentum accedant (cf. can. 595, §1, no. 3). Qui autem hoc facere neglexerit, per Superiorem publice puniatur.»

[65] Can. 664: «In animi erga Deum conversione insistant religiosi, conscientiam etiam cotidie examinent et ad paenitentiae sacramentum frequenter accedant.»

Constitutions, which, similar to the Code, recommend «frequent» confession for all the members.⁶⁶

Mention must also be made of the choice given to the Brothers regarding the personal confessor. Confessors are to be made available to the community so that members can celebrate the sacrament.⁶⁷ The superior is evidently the one responsible for arranging for this service in those communities where it is necessary. But an individual is in no way obliged to go to confession to that particular priest.⁶⁸ (Often, because of the location of the house, or the make-up of its members, there is no need to bring in confessors, since the Brothers already have readily available access to confessors.) In any case, the superior is encouraged to promote an appreciation for this sacrament among the members of his community.⁶⁹

One concrete way in which the Prior can encourage such appreciation is foreseen in the Constitutions within the context of communal celebrations of reconciliation:

> Penitential celebrations where the proclaimed word of God is an invitation to conversion and renewal of life should be held.

---

66 *Constitutiones,* no. 92: «... Frequens et diligens huius sacramenti usus assiduum studium est gratiam baptismi perficiendi, ut magis magisque vita Iesu manifestetur in nobis...» The usual interpretation given to «frequenter» is «twice a month». One official source in which this is found is a letter written by the SCRSI to the Order, in response to the new Constitutions published in 1968: «Circa confessionem, Religiosi frequenter, i.e. sexto saltem decimo quoque die, ad eam accedant...» (See Letter SCRSI, 18 March, 1969, Prot. N. 4063/68).

67 Can. 630, §2: «Solliciti sint Superiores ad normam iuris proprii, ut sodalibus idonei confessarii praesto sint, apud quos frequenter confiteri possint.»

68 Can. 630, §3: «In monasteriis monialium, in domibus formationis et in communitatibus numerosioribus laicalibus habeantur confessarii ordinarii ab Ordinario loci probati, collatis consiliis cum communitate, nulla tamen facta obligatione ad illos accedendi.»

69 *Constitutiones,* no. 92a: «... Superiores vero ardentem erga hoc sacramentum amorem promoveant, debitam libertatem quoad eius receptionem relinquentes.»

Such celebrations express the ecclesial aspect of penance and could fittingly form part of chapters of renewal.[70]

Superiors are not to hear the confession of the Brothers unless they are spontaneously requested to do so.[71] This, in principle, is another means of protecting the individual members from having to reveal matters of conscience to the superior. There may also be situations in which the Prior will not want to be bound by the seal of confession, in order to exercise freely his authority. He may therefore even decide to refuse to hear the confession of a member of the community in a situation wherein he believes that information revealed in the context of the sacrament will in some way compromise his ability to act as he ought. If it does happen that a Prior receives in the context of the sacrament information upon which he would ordinarily have to act, he cannot do so.[72] The inviolability of the seal of confession must always be protected regardless of the circumstances.

Another aspect of the sacrament of penance which enters into the discussion of the local Prior is that of the «faculties» required to hear confessions.[73] Legislation which concerns the faculties

---

70 *Constitutiones*, no. 92b: «Habeantur celebrationes paenitentiales, ubi Verbum Dei proclamatum ad conversionem et vitae renovationem invitet. Hae celebrationes aspectum ecclesialem paenitentiae exprimunt et locum optium habere possunt in Capitulis renovationis.» (Regarding the Chapter of Renewal, see pp. 123-125).

71 Can. 630, §4: «Subditorum confessiones Superiores ne audiant, nisi sponte sua sodales id petant.»

72 Can. 983, §1: «Sacramentale sigillum inviolabile est; quare nefas est confessario verbis vel alio quovis modo et quavis de causa aliquatenus prodere paenitentem.» Can. 984, §1: «Omnino confessario prohibetur scientiae ex confessione acquisitae usus cum paenitentis gravamine, etiam quovis revelationis periculo excluso.» Can. 984, §2: «Qui in auctoritate est constitutus, notitia quam de peccatis in confessione quovis tempore excepta habuerit, ad exteriorem gubernationem nullo modo uti potest.»

73 A priest, in order to absolve validly from sins, must have, in addition to the *potestas ordinis*, the «facultas» to exercse that power over the faithful. See can. 966, §1.

has been greatly simplified in the new Code. This simplification is due in large part to the new provision that allows a confessor, who by virtue of his office or through delegation from his local ordinary has received faculties to hear confessions, to absolve validly anywhere, unless such is specifically denied by a particular local ordinary.[74]

Local Priors, by virtue of their office, enjoy the faculty to hear confessions according to canon 968, §2:

> In virtue of their office superiors of a clerical religious institute or society of apostolic life of pontifical right who in accord with the norms of their constitutions possess executive power of governance enjoy the faculty to hear the confessions of their subjects and others staying in the religious house day and night, with due regard for the prescription of can. 630, §4.[75]

---

74 Can. 967, §2: «Qui facultate confessiones habitualiter excipiendi gaudent sive vi officii sive vi concessionis Ordinarii loci incardinationis aut loci in quo domicilium habent, eandem facultatem ubique exercere possunt, nisi loci Ordinarius in casu particulari renuerit, firmis prescriptis can. 974, §§2 et 3.» According to the new Code, religious have a domicile in the place where they are assigned; can. 103: «Sodales institutorum religiosorum et societatum vitae apostolicae domicilium acquirunt in loco ubi sita est domus cui adscribantur; quasi-domicilium in domo ubi, ad normam can. 102, §2, commorantur.»

75 Can. 968, §2: «Vi officii facultate gaudent confessiones excipiendi suorum subditorum aliorumque, in domo diu noctuque degentium, Superiores instituti religiosi aut societatis vitae apostolicae, si sint clericales iuris pontificii, ad normam constitutionum potestate regiminis exsecutiva fruentes, firmo tamen praescripto can. 630, §4.» See footnote no. 71 for the text of can. 630, §4; it states that superiors are not to hear the confessions of their subjects unless spontaneously requested. Regarding those who «stay in the house day and night», it is commonly accepted that those who have stayed in the religious house at least one night are in this category. Thus, even guests can be considered in these terms, so that if need arises, they can be absolved by one who has faculties to hear the confessions of members of the house «aliorumque in domo diu noctuque degentium.»

By virtue of the Code, this faculty can be used anywhere for hearing the confessions of other Augustinians, and for others who stay day and night in a house of the Order:

> Those who have been granted the faculty to hear confessions in virtue of an office or by a grant from a competent superior in accord with the norms of cann. 968, §2 and 969, §2 can by the law itself use the faculty anywhere in respect to members and others who stay day and night in a house of the institute or society; such persons also exercise this faculty licitly unless some major superior has denied it concerning his own subjects in a particular case.[76]

A Prior can also delegate the faculty to hear confessions to any priest, for the confessions of members of that community or of those who live day and night in the house.[77] Although this power to delegate would be used rather seldom, there may be cases where a priest does not have faculties and so this possibility is an available option. Before delegating the faculties to a priest, the Prior must be reasonably certain that the priest is competent to hear confessions.[78]

---

76 Can. 967, §3: «Ipso iure eadem facultate ubique potiuntur erga sodales aliosque in domo instituti aut societatis diu noctuque degentes, qui vi officii aut concessionis Superioris competentis ad normam cann. 968, §2 et 969, §2 facultate confessiones excipiendi sunt instructi; qui quidem eadem et licite utuntur, nisi aliquis Superior maior quoad proprios subditos in casu particulari renuerit.»

77 Can. 969, §2: «Superior instituti religiosi aut societatis vitae apostolicae, de quo in can. 968, §2, competens est qui facultatem ad excipiendas confessiones suorum subditorum aliorumque in domo diu noctuque degentium presbyteris quibuslibet conferat.»

78 Can. 970: «Facultas ad confessiones excipiendas ne concedatur nisi presbyteris qui idonei per examen reperti fuerint, aut de eorum idoneitate aliunde constet.» A final note: if the Prior is not a priest, he cannot delegate faculties to hear confessions, because he does not possess (at least fully) the ecclesiastical power of governance.

CHAPTER FIVE

5. Care of the sick

The sick among us are a special sign of Christ's redeeming suffering; they invite the Brothers to care for them by providing both physical and spiritual comfort.[79]

So that they may bear their difficulties more patiently and more fruitfully, we should show the greatest concern and fraternal love in the care of the sick and the aged, for in them we serve Christ.[80]

In caring for the sick, the Prior is charged by the Constitutions with direct responsibility to see to it that all the sick Brother's needs are taken care of. «Priors should see that all their spiritual and material necessities are generously provided for, and without denying, because of poverty, whatever the doctor judges necessary for the sick.»[81] It would be a false sense of the vow of poverty to deprive a sick member of the community of some prescribed treatment because of a desire to save money or to create an image of being poor. In addition, the Prior is expected to inform all the communities of the Province of a grave illness of one of the Brothers, so that all of the members of the Province can pray for that Brother.[82]

---

79 *Constitutiones*, no. 94a: «... Infirmi in nostris Communitatibus signum singulare nobis praebent dolorum Christi nos redimentium, fratresque invitant, ut ipsos physicis adiuvent subsidiis et spirituali confortatione reficiant.» Cfd. Ordo Unctionis infirmorum, nn. 4-5, in *Notitiae* 9(1973)57.

80 *Constitutiones*, no. 122: «In curam infirmorum et senium, cum Christo serviamus in illis, quam maximam sollicitudinem et fraternam caritatem impendere debemus, quo sua incommoda patientius et fructuosius tolerare possint...»

81 *Constitutiones*, no. 122: «... Priores igitur invigilent ut omnia necessaria sive spiritualia sive materialia eis benigne subministrentur, nec denegetur, ratione paupertatis, quod, medicorum iudicio, infirmis opus fuerit.» (Cf. Ratisbon Constitutions, c. 13, no. 79.)

82 *Constitutiones*, no. 94b: «... Prior Localis omnes Communitates Provinciae opportune de hoc certiores faciat, ut omnes Fratres pro infirmo orent...»

In providing for the spiritual welfare of the ill, one of the most appropriate signs of God's healing grace is realized in the sacrament of the Anointing of the Sick. This sacrament «perpetuates the concern that the Lord himself had for the sick.»[83] In the cases in which a Brother is seriously ill the reception of this sacrament is not only advised, but encouraged so that the Brother might receive the special help of God's grace. «Care should be taken that a sick Brother receives the sacrament at an opportune time and, insofar as possible, in the presence of other Augustinians and family members.»[84]

While the Constitutions do not specify who is ordinarily the minister of the sacrament, it would seem that the Prior is to administer the sacrament if he is a priest. This conclusion is based upon canon 1003, §2, along with what has already been discussed above regarding the Prior's role in being entrusted with the care of souls:[85]

> All priests to whom the care of souls has been committed have the duty and the right to administer the anointing of the sick to all the faithful committed to their pastoral care . . .[86]

In the *Ordo unctionis infirmorum eorumque pastoralis curae*, in discussion on the ordinary minister of the sacrament, the following is stated:

---

83 *Constitutiones*, no. 94a: «In Unctione infirmorum cura a Domino erga infirmos adhibita continuat . . .»

84 *Constitutiones*, no. 94b: «Tempore opportuno provideatur ut infirmis sacramentum Unctionis recipiat, praesentibus, quatenus possible sit, ceteris Augustinensibus fratribus et familiaribus infirmi . . .»

85 The discussion on the care of souls is at the beginning of this chapter; cf. p. 113 ss.

86 Can. 1003, §2: «Officium et ius unctionis infirmorum ministrandi habent omnes sacerdotes, quibus demandata est cura animarum, erga fideles suo pastorali officio commissos . . .»

This office is ordinarily exercised by bishops, pastors and their assistants, priests who care for the sick or aged in hospitals, and superiors of clerical religious institutes.[87]

Since, according to canon 2,[88] liturgical norms are not changed by the Code unless they are contrary to the Code, this norm is still in effect. Thus, when the Prior is a priest, he as spiritual leader of the community should be the one to administer the sacrament of the anointing of the sick to those who request it or to those whose condition indicates that they should receive it.

In addition, when members of the community are ill, the Prior should see to it that their other spiritual needs are met. If they wish to receive the Eucharist or celebrate the sacrament of penance, the Prior should see to it that their requests are fulfilled. It is in fact the duty of the Prior to bring the Eucharist to the sick in the form of Viaticum.[89]

---

87 *Ordo unctionis infirmorum eorumque pastoralis curae* (Vatican City: Typis Polyglottis Vaticanis, 1975), no. 16: «Minister proprius Unctionis infirmorum est solus sacerdos. Episcopi, parochi et eorum cooperatores, sacerdotes quibus mandata est cura infirmorum vel senium in valetudinariis, et superiores communitatum religiosarum clericalium, huius ministerii munus ordinarie exercent.» English trans. from *The Rites*, vol. 1 (New York: Pueblo Pub. Co., 1983). Reference is made in the *Ordo* to v. can. 938, which in turn refers to v. can. 514; §§1-3. Of immediate interest is v. can. 514, §1: «In omni religione clericali ius et officium Superioribus est per se vel per alium aegrotis professis, novitiis, aliisve in religiosa domo diu noctuque degentibus causa famulatus aut educationis aut hospitii aut infirmae valetudinis, Eucharisticum Viaticum·et extremam unctionem ministrandi.» While the new Code does not contain this provision for the anointing of the sick, for the reasons indicated above the same conclusion can be drawn. Also, see the following footnote, regarding the superior's responsibility to bring Viaticum to the sick.

88 [Editor's note: There is no footnote in the manuscript corresponding to the callout 88.]

89 Can. 911, §1: «Officium et ius sanctissimam Eucharistiam per modum Viatici ad infirmos deferendi habent parochus et vicarii paroeciales, cappellani, necnon Superior communitatis in clericalibus institutis religiosis aut societatibus vitae apostolicae quoad omnes in domo versantes.» This canon is found in the section of the Code which

Obviously, all other needs that a sick member of the community has should be attended to by the Prior, either personally or by someone designated by him, in order to insure that the sick person receive the proper treatment during his illness.

6. For the deceased

Outlined in the Constitutions are a number of occasions on which Mass is to be offered for specific intentions, such as on the death of the Pope or of the Prior General.[90] In addition to these Masses, there are a couple of responsibilities which must be taken care of by the Prior. Upon the death of a member of the community, whether professed, novice or a person who lived day and night in the monastery, the community is to remember him in prayer and in the celebration of the Eucharist.[91] That same community, furthermore, is responsible for the funeral arrangements.[92] All the communities of the Province are to be notified as soon as possible when a Brother has died; «prayers for the deceased ought not to be delayed.»[93]

---

treats the sacrament of the Eucharist, and not in the portion on institutes of consecrated life.

90 *Constitutiones,* no. 111d: «In obitu Summi Pontificis in omnibus Communitatibus Missa offeratur. Id ipsum fiat pro Priore Generali actuali vel absoluto.»

91 *Constitutiones,* no. 111b: «Hac de causa, defuncto professo, vel novitio vel aliquo ex iis qui nobiscum diu noctuque degunt, Communitas, de cuius familia erat, ad orationes et ad celebrationem Sacrificii Eucharistici eum commemoret curamque de funere fraterne gerat.»

92 Ibid.

93 *Constitutiones,* no. 94b: « . . . Fratre defuncto, Provinciae nuntius statim mittatur, ne suffragia differantur.»

CHAPTER SIX

THE MUNUS REGENDI

Continuing the analogical presentation of *Mutuae relationes*, this study now turns to the Prior's duties in ordering the life of the community. From the point of view of the daily life of the local community, many of the small details which in and of themselves are seemingly insignificant are at times major factors in creating an overall sense of well-being in the community. Ability on the part of the Prior to sense what needs to be done and to impart to others this same capability can lead to a life in which all the members are duly concerned about the community and out of which each man can more effectively offer to the Church fruitful service in the apostolate. Realistically speaking, it is probably this dimension of the Prior's role which is most immediately felt and appreciated by the community. If by means of good leadership he is instrumental in uniting the community, in attending to the needs of the community which require his attention, and in watching over their adherence to the Augustinian life, he will fulfill his office of governing in the community.

Concrete realities must be dealt with in the situation in which they arise, and it would be impossible here to try to present every possibility that may present itself in the context of the community's life. Nevertheless, there are some general categories which cover a great many of the situations with which a Prior has to deal. This chapter will present these aspects of the Prior's office of governing; since this is indeed such a general duty, the result may seem somewhat of a potpourri. The Code itself has no book entitled "De munere regendi", since in effect the entire Code is an expression of the governing office of the Church. Much the same could be said of this study as well. However, there are some specific dimensions to be presented that can easily be conceived of as making up part of the Prior's role of governance in the local community.

Apart perhaps from theoretical studies, the Prior's role can never be seriously considered in isolation from his community, nor must a Prior ever try to fulfill his office as if he were set apart from the other members. Juridically, two specific groups are mandated which offer the Prior an aid in his administration and direction of the community, and which ensure a voice for all the Brothers in the making of certain decisions. These two groups are the Council and the House Chapter; each will be looked at in turn to see how they interact with the Prior's leadership in the life of the community.

While every community is to have a Treasurer who has immediate responsibility for the material well-being of the community and house, he is appointed with the understanding that he work "under the direction of the Prior."[1] Thus, a brief look will be taken at the administration of the material goods of the community.

Finally, the last section of this presentation of the *munus regendi* will discuss what may be one of the most difficult of all the Prior's duties. *De vitae communitatis tutela*, the safeguarding of

---

[1] *Constitutiones*, no. 321: "Oeconomus: Ipsius est bonorum Domus accurata administratio . . . sub moderamine Prioris . . ."

the life of the community, deals with the unfortunate situations in which difficulties enter into the community's life due to some violation by one of the Brothers. Surely no one looks forward to the occurrence of such cases, but if and when problems arise because of the difficulties which one of the Brothers is undergoing, the Prior must not hesitate to step in, in order to prevent the possibility that greater damage be done because too much time was allowed to pass before action was taken.

Obviously, in all of the topics treated here, there is a great deal of responsibility that rests on the shoulders of the Prior. But at the same time, there is a call to each member of the community to invest himself and to cooperate as much as possible in contributing to the smooth-running and effective living of the community. Recognition must be given within each community of the particular conditions present, and this requires a certain flexibility in arranging the common life. Where additional norms are thought to be necessary, this is to be done at the level of the Provincial Statues or by the individual community.[2]

1. The Local Prior and his Council

Canon law mandates that "according to the norm of the constitutions, superiors are to have their own council, whose assistance they are to use in carrying out their office."[3] This general norm indicates the requirement of a group whose task it is to advise the

---

2 *Constitutiones*, no. 113: "In actibus vitae communis ordinandis, pro condicionum et occupationum diversitate, liberalitas quaedam adhibeatur. Normae igitur particulares . . . pro bono Communitatis et singulorum, vel Statutis Provincialibus vel a Communitate locali determinandae sunt, ita tamen ut vitam communem et apostolicam revera foveant."

3 Can. 627, §1: "Ad normam constitutionum, Superiores proprium habeant consilium, cuius opera in munere exercendo utantur oportet."

Prior in decision-making and in giving direction within the community. Specifics of how the members of the Council are chosen and of what exactly their task is to be are left up to particular law. In the Constitutions, certain provisions are made:

> All [Superiors] have their Counselors, whose consent or advice is required according to the norms of the Constitutions and the common law.[4]

> It is the duty of the Counselors, who may not be more than four in number, to assist both the Prior and the Brethren with their advice and work, and to deliberate and offer their judgement about more important business.[5]

a) Membership

Province Statutes are to determine the way in which the Counselors are chosen, and the number that are to be chosen in each community, according to the needs of the particular house.[6]

---

4 *Constitutiones*, no. 242: " . . . Omnes [Superiores] habent Consiliarios suos, quorum consensus vel consilium, ad normam Constitutionum et iuris communis, exquirere debent . . . "

5 *Constitutiones*, no. 319: "Munus est Consiliariorum, qui ad maximum quattuor esse possunt, tam Priori quam Fratribus, consilio et opera assistere simulque negotia maiora perpendere et suam de iis sententiam dicere."

6 *Constitutiones*, no. 317: "In singulis Domibus, iuxta loci necessitates et ad normas Statutorum Provincialium, uti officiales eligantur aliqui Fratres qui Priorem in servitium Communitatis adiuvare debent et sub eius moderamine munus suum adimplere." (See above, footnote no. 5, for the description of the Counselor's role.) The English translation of no. 317 uses the word "elected" for "eligantur". A more accurate translation would be "chosen", since in fact the house officials are frequently appointed. In fact, in the case of the house Treasurer, the Provincial appoints him according to the norm of the Constitutions. The reading "elected" results in an apparent contradiction in the Constitutions between no. 317, and no. 363, which describes the choosing of Priors, Treasurers, and other officials by the Provincial and his Council after the Provincial Chapter. While "elected" does also have the meaning of "chosen", its modern usage is primarily that of being chosen by popular vote.

There are several possible ways of selecting the Counselors. One would be by direct voting of the Chapter members: the members who receive an absolute majority of votes would be chosen. Another method would be for the Prior to nominate men and seek the ratification or approval of these nominations from the House Chapter. Thirdly, the Prior could consult with the community, and based upon this consultation, choose his counselors. Provincial Statutes could determine that different methods be used, depending upon the number of men in the given community. While the Counselors are not necessarily elected by all the members of the Chapter, it is important that there be some form of consultation with the community so that the principle of equality of the Brothers be maintained and realized.

Regarding eligibility, any member of the house Chapter can be elected to the office of Counselor, except obviously for the Prior and students in formation if the Province Statutes have limited their possession of passive voice.[7]

b) Procedure

Ordinarily, the Council must be convoked by the Prior, and as a group. This is to be done in accordance with canon 166, which indicates that every member must be given notice of the convocation; if a Counselor is overlooked and therefore absent, any action on the part of the Council is valid, unless, however, the overlooked Counselor makes recourse within three days of his receiving notice of the meeting, giving proof of the oversight

---

7 See *Constitutiones*, no. 293, which gives the possibility to Provincial Statutes of limiting the exercise of active and passive voice until formation is completed.

and absence.⁸ Such recourse would be made to the Prior himself, and if not acknowledged, to the Major Superior. While such action would be very rare in the working of a local community (principles given in this entire section on Councils are generally the same at any level of government), there are cases in which the consent of the Council is required in order for the Prior to act validly (to be discussed below), and where the absence of one of the Counselors might be crucial.

The Council must be consulted as a group, not as individuals, unless particular law makes other provisions for given cases. In all the instances where the Council's advice or consent is required to the Constitutions, there is no such provision, and therefore the Council is to meet as a group. It is not sufficient for the Prior to go from one Counselor to another, individually, to ask for their opinion on matters.

As already indicated above, it is the duty of the Council to assist the Prior in directing the community, offering him advice especially about more difficult matters which may need to be decided. Juridically speaking, there are certain questions which require that the Prior seek the advice or the consent of his Council before he can validly act. Such cases are prescribed either by universal law, or by proper law, and the advice or consent is to be obtained in the manner given in canon 127:

---

8 Can. 166, §1: "Collegii aut coetus praeses convocet omnes ad collegium aut ad coetum pertinentes; convocatio autem, quando personalis esse debet, valet, si fiat in loco domicilii vel quasi-domicilii aut in loco commorationis." §2: "Si quis ex vocandis neglectus et ideo absens fuerit, electio valet; attamen ad eiusdem instantiam, probata quidem praeteritione et absentia, electio, etiam si confirmata fuerit, a competenti auctoritate rescindi debet, dummodo iuridice constet recursum saltem intra triduum ab habita notitia electionis fuisse transmissum."

When the law determines that in order to place certain acts a superior requires the consent or counsel of a college or group of persons, the college or group must be convoked according to the norms of can. 166, unless particular or proper law provides otherwise when counsel only is to be sought; however, for such acts to be valid it is required that the consent of an absolute majority of those present be obtained or that the counsel of all . . . be sought.[9]

The determination of absolute majority is different in the new Code than it was in the old, and it therefore merits a moment's attention. In the old Code, absolute majority was determined upon the number of valid votes cast.[10] On the other hand, the new Code states that absolute majority is calculated upon the number of voters who are present.[11] A practical example will clearly indicate the difference. A council of four members meets, all members are present. On an issue which requires the consent

---

9 Can. 127, §1: "Cum iure statuatur ad actus ponendos Superiorem indigere consensu aut consilio alicuius collegii vel personarum coetus, convocari debet collegium vel coetus ad normam can. 166, nisi, cum agatur de consilio tantum exquirendo, aliter iure particulari aut proprio cautum sit; ut autem actus valeant requiritum ut obtineatur consensus partis absolute maioris eorum qui sunt praesentes aut omnium: exquiratur consilium." The English translation of this canon is of the CLSA, but it will be noticed, there is a small omission (. . .). The English reads "the counsel of all who are present be sought." The Latin would be better translated "the counsel of all be sought." This is an important distinction, since the interpretation can certainly be made that the advice must be asked even of those Counselors who are not present at the meeting. The translation of the Canon Law Society of Great Britain and Ireland reads "that the advice of all be sought." Whether the Prior would need, ad validitatem, to seek the advice of a Counselor who was unable to attend the meeting is doubtful. It is advisable, however, that he seek the opinion of all Counselors in order to make wise and prudent decisions.

10 V. Can. 101, §1: "Circa actus personarum moralium collegialium: no. 1: Nisi aliud expresse iure communi aut particulari statutum fuerit, id vim iuris habet, quod, demptis suffragiis nullis, placuerit parti absolute maiori eorum qui suffragium ferunt . . . "

11 Can. 127. (Text is in footnote no. 9, above.) For voting in collegiate acts, can. 119, the same is true: absolute majority of those who are present is required.

of the council, only three members vote; two vote in favor and one against. Under the old Code, the consent would have been granted, since two out of three valid is certainly absolute majority. In the new Code, there is no consent: to receive absolute majority, more than half must be in favor. In this case, there are only two votes out of four voting members present. The Prior would be unable to act validly.

Another problem arises in the case where the Prior does not receive an absolute majority, but in which two Counselors are in favor and two opposed. Can the Prior cast a deciding vote in order to break the tie? Since there is not agreement among the authors, it is worth a moment to consider the various opinions which have been expressed on this matter.

Some argue that, based upon canon 119, the Prior can cast the deciding vote, but only after two ballots have already been taken:

> With regard to collegial acts, unless provision is made otherwise by law or statutes:
>
> no. 2: if it is a question of other matters [not elections], that action will have the force of law which, when a majority of those who must be convoked are present, receives the approval of an absolute majority of those who are present; if after two ballots it is a tie vote, the presiding officer can break the tie by his or her vote.[12]

---

12 Can. 119: "Ad actus collegiales quod attinet, nisi iure vel statutis aliud caveatur: no. 2 – si agatur de aliis negotiis, id vim habet iuris, quod, praesente quidem maiore parte eorum qui convocari debent, placuerit parti absolute maiori eorum qui sunt praesentes; quod si post duo scrutinia suffragia aequalia fuerint, praeses suo voto paritatem dirimere potest." This canon is parallel to v. can. 101, upon which Goyeneche based his agreement to this side of the argument: "Potestne superior suo voto paritatem suffragiorum dirimere?" in CpR 8(1927)31-32.

This argument would affirm that a Prior can vote, not because he is a member of his Council, but because he is the presiding officer, and that, therefore, after the second attempt, if a tie vote still results, he may cast the deciding vote.

A second argument is, in effect, the exact opposite: a Prior cannot vote with his Council, nor can he break a tie vote even after the second ballot. This opinion is based on the following: a Prior is not a member of his Council. The reason for the Council's existence is to give advice to the Prior; it makes no sense that the Prior advise himself in this context. And, as to the effect of canon 119, those who hold this opinion argue that canon 119 is not applicable to this situation. Canon 119 is describing the procedure which a collegial body must take in order to perform a juridical act. If the action is approved, it must be performed. On the other hand, canon 127 refers to the consent that is necessary in order for a superior to perform a juridical act. However, the fact that consent is given by a council does not oblige the superior to act. He is free to decide himself whether or not to carry out the action. (Obviously the contrary is not true: if the council does not grant the consent, the superior cannot act.) Thus, the authors who support this argument state that canon 119, which refers to collegial acts, is not applicable to the seeking of consent which the superior must do in those cases specified by law.[13] There is, nevertheless, the possibility acknowledged by these authors that proper law gives the superior the faculty to break a tie vote in matters which require the consent of the council as prescribed in the same proper law. In other words, this faculty cannot be given for those matters which, in common law, require the consent of

---

13 This opinion is proposed by A. GUTIÉRREZ, "Facultas superioris dirimendi paritatem in actibus consilii" in CpR 63(1982)35-38, and in "De superiore et consilio triplex quaestio" in CpR 54(1973)122-134.

the council. But if proper law establishes cases of this type, it can also give the superior the faculty to break tie votes. There are no such cases in the Order's Constitutions, although Province Statutes could make such determinations.

A third opinion on this question claims that the superior can break a tie vote, and moreover, if so determined in the constitutions, the superior can even vote as a member of the council. Primary support for this position is given by the fact that the Congregation for Religious and Secular Institutes has approved the constitutions of many different groups which express that the superior is a member of his or her council with the right of vote, as well as the presiding officer.[14] The fact, too, that the number of counselors is almost always even leads to the conclusion that a tie vote can be avoided by the decisive vote of the superior.

Now, in the case of the Augustinian Order, what can be said as to the Prior's relationship and power to vote with his Council? There is no specific statement in the Constitutions that says that the Prior is a member of the Council. However, by reason of analogy, he can be considered a member: both on the Provincial and General levels, the superior is a member of the Council.[15] Thus, in practice, a Prior may follow the opinion that he does have the right to vote with the House Council.

There is, unfortunately, a lack of precision in the Constitutions in this matter. The Code of Canon Law makes a distinction between cases in which a superior and his council vote as a collegiate body, and cases where a superior needs the consent of his

---

14 See E. GAMBARI, *Il nuovo codice e la vita religiosa* (Milan: Ancora, 1984), p. 154.

15 *Constitutiones*, no. 391: "Consiliariorum munus est Priorem Provincialem in Provinciae regimine prudenti consilio et actuosa opera adiuvare. Iidem una cum Priore Provinciali Consilium Provinciae constituunt." A parallel determination is made regarding the General and the Council of the Order in no. 468.

council in order to act.[16] While there are distinctions made in the Constitutions as to those times when a superior must act "with the consent of his council" and other cases when it is the Council that acts, there is not a great deal of clarity as to the mind of the legislator on the question of whether the superior can always vote with the council, and as to the distinction of when the Council acts collegially and when as an advisory board to the superior. According to the opinion of this writer, the Constitutions should establish more clearly the procedure to be followed when the council's intervention is required.[17]

In the meantime, because of existing practice and due to the various opinions which do exist on these matters, the Prior can follow the opinion that he has the right to vote as a member of the Council, even in those cases where he needs the consent of the Council in order to act.

There are also cases specified by law in which the Prior must, for validity of an act, seek the advice of his Council. He is required to hear the opinion of every member, even though he does not have to follow their advice. Nevertheless, in cases where the opinion of the Council is unanimous, he should not act contrary to the

---

16 Among the many cases where the Code specifies that the superior must have the consent of his council: can. 638, §3: "... Superioris competentis cum consensu sui consilii ... " On the other hand, can. 699, §1 reads: "Supremus Moderator cum suo consilio ... collegialiter procedat ... "

17 There are actually very few cases specified in law which require the consent of the Council in order for the Prior to act validly. Such is the case, however, on the Provincial and General levels. In order to provide more clarity, it would be sufficient to state, for example, that the superior can vote with the Council in all matters (which some authors believe to be invalid); or that in matters decided by the "Council", the Superior has a vote, whereas in matters in which the superior can only act "cum consensu sui consilii", he does not have a vote, except (if so decided by the legislator, i.e. a General Chapter) after two tie ballots. This latter solution would seem to lend more credibility to the very reason for which such consent is required: at times, a kind of braking force exercised by a Council might well be called for.

judgment except with good reasons which he considers sufficient to override the Council's recommendation.[18]

Concerning the Prior's obligation to hear the Council, there has been a noteworthy change put into the new Code. In the old Code, because of a lack of uniformity in vocabulary, there was a certain amount of doubt established as to the question of what was required for validity and what requirements were for liceity. The question of a superior's obligation to seek the advice of his council, while seemingly necessary for validity, was reduced to a requirement for liceity because of the doubt established.[19]

The new Code, however, has remedied the doubt, primarily by following a norm of consistency in the language it uses for requirements *ad validitatem*.[20] Therefore, there is no longer any doubt that the Prior must hear the opinion of his Council for the validity of those acts specified in the law which require such consultation.

Just as an obligation rests upon the Prior to hear the opinion of every member of the Council, so too there is the obligation placed on each Counselor to express honestly his own judgment on the

---

18 V. can. 105, no. 2: "si consilium exigatur, invalidus est actus Superioris easdem personas non audientis; Superior, licet nulla obligatione teneatur accedendi ad earundem votum, etsi concors, tamen sine praevalenti ratione, suo iudicio aestimanda, ab earundem voto, praesertim concordi, discedat."

19 V. can. 105, no. 1: "... si consilium tantum, per verba, ex.gr.: 'de consilio consultorum', vel 'audito Capitulo', 'parocho', etc., satis est ad valide agendum ut Superior illas personas audiat ... " Here, it seems clear that the requirement is for validity. But because there are other canons which call for the advice of a council in which the requirement is *ad licitatem*, a lack of clarity results. See, for example, v. can. 1653, §1: "Ordinarii locorum possunt ... ; sed, ut *licite agant*, debent audire Capitulum cathedrale ... "

20 Can. 10: "Irritantes aut inhabilitantes eae tantum leges habendae sunt, quibus actum esse nullum aut inhabilem esse personam expresse statuitur." (Cf. v. can. 11, the difference being the removal of the words *vel aequivalenter* after *expresse*.) Can. 127 (see footnote 9) has been reworded, and those canons which call for advice of the council or similar body have been written in such a way as to avoid contradictory language.

matter at hand. Where the seriousness of the matter demands it, secrecy must be observed by all the Counselors· so as to protect the right of all the parties involved in the discussion.[21]

c) Matters requiring the consent/advice of the Council

Canon law establishes two instances in which the superior must seek the consent of his Council in order to act. The first is in regards to acts of alienation and other business transactions in which the financial condition of the community can be adversely affected.[22] Specific limits in terms of ordinary and extraordinary administration are set in proper law, and there may even be subdivision within the category of extraordinary administration. Those acts which are beyond the established limits of the Treasurer's purview have to be approved by the Prior with the consent of his Council.

A second instance in which canon law requires that the Council be heard is when there is the necessity, due to serious exterior scandal or very grave imminent harm to the Order, of expelling a Brother from the religious house, and where there is even danger in delay to the extent that the matter cannot be immediately

---

21 Can. 127, §3: "Omnes quorum consensus aut consilium requiritur, obligatione tenentur sententiam suam sincere proferendi atque, si negotiorum gravitas id postulat, secretum sedulo servandi; quae quidem obligatio a Superiore urgeri potest."

22 Can. 638, §3: "Ad validitatem alienationis et cuiuslibet negotii in quo condicio patrimonialis personae iuridicae peior fieri potest, requiritur licentia in scripto data Superioris competentis cum consensu sui consilii . . . " This case is also presented in the Constitutions; treasurers are to administer the goods of the community under the direction of the Prior and his Council. *Constitutiones*, no. 492: "Eorum [Oeconomorum] munus praecipuum est Domus . . . curam gerere, sub directione Superiorum eorumque Consiliorum eadem administrare et omni tempore Superiores ipsos eorumque Consilia, de rebus ad quaestiones oeconomicas directe vel indirecte attinentibus, considerato iudicio adiuvare . . ." This entire topic will be discussed in further detail in the section of this chapter "The administration of the material goods of the house."

CHAPTER SIX

dealt with by the major superior.²³ In this case, the Prior with the consent of his Council may decide to expel the member from the house. Upon such action, the whole matter must be referred to the Provincial who will have to decide upon subsequent action to be taken.²⁴

In the constitutions, several matters are designated which require the intervention of the Council. Before a meeting of the local Chapter, the Prior should discuss the more serious business or concerns with his Counselors before they are presented to the Chapter for decision.²⁵ It is also possible for Chapter members to present to one of the Counselors matters which he would like considered in the Chapter; the Counselor should present these in the meeting with the Prior before the order of business is prepared for the Chapter.²⁶

Priors have, by virtue of the Constitutions, the power to dispense from disciplinary laws of the Order for their own jurisdiction. They may dispense in single cases, if there is just cause, any of the Brothers individually, or "with the consent of his Council, all together."²⁷

23 Can. 703: "In casu gravis scandali exterioris vel gravissimi nocumenti instituto imminentis, sodalis statim a Superiore maiore vel, si periculum sit in mora, a Superiore locali cum consensu sui consilii e domo religiosa eici potest . . . "

24 Can. 703: " . . . Superior maior, si opus sit, dimissionis processum ad normam iuris instituendum curet, aut rem Sedi Apostolicae deferat." This case will be further investigated in the last section of this chapter, "Safeguarding the life of the community."

25 *Constitutiones*, no. 302: "Capitulum Locale ordinarie semel in mense celebretur. Congruo tempore antea, una cum expositione argumenti, communicetur omnibus Capitolaribus, praesertim vero Consiliariis qui, cum Priore et officialibus, negotia graviora perpendant, antequam omnibus in Capitulo definienda proponantur."

26 *Constitutiones*, no. 303: " . . . Singulorum vero Fratrum Capitularium ius est quidquid, suo iudicio, bono communi faveat, Priori et Consiliariis tradere, ut de eo in Capitulo agatur, dummodo communicatum fuerit antequam ordo Capituli conficiatur . . . " The next section in this chapter discusses this topic further.

27 *Constitutiones*, no. 280a: "Quoad Constitutiones Ordinis, omnes Superiores etiam Locales, in sua quisque iurisdictione, nisi expresse vetiti sint, iusta de causa, a

In order to carry out his duty of protecting the life of the community, a Prior may impose a precept upon a member of the community. To do so validly, he must have the consent of his Council, unless the matter is entirely secret.[28] In more serious cases, if one of the house officials has violated the common life, the Prior, with the consent of his Council, can suspend the official from office.[29]

Any other cases where the advice or consent of the Council is to be sought by the Prior are to be determined by the Provincial Statutes. A Prior should certainly not hesitate to consult his Council about matters which are of concern to the whole community and which are serious in nature. Although the Council's role is primarily advisory, it can be of great help to the Prior when the Counselors are chosen wisely, and when the Prior knows how to profit by the assistance offered to him in the form of wise counsel.

2) The Local Chapter

When speaking continually on the topic of the local superior, one might too easily forget or lose proper perspective of the value which must be found in the dimension of fraternal equality in the Augustinian Order. "Our Order is one of apostolic fraternity, that is a community of Brothers who live with the People of

---

legibus ad observantiam regularem pertinentibus Fratres, etiam hospites, vel singulos vel etiam, de consensu sui Consilii, omnes simul, in singulis casibus, dispensare possunt." Other examples of the power to dispense can be mentioned: the Liturgy of the Hours (see p. 119); attendance at local Chapters (see p. 163); from fast and abstinence (*Paenitemini*, 17 feb. 1966, AAS 58 [1966] 177-198, no. 7).

28 *Constitutiones*, no. 286b: "Praeceptum suam non obtinet vim, si a Priore Locali imponatur toti Communitati sine praevio consensu Superioris Maioris, vel singulis Fratribus sine consensu sui Consilii, nisi agatur de casibus omnino secretis ... "

29 *Constitutiones*, no. 512: " ... Prior Localis, de consensu sui Consilii, officiales Domus ab officio suspendere potest ... " Both cases mentioned in this paragraph are considered in the last section of this chapter, "Safeguarding the life of the community."

God ... "³⁰ "Brotherhood in the Order, therefore, ought to be singularly evident in the equality of all the Brothers, admitting of no privilege or honorary title."³¹ It is within the context of the local community that the Prior offers his service, and in terms of governance of the community, it is the Prior as "first among equals" with the Chapter that best demonstrates this fraternity of the local level.³² In guiding the community, the Prior must never try to work in isolation from the Chapter. Nor must he use the Chapter merely as a juridical structure within which certain business items are approved. Properly developed, the Chapter can become an integral part of the community's life, providing real consensus among the Brothers based upon the principle of fraternal equality that is part of the Order's nature.

Legislation which determines the membership, the procedure to be followed and the authority of the local Chapter is left primarily to proper law. In fact, the Code of Canon Law has virtually nothing to say about this important aspect of Augustinian life. Chapters are discussed in canons 631 to 633; canon 631 refers to the General Chapter; canon 632 states:

> Proper law is to determine clearly what pertains to other chapters of the institute and other similar gatherings, namely,

---

30 *Constitutiones*, no. 10: "Religio enim nostra Ordo est fraternitatis apostolicae seu Communitas Fratrum, quae cum populo Dei vivit ... "

31 *Constitutiones*, no. 12: "Fraternitas ergo in Ordine singulariter manifestari debet in aequalitate omnium Fratrum, nullo privilegio vel titulo honorificio admisso ... "

32 *Constitutiones*, no. 13: "Ordinis structura eamdem fraternitatem bene commonstrat. Potestas suprema regendi tribuitur Capitulo Generali, quod totum Ordinem repraesentat, eamque Capitula Provincialia, Viceprovincialia et Localia, in suo quaeque ambitu, iuxta Constitutiones participant. Ideo magni momenti est conceptus electionis et repraesentationis in Ordine."

regarding their nature, authority, composition, mode of procedure and time of celebration.[33]

The third canon of this article presents the possibility of other organs of participation or consultation.[34] Because of the nature of the local Chapter in the Augustinian Order there is as such no general need to establish other structures of a similar nature. Province Statutes could, if the need arises, establish such forms of participation in government.

a) Membership

As already highlighted in the introductory remarks to this section, the Chapter holds importance as a structure which gives expression to the fraternal nature of the Order. Thus, all Brothers with active voice are members of the Chapter, and no distinction is made between ordained and non-ordained Brothers as was done in the old Constitutions.[35] Generally speaking, all Brothers in

---

33 Can. 632: "Ius proprium accurate determinet quae pertineant ad alia instituti capitula et ad alias similes coadunationes, nempe ad eorum naturam, auctoritatem, compositionem, modum procedendi et tempus celebrationis."

34 Can. 633, §1: "Organa participationis vel consultationis munus sibi commissum fideliter expleant ad normam iuris universalis et proprii, eademque suo modo curam et participationem omnium sodalium pro bono totius instituti vel communitatis exprimant." §2: "In his mediis participationis et consultationis instituendis et adhibendis sapiens servetur discretio, atque modus eorum agendi indoli et fini instituti sit conformis."

35 *Constitutiones,* no. 301: "Congressio Fratrum Communitatis vocem activam habentium, eo fine convocata ut, consilio fraterno, de communis omnium Fratrum boni causa, sub moderamine Prioris agat, Capitulum Locale constituit." Cf. *Constitutiones* (1926), no. 891: "Capitulum Conventus, semel saltem in mense celebrandum, constat ex omnibus vocem habentibus, nempe Sacerdotibus triennio ante solemniter in Ordine professis, qui etiam triennio ante studiorum curriculum absolverint; omnes autem in Capitulum vocati eidem interesse tenentur." In *Ecclesiae sanctae,* II (6 aug. 1966, AAS 58 [1966] 757-787), no. 27: "Capitula generalia et Synaxes monum explorent, vi cuius sodales qui conversi, cooperatores vel alio nomine vocantur, gradatim in determinatis actibus communitatis et in electionibus votum obtineant activum et, in quibusdam muneribus, etiam passivum; ita revera fiet ut ipsi cum vita et communitatis operibus arcte

CHAPTER SIX

solemn vows possess active voice, although there is one possible limitation, left up to the determination of the Provincial Statutes. This has to do with those Brothers who have not completed the time of initial formation:

> Provincial Statutes are to determine the conditions under which [rights of active and passive voice] are to be exercised, either by deferring their exercise up to the end of the time of formation, or by restricting it to specified matters during formation.[36]

Even in cases where a Brother does not have active voice, the Prior or Chapter itself should ask his opinion in matters where it would be deemed helpful.[37] Those Brothers who have no voice in the Chapter may submit, in writing, suggestions or questions which must be considered by the Chapter, as long as they were

---

coniungantur, et sacerdotes liberius in ministeria propria incumbere possint." Thus, the 1968 Constitutions gave all Brothers active and passive voice from the time formation was completed: no. 292: "Omnes Fratres votorum sollemnium, tempore formationis expleto, voce activa et passiva fruuntur. Tempus vero formationis pro clericis usque ad absolutionem curriculi theologici et pastoralis extenditur; pro non-clericis vero quattuor annos post tempus probationis, nisi in Constitutionibus vel statutis provincialibus aliter provisum sit." This was further modified at the General Chapter of 1977 to read (now no. 293): "Omnes fratres votorum sollemnium voce activa et passiva fruuntur. Sub quibus vero condicionibus, aut post tempus formationis differendo aut, intra tempus formationis, ad materias speciales restringendo, haec iura exerceantur, Statuta Provincialia determinent." Once again, at the General Chapter of 1983, a modification was made, substituting the words, "usque ad finem formationis temporis differendo," for "post tempus formationis differendo." (*Acta OSA* 28 [1983] 117).

36 *Constitutiones*, no. 293: ". . . Sub quibus vero condicionibus, aut usque ad finem formationis temporis differendo, aut, intra tempus formationis, ad materias speciales restringendo, haec iura exerceantur, Statuta Provincialia determinent."

37 *Constitutiones*, no. 303: ". . . Singulorum vero Fratrum Capitularium ius est quidquid, suo iudicio, bono communi faveat, Priori et Consiliariis tradere, ut de eo in Capitulo agatur, dummodo communicatum fuerit antequam ordo Capituli conficiatur, salvo casu urgentis necessitatis. Si opportunum videtur, audiantur etiam Fratres non Capitulares."

submitted before the formulation of the order of business, or even afterwards if they are cases of urgent necessity.[38]

Two final comments are in order regarding the membership of the Chapter. Unlike the case of the Council, the Prior is a member of the Chapter, and does certainly have the right to vote. Secondly, in order to hold a house Chapter, there must be at least three solemnly professed Brothers assigned *de familia* to that community.[39] If there are not three such members, important matters must be referred to the Provincial and his Council, unless the Provincial Statutes make other provisions.[40]

b) Authority

There is a very important relationship between the local Chapter and the Prior in terms of governing the community. Theologically, an Augustinian community is an attempt to reconstitute the conditions of the first Christian community as described in the Acts of the Apostles and as adopted by Augustine in his Rule.[41] In this

---

38 *Constitutiones*, no. 294: "... Fratres autem qui partem in Capitulo non habent, possunt libere petitiones, quaestiones vel suggestiones per litteras ipsi proponere: quae omnia Capitulum attente perpendere debet, dummodo communicata fuerint antequam ordo Capituli conficiatur, salvo casu urgentis necessitatis." Note that while no. 303 (see preceding footnote) speaks of the right of Chapter members to submit suggestions to the Chapter, this number gives the right to non-members making no specification as to whether or not active voice is a requirement. This number is found in the general introduction, chapter 13, *De Capitulis*. There is also an error in the translation of the text into English, where "per litteras" is translated "by mail"; "in writing" would be more accurate.

39 *Constitutiones*, no. 305: "Ubi Capitulum Locale celebrari non potest, quia tres saltem Fratres voce activa gaudentes de familia non sunt..."

40 *Constitutiones*, no. 305: "Ubi Capitulum Locale celebrari non potest, quia tres saltem Fratres voce activa gaudentes de familia non sunt, omnia maioris momenti negotia, quae eidem deliberanda sunt, Superioris Maioris eiusque Consilii remittantur iudicio, nisi Statuta Provincialia aliter provideant."

41 See p. 24.

community, authority is service, and that service is rendered within a context of listening to what the Spirit is saying in His people so that His projects can be carried out freely and willingly. The Prior then is called to listen, so that together they can discern and implement what the Spirit inspires. This theology of listening as the Spirit welds the group into community provides a framework within which the Chapter's authority can be understood.

With this as a general introduction to the question of the Chapter's authority, it is now possible to look more closely at what the Code of Canon Law and the Constitutions specify in this regard. According to canon 596, §2, "chapters possess ecclesiastical power of government for both the external and internal forum."[42] While the major impact of this provision lies on the level of the General Chapter, within the limits of local community the house Chapter has what could be considered a quasi-legislative authority. While canon 596 does recognize the Chapter's possession of ecclesiastical authority, canon 632 leaves the determination of the power of other chapters (those that are not general) to proper law.[43] In the Order's Constitutions, chapter twelve, "The Law by Which Our Order is Governed", no power of legislation as such is given to the Local Chapter. In fact, Local Chapters are totally omitted.

It must be stated at the same time, however, that a certain authority is given to the Local Chapter by the Constitutions. The Constitutions state that particular norms for the good of the community and of individuals are to be determined by either the

---

42 Can. 596, §2: "In institutis autem religiosis clericalibus iuris pontificii pollent insuper potestate ecclesiastica regiminis pro foro tam externo quam interno."

43 Can. 632: "Ius proprium accurate determinet quae pertineant ad alia instituti capitula et ad alias similes coadunationes, nempe ad eorum naturam, auctoritatem, compositionem, modum procedendi et tempus celebrationis."

Provincial Statutes or the local community.⁴⁴ This is not, strictly speaking, legislative power, but it is a definite authority possessed by the local Chapter to take action in making norms (to be distinguished from laws) which guide the life of the community. This is stated, though, with the understanding that the local Chapter cannot be considered as a kind of "mini" Provincial Chapter, which, in making statutes, does exercise real legislative authority.

Several things can be stated about the local Chapter's authority. Its areas of competence are presented below in section (d), "Matters to be discussed by the Local Chapter." It has no authority to make decisions which are contrary to the law, whether common or proper. Also, as the direction of the house Chapter pertains to the local Prior,⁴⁵ who is not elected by the Chapter but appointed by the Provincial, a certain accountability is due to the Provincial for the actions taken by the Chapter. Thus, any extraordinary decisions made by a Chapter are subject to confirmation by the Major Superior. Province Statutes may specify what matters are to be submitted for such approval.

Unlike the deliberations of the Prior's Council,⁴⁶ the decisions made by the house Chapter in areas of its competence must be considered as binding. At the same time, the Chapter cannot interfere in those matters which are entrusted to the Prior in

---

44 *Constitutiones,* no. 113: " . . . Normae igitur particulares, pro bono Communitatis et singulorum vel statutis Provincialibus vel a Communitate locali determinandae sunt . . . " It is worth noting that this number speaks of the community and not of the Chapter.

45 *Constitutiones,* no. 301: "Congressio Fratrum Communitatis vocem activam habentium, eo fine convocata ut, consilio fraterno, de communis omnium Fratrum boni causa, sub moderamine Prioris agat Capitulum Locale constituit."

46 See above p. 149.

virtue of his authority.[47] An example, even if extreme, would be helpful to illustrate the point. If the Prior validly gives a precept to a member of the community,[48] and other Brothers for some reason think it unreasonable, the Chapter does not have the authority to negate the action that the Prior has taken.[49] At this point a certain difficulty arises. It is the opinion of this writer that the Constitutions are not always sufficiently clear about the relationship between the Prior and the Chapter. As already mentioned, the direction of the Chapter pertains to the Prior, yet at the same time, the Constitutions state that the Superior's "administration is subject to the Chapter in order to render common life more effective."[50] This apparently refers to superiors at any level of government, and the conclusion can therefore be drawn that the Prior is accountable to the local Chapter in his direction of the Community. While it is actually a distortion to conceive of the Chapter in conflict with the Prior, the reality is that there are times where such conflicts do arise. While the Prior cannot act in total isolation from the Chapter, neither may he be considered as a mere executor of the Chapter's decisions. It seems then that there is need for clearer specification of the various dimensions of the Prior-Chapter relationship.

---

47 Refer to chapter two of this study for an analysis of the personal authority of the local Prior.

48 See pp. 179-180.

49 There is always the right of appeal that rests with the member upon whom the precept was imposed. Appeal would be made to the Major Superior.

50 *Constitutiones*, no. 14: "Superior proinde Frater est ad quem pertinent Fratres, quorum cura ei ab Ordine est commissa, qua filios Dei regere, eiusque administratio Capitulo submittitur ad vitam communitariam efficaciorem reddendam..."

c) Procedure

Chapters are to be convoked by the Prior at least once a month.[51] This is done either by the Prior at his own initiative, or at the request of a majority of the Chapter members.[52] Each member should receive, before the meeting, an agenda which has been prepared by the Prior in conjunction with his Council[53] and with the other officials of the House.[54] Preparation by all of these community members can greatly aid the successful and fruitful outcome of any Chapter deliberations.

Members must be convoked in accordance with canon 155,[55] and the Chapter cannot be held unless more than half the members are present. At least one of the Counselors must also be there.[56] Because of the importance of this moment in the life of the community, "all who are convoked are obliged to attend."[57] In the case of the advanced age of one of the Brothers, the Prior can dispense from this obligation.[58] Such a dispensation can evidently be given habitually; it is unnecessary for the older Brother to ask

---

51 *Constitutiones*, no. 302: "Capitulum Locale ordinarie semel in mense celebratur."

52 *Constitutiones*, no. 303: "Ius Capituli convocandi ad Priorem pertinet, qui vel sua sponte vel maioritatis Capitularium rogatu illud indicit . . . "

53 See above, p. 154. Any serious question to be discussed in the Chapter should be considered by the Prior and his Council before the agenda is finalized.

54 *Constitutiones*, no. 302: " . . . Congruo tempore antea, una cum expositione argumenti, communicetur omnibus Capitularibus, praesertim vero Consiliariis qui, cum Priore et officialibus, negotia graviora perpendant, antequam omnibus in Capitulo definienda proponantur."

55 Can. 166, §1: "Collegii aut coetus praeses convocet omnes ad collegium aut ad coetum pertinentes . . . " The procedure in this regard is basically the same as that discussed above for convoking of the Council. See pp. 145-146.

56 *Constitutiones*, no. 304: " . . . sine praesentia maioris partis Capitularium et cuiusdam ex Consiliariis, Capitulum celebrari nequeat . . . "

57 *Constitutiones*, no. 304: "Omnes convocandi eidem interesse tenentur . . . "

58 *Constitutiones*, no. 304: " . . . Fratres, qui propter provectam aetatem aegre ferant Capitulo adesse, a Priore Locali dispensari possunt."

every time to be excused from attending the meeting. In the case of other members of the Chapter, the Prior can also excuse them in individual cases when there is sufficient reason.[59]

Generally speaking, the Prior is responsible for chairing the meeting of the Chapter, although there may be exceptions to this. One example of this would be if the Prior Provincial is present at the meeting; he has the right to preside if he so wishes.[60] With the exception of the manner to be used in voting, the Constitutions give no specific prescriptions about the way the Chapter is to be run.[61] Thus, the custom of the place can be followed.

In those deliberations where a vote is to be taken, the following procedures are outlined:

> Voting in matters of greater importance is ordinarily to be done by secret ballot. Voting by another method may be employed in matters of small importance, provided all are agreed.[62]

This last item is of great importance. It indicates that if even one member objects to using some method other than a secret ballot, his wishes must be respected; otherwise the entire votation could be invalid.[63] In addition to assuring the right to a secret ballot if so

---

[59] The Prior has the power to dispense in individual cases from laws in the Constitutions regarding the discipline of the common life. Attendance at Chapter would therefore be one of the cases from which the Prior can dispense. See no. 280a, quoted in footnote 27, above.

[60] *Constitutiones*, no. 383: " . . . In omnibus Capitulis Localibus suae Provinciae voce gaudet eisque praeesse potest."

[61] The former Constitutions (1926) included several numbers about the opening of the meeting, the procedure to follow, voting, etc. (see nn. 896-901).

[62] *Constitutiones*, no. 295: "Votationes in rebus maioris momenti per secreta suffragia ordinarie fiant. Votatio autem per alium methodum fieri potest in rebus minoris momenti, omnibus consentientibus."

[63] The casting of one invalid vote does not in and of itself nullify the election or votation. However, by analogy, if it is clear that by subtracting that vote the decision made did not receive the required absolute majority, the votation is invalid. This

desired, the Prior should also ascertain that the other canonical requirements for voting and elections are followed: votes must be free, certain, absolute and determinate.[64]

Approval of any business or proposal brought to the Chapter must be by absolute majority.[65] Ideally, a consensus ought to be reached by the whole community, but realistically that is frequently not possible. But no decision can be made with only a minority of the Brothers in its favor.

In an election where several candidates are presented by the Prior (for example, if this is the method being used for the selection of the Counselors), the candidates themselves may be present and may vote.[66] In the old Code, a vote cast for oneself was invalid,[67] but this is no longer found in the new Code. In part, this could well be because of the difficulty in determining if such a vote was indeed cast. And there are valid arguments for and against the morality of voting for oneself. The decision is now left to the individual.

---

conclusion is based upon can. 171, §2, which speaks of the presence of ineligible voters in an election: "Si quis ex praedictis admittatur, eius suffragium est nullum, sed electio valet, nisi constet, eo dempto, electum non rettulisse requisitum suffragiorum numerum." By virtue of another argument as well the votation may be considered invalid: canon 170 states: "Electio, cuius libertas quoquo modo reapse impedita fuerit, ipso iure invalida est." If a voter's freedom was impaired because of the lack of a secret ballot, the vote is invalid. But if a majority of the voters are denied the right to the secret ballot, then the whole election or votation would be invalid.

64 Can. 172, §1, no. 1: "Suffragium, ut validum sit, esse debet: liberum; ideoque invalidum est suffragium eius, qui metu gravi aut dolo, directe vel indirecte, adactus fuerit ad eligendam certam personam aut diversas personas disiunctive . . ." For no. 2 of this paragraph, see footnote 63, above.

65 *Constitutiones*, no. 308: "Ut negotia pertractata in Capitulo approbata habeantur, maioritas absoluta suffragiorum Fratrum vocalium requiritur." See p. 148 regarding the determination of absolute majority in the new Code.

66 *Constitutiones*, no. 296: "Ubi, ad normam Constitutionum, plures candidati a Superiore proponendi sunt, candidati propositi, si vocales sunt, in electione suffragium ferre possunt . . ."

67 V. can. 170: "Suffragium sibimetipsi nemo valide dare potest."

If the election is to be by vote casting for a single candidate, that person cannot vote, nor can he be present during the voting.[68]

All matters that are discussed and all decisions made in the Chapter are to be recorded in a book of acts, or written and kept in some other manner, and signed by all who were present at the meeting.[69] Finally, all those who participate in the Chapter are to observe secrecy about what was discussed in the session "if divulging of these matters would do harm to the good of the community or individual persons."[70] Likewise, if a majority of the Chapter members ask that a certain matter be kept secret, the obligation to maintain secrecy applies. If necessary, the Prior should remind the Brothers of their responsibility in this regard.[71]

d) Matters to be discussed by the local Chapter

Although the new Constitutions are less specific than the former in terms of the various questions which must be presented to the Chapter for discussion or approval,[72] there are several items

---

68 *Constitutiones*, no. 296: "... In electione autem per ballotationem, unicus candidatus a Superiore propositus nec suffragium dare nec praesens esse potest."

69 *Constitutiones*, no. 300: "Quod in Capitulis actum et conclusum erit, in Actorum libro adnotetur vel saltem scripto servetur, et ab omnibus, qui Capitulo interfuerint, subsignetur."

70 *Constitutiones*, no. 299: "Capitulum participantes secretum servare tenentur circa argumenta in Capitulo acta, si ex divulgatione bonum commune vel privatum laedi potest; idem fiat in casibus specialibus, si maioritas Vocalium hoc necessarium vel utile iudicet."

71 Ibid. See also can. 127, §3: "Omnes quorum consensus aut consilium requiritur, obligatione tenentur sententiam suam sincere proferendi atque, si negotiorum gravitas id postulat, secretum sedulo servandi; quae quidem obligatio a Superiore urgeri potest."

72 See *Constitutiones* (1926), no. 894: although fewer points are enumerated in the new Constitutions, most of the items of the old are actually included in the new, at least by general category.

enumerated which may not be decided without the Chapter's express consent:

> In the local Chapter the following must be discussed and, without its express consent, may not be decided:
> a) matters of greater importance regarding the life of the community;
> b) any extraordinary contract;
> c) the report of the Prior and the other officials about income and expenses;
> d) the daily schedule of the House;
> e) all matters assigned to the Chapter by the Constitutions or Provincial Statutes.[73]

Each of these categories merits a moment's attention especially in light of what has been said about the Chapter's place in the life of the community and its authority in areas specified by the Constitutions.

Matters of greater importance regarding the life of the community: a general category which is to be used widely by the Prior in presenting matters to the Chapter, this heading should include such things as promoting and protecting the patrimony of the Order.[74] Moreover, all those aspects of the community's life which

---

73 *Constitutiones*, no. 306: "In Capitulo Locali perpendi debent, et, sine eius expresso consensu, decerni non possunt:
a) negotia maioris momenti ad vitam communem attinentia;
b) quilibet extraordinarius contractus;
c) relatio a Priore ceterisque officialibus de proventibus et expensis;
d) horarium Domus;
e) omnia alia negotia quae eidem Constitutiones vel Statuta Provincialia mandant."

74 Can. 578 defines "patrimony": "Fundatorum mens atque proposita a competenti auctoritate ecclesiastica sancita circa naturam, finem, spiritum et indolem instituti, necnon eius sanae traditiones, quae omnia patrimonium eiusdem instituti constituunt, ab omnibus fideliter servanda sunt." Discussion on concrete topics by the local Chapter,

form part of its responsibility to the Order or to the Church could well be formulated and discussed in the context of the Chapter. Such topics as hospitality[75] and the community's role in fostering vocations[76] could also be included in this category. The actual content of this category will always depend, however, upon the concrete circumstances of the given community.

The second major heading of business that requires the Chapter's consent is *any extraordinary contract*. "Contract" is to be understood as any agreement between two or more parties which in some way changes the financial conditions of the community: buying, selling, taking out or making loans, accepting obligations, etc. "Extraordinary" refers to limits which must be set by Provincial Statutes regarding what is within the Treasurer's capacity to act, and what exceeds it. More will be said about the administration of material goods in the following section; at this point, the major emphasis rests on the fact that when a significant amount of the community's funds or property is in question, the whole community must be consulted before action is taken. It is even possible for the local Chapter to set limits upon the Treasurer's juridical capability to incur expenses.[77] This should

---

or better, by all members of the local community, will lead to a more concrete understanding of what the community can do to foster and protect these values.

75 *Constitutiones*, no. 120a: "Memores exempli S.P. Augustini, qui 'hospitalitatem semper exhibuit' (Vfr. 4, 8, p. 413), et nostrae amicitiae in Christo fundatae, hospitalitatem erga omnes, maxime autem erga nostrates, apte comiterque exerceamus." The Prior has special responsibility in matters of hospitality, but all the Brothers should be aware of their role as generous hosts to any guests that are staying with the community.

76 *Constitutiones*, nos. 200-201. Note that it is not only the director of vocations who must work to foster vocations, but every member of the Order: "Meminerint autem Fratres continuam apud Deum orationem, exemplum propriae vitae et suam in vinea Domini actuositatem optimam esse commendationem nostri Ordinis et invitationem ad vitam augustinianam amplectendam . . . " (no. 201).

77 *Constitutiones*, no. 494: "Expensas et actus iuridicos ordinariae administrationis, ratione sui muneris, Oeconomi valide facere possunt intra fines ipsis a Capitulis

be done, however, with a sense of balance, trying to avoid an exaggerated limitation upon the normal operations which must be performed for the efficient maintenance of the house and the well-being of the Brothers.

Related to the subject of extraordinary contracts is the following item which must be submitted to the local chapter for its approval, *the report of the Prior and the other Officials about income and expenses*. Although the Prior and Treasurer have the authority to incur expenses within the limits of ordinary administration, they must still make a report each month to the Chapter about the financial state of the community.[78] This serves two purposes: the Prior and Treasurer are accountable to the community for the actions taken in directing the community's financial matters. At the same time, presenting a report to the community will help raise an awareness among the members of certain economic realities, thereby encouraging greater responsibility on the part of all the Brothers as regards each one's role in this aspect of the community's life.

Consent of the Chapter is also required in establishing *the daily schedule of the House*, or in making any changes in what has already been decided. The Constitutions offer a very important principle which should be kept in mind as the horarium of the community is decided upon: "the arrangement of the common life should be managed with a certain flexibility, according to

---

respectivis determinatos: pro expensis et actibus iuridicis extraordinariis indigent in singulis casibus consensu Capituli Localis, vel Superiorum Maiorum vel istorum cum suo Consilio."

78 *Constitutiones*, no. 498: "Oeconomi relationem accuratam de statu oeconomico Domus vel Provinciae vel Ordinis, quoties a Superioribus eorumque Consilio requiratur praesentent: . . . Capitulo vero Locali semel saltem in mense."

differences of surroundings and occupations."[79] In formulating the schedule, the community should keep in mind those common acts which are mandated or suggested by the Constitutions: the Liturgy of the Hours,[80] community Mass,[81] common recreation,[82] as well as any other moment decided upon by the community. In addition, it is frequently helpful to decide upon a given day each month for the meeting of the House Chapter itself. In this way, plans can be made in advance so that conflicts in schedules are more readily avoided.

All matters assigned by the Constitutions or Provincial Statutes to the Chapter must be submitted for the necessary approval. Besides those matters which have already been mentioned in the sections above, the Constitutions require that the following items be considered in the House Chapter: the budget of the maintenance and new acquisitions of the house library;[83] if there are candidates in formation in the community, they must be presented to the House Chapter for advancement to subsequent periods of formation, for renewal of vows and for solemn vows;[84] likewise, presentation of candidates for ministries and orders must be made to the Chapter before submitting them to the Provincial and his

---

79 *Constitutiones,* no. 113: "In actibus vitae communis ordinandis, pro condicionum et occupationum diversitate, liberalitas quaedam adhibeatur . . ."

80 See *Constitutiones,* no. 97, pp. 119-121 of this study.

81 See pp. 127-128.

82 *Constitutiones,* no. 116: "Communis recreatio: In omnibus Domibus, tempore in Capitulo Locali definiendo, fiat in communio recreatio, qua vincula Communitatis in familiari conversatione et gaudio firmentur."

83 *Constitutiones,* no. 148: ". . . Capitulum Locale quotannis statuat, vel a Priore Provinciali cum suo Consilio petat, summam pecuniae in libros bibliothecae conservandos et augendos necessariam."

84 *Constitutiones,* no. 227: "Admissio candidatorum ad tempus probationis, ad Novitiatum et ad professionem tum annualem tum sollemnem ad Superiorem Maiorem pertinet de consensu sui Consilii, habita ratione suffragii Capituli Localis, ubi candidati degunt, et praesertim, Coetus Formationis, si iuxta Statuta Provincialia adest . . ."

Council;[85] in preparation for the Ordinary Provincial Chapter, the Prior must submit a report on the state of the house which must be signed (and, in effect, approved) by all the members of the House Chapter;[86] any planning or development regarding the community's financial affairs should be done in conjunction with the House Chapter.[87]

While the House Chapter has a definite juridical function, its purpose should not remain only on that level. If the Prior and the other community members give careful consideration to the value of this fraternal expression of coresponsibility, the Chapter can become a true source of strength for the common life. This requires, however, a sense of commitment and cooperation on the part of all the members, as well as good planning on the part of the Prior.

3. Administration of temporal goods

Houses of the Order have the right to acquire, possess, administer and alienate temporal goods.[88] Administration of these goods is

---

85 *Constitutiones*, no. 233: "... Fratres ergo ad Ministeria et Ordines recipienda a Superiore maiore de consensu sui Consilii ne proponantur, nisi de eorum scientia, moribus aliisque iure requisitis plene constiterit, habita ratione suffragii Capituli Localis et praesertim Coetus Formationis ..."

86 *Constitutiones*, no. 339: "Priores locales Capitulo exhibere debent, vel si praesentes non sint, per Discretum vel scriptis mittere: a) Relationem duplici exemplari exaratam de statu personali et oeconomico Domus, a Fratribus Capituli Localis subsignatam ..."

87 *Constitutiones*, no. 496: "Planificationes maioris momenti ordinarie fiant a Capitulis vel, si necessarium fuerit, a Superioribus Maioribus de consensu respectivi Consilii, semper tamen praehabito voto consultivo Commissionis de re oeconomica ..."

88 *Constitutiones*, no. 486: "Dum in hoc mundo peregrinamur a Domino (cf. 2 Cor. 5,6) bonis temporalibus uti tenemur tamquam Dei donis necessariis ad vitam temporalem sustentandam et ad opera apostolica, praesertim erga egenos, exercenda. Qua de causa ad proprios fines prosequendos Domibus, Provinciis et Ordini licet bona temporalia acquirere, possidere et administrare, quod in bonum Ecclesiae cedit." Can. 634,

to be carried out in accordance with the norms found in Book Five of the Code, *De bonis Ecclesiae temporalibus*,[89] norms given in Book Two, Article Three, which regard the temporal goods of religious institutes,[90] and norms established by the Order for this purpose.[91] Primary responsibility for the administration of these goods is entrusted to the House Treasurer, who is to work under the direction of the Prior.[92] Canon law recommends that these two offices be filled by distinct persons "to the extent that it is possible."[93] Thus, while such separation is not mandatory, it is advisable, especially in larger communities, in order to relieve the Prior from too many concerns about temporal administration when his primary responsibility is much broader in scope.[94] Local Priors, however, do have the right to carry out ordinary acts of administration just as the Treasurer. Given, nevertheless, normal

---

§1 also acknowledges this capacity, including the right of alienation, which, although not mentioned in the Constitutions, is not explicitly excluded. According to this canon, houses have the right of alienation unless the capacity has been excluded or restricted by the Constitutions. Can. 634, §1: "Instituta, provinciae et domus, utpote personae iuridicae ipso iure, capaces sunt acquirendi, possidendi, administrandi et alienandi bona temporalia, nisi haec capacitas in constitutionibus excludatur vel coarctetur."

89 Can. 635, §1: "Bona temporalia institutorum religiosorum, utpote ecclesiastica, reguntur praescriptis Libri V *De bonis Ecclesiae temporalibus*, nisi aliud expresse caveatur."

90 See canons 634-640.

91 Can. 635, §2: "Quodlibet tamen institutum aptas normas statuat de usu et administratione bonorum, quibus paupertas sibi propria foveatur, defendatur et exprimatur."

92 Can 636, §1: "... Etiam in communitatibus localibus instituatur, quantum fieri potest oeconomus a Superiore locali distinctus." Also, *Constitutiones*, no. 321: "Oeconomus; Ipsius est bonorum Domus accurata administratio, iuxta normas·nn. 486-499, sub moderamine Prioris..."

93 Can. 636, §1 (see footnote no. 92). On higher levels of government, the separation of the offices of Superior and Treasurer is obligatory, but since realistically it is often difficult to do so in small communities, the law allows for the case of one man having both offices.

94 See above, especially regarding the *cura animarum*, pp. 114-117.

circumstances, the house Treasurer should generally be the person to take care of such activities.[95]

Without going into too much detail about the role of the Treasurer and Prior's direction of the administration of the community's temporal goods, a few points are too important to leave out of this study. Canon 1284 gives a general outline of the duties of financial administrators; both Priors and Treasurers should be well aware of these responsibilities.

§1 - All administrators are bound to fulfill their office with the diligence of a good householder.

§2 - For this reason they must:
1) take care that none of the goods entrusted to their care is in any way lost or damaged and take out insurance policies for this purpose, insofar as such is necessary;
2) take care that the ownership of ecclesiastical goods is safeguarded through civilly valid methods;
3) Observe the prescriptions of both canon and civil law or those imposed by the founder, donor or legitimate authority; they must especially be on guard lest the Church be harmed through the non-observance of civil laws;
4) accurately collect the revenues and income of goods when they are legally due, safeguard them once

---

95 A Prior, in this regard, actually has more authority than a bishop in his diocese. A Prior has actual direction, which would include the capacity to administer the goods of the community. A bishop in his diocese has the role of supervising the administration of the temporal goods: the right to demand reports, inspect the [Ed. note: The end of the sentence is not present]. Can. 1276, §1: "Ordinarii est Sedulo Advigilare administrationi omnium bonorum, quae ad personas iuridicas publicas sibi subiectas pertinent, salvis legitimis titulis quibus eidem Ordinario potiora iura tribuantur." See V. DE PAOLIS, "Temporal Goods of the Church in the New Code with Particular Reference to Institutes of Consecrated Life" in *The Jurist* 43(1983)353.

collected and apply them according to the intention of the founder or according to legitimate norms;

5) pay the interest on a loan or mortgage when it is due and take care that the capital debt itself is repaid in due time;

6) with the consent of the ordinary invest the money which is left over after expenses and which can be profitably allocated for the goals of the juridic person;

7) keep well ordered books of receipts and expenditures;

8) draw up a report on their administration at the end of each year;

9) duly arrange and keep in a suitable and safe archive the documents and deeds upon which are based the rights of the Church or the institution to its goods; deposit authentic copies of them in the archive of the curia when it can be done conveniently.

§3 - It is strongly recommended that administrators prepare annual budgets of receipts and expenditures; however, it is left to particular law to issue regulations concerning such budgets and to determine more precisely how they are to be presented.[96]

---

[96] Can. 1284, §1: "Omnes administratores diligentia boni patrisfamilias suum munus implere tenentur." §2: "Exinde debent: 1) vigilare ne bona suae curae concredita quoquo modo pereant aut detrimentum capiant, initis in hunc finem, quatenus opus sit, contractibus assecurationis;

2) curare ut proprietas bonorum ecclesiasticorum modis civiliter validis in tuto ponatur;

3) praescripta servare iuris tam canonici quam civilis, aut quae a fundatore vel donatore vel legitima auctoritate imposita sint, ac praesertim cavere ne ex legum civilium inobservantia damnum Ecclesiae obveniat;

4) reditus bonorum ac proventus accurate et iusto tempore exigere exactosque tuto servare et secundum fundatoris mentem aut legitimas normas impendere;

5) foenus vel mutui vel hypothecae causa solvendum, statuto tempore solvere, ipsamque debiti summam capitalem opportune reddendam curare;

In connection with this last item of preparing an annual budget, but also within the overall realm of the administration of temporal goods, each Province should formulate statutes which regulate the specific manner in which the direction and administration of these goods is to be performed.[97]

Civil law is "canonized" in the Code, and Priors and Treasurers must pay careful attention to the requirements made by these laws. Only in cases in which the civil law is contrary to divine or canon law may it be violated.[98]

Finally, in presenting these general guidelines, the principle found in the Constitutions merits consideration, not only by the Prior and Treasurer, but by every member of the community;

> It is well to remember that it is our duty to offer a good example to others also in the administration of temporal goods by not holding on to resources that are not being used, since we

---

6) pecuniam, quae de expensis supersit et utiliter collocari possit, de consensu Ordinarii in fines personae iuridicae occupare;

7) accepti et expensi libros bene ordinatos habere;

8) rationem administrationis singulis exeuntibus annis componere;

9) documenta et instrumenta, quibus Ecclesiae aut instituti iura in bona nituntur, rite ordinare et in archivo convenienti et apto custodire; authentica vero eorum exemplaria, ubi commode fieri potest, in archivo curiae deponere.

§3: "Provisiones accepti et expensi, ut ab administratoribus quotannis componantur, enixe commendatur; iuri autem particulari relinquitur eas praecipere et pressius determinare modos quibus exhibendae sint."

97 *Constitutiones*, no. 499; "Quoad alia particularia decernenda ad bona conservanda et promovenda, singulae Provinciae et Viceprovinciae statutum speciale condant et in omnibus Capitulis Provincialibus et Viceprovincialibus, saltem Ordinariis, illud recognoscant."

98 Besides can. 1284, §2, no. 3 (see footnote 96, above), civil law is discussed in can. 1290, with reference to contracts and alienation: "Quae ius civile in territorio statuit de contractibus tam in genere, quam in specie et de solutionibus, eadem iure canonico quoad res potestati regiminis Ecclesiae subiectas iisdem cum effectibus serventur, nisi iuri divino contraria sint aut aliud iure canonico caveatur, et firmo praescripto can. 1547." (Can. 1547 regards witnesses as being admissible for proof in every kind of canonical process, even if contrary to civil law.)

are obliged to give witness to both individual and collective poverty, and we know that in this matter of careful and conscientious administration both defect and excess are equally contrary to poverty.[99]

4. Safeguarding the life of the community

Already in Chapter One, the Prior's role as guardian of the community has been presented, both as understood by St. Augustine and as mandated by the Code of Canon Law and the Constitutions.[100] In order to maintain a certain peace and harmony within the community, the Prior is expected to ensure that the precepts of the Rule and Constitutions are observed. Unfortunately, one of the most difficult tasks that falls upon the Prior in his office comes about as a result of the loss of that discipline or commitment on the part of a community member which is essential to the religious life. It is at these moments that the Prior must exercise his authority, always with a great amount of concern for the Brother who is in difficulty, prudently seeking what is best for the entire community. Chapter Twenty-six of the Constitutions addresses this situation, and as will be seen, the procedure to be taken in these cases rests heavily upon the local Prior. It is therefore necessary for him to be aware of his duties, of his responsibility both to the community and to the individual who finds himself in difficulty, so that unhealthy situations can be readily rectified.

---

[99] *Constitutiones*, no. 489: "Meminisse iuvat nostrum officium esse, etiam in administratione bonorum temporalium, exemplum aliis praebere, opes nostras infructuosas non retinendo, quia testimonium paupertatis et individuale et etiam collectivum dare debemus, scientes hac in re, fere similiter contra paupertatem esse curam et sollicitudinem parvam vel nimiam in administratione adhibere."

[100] See pp. 12-13, 31-32.

Although religious families offer to their members helps by which they, through love and joyful confidence in the Spirit, can securely and faithfully protect their religious profession, nevertheless, while we are in exile from the Lord, not even the religious family is an altogether safe place, so that some may labor under troubles and difficulties and even fall from their first fervor.[101]

Charity which should reign in our hearts and love for the reputation for the Order should cause the whole community, Superiors and individual Brothers, to aid with the help of God those Brothers who may be in trouble, remembering the words of our Father Augustine—we are human and might have had the same fault; let mercy go before reprimand.[102]

Hence, if any of us should be aware that some Brother is in difficulties, he should be concerned about the other's spiritual welfare and should, if possible, immediately correct or admonish him in a fraternal way with great kindness, charity and patience. If the problem is not known to others, he should keep it secret for the sake of the Brother's honor and good name. "Let not the beginnings of evil go unchecked, but correct them as soon as they appear."[103]

---

101 *Constitutiones*, no. 500: "Quamvis familiae religiosae sodalibus suis subsidia conferant, quibus caritatis via, spiritu gaudentes, religiosam professionem secure et fideliter custodire valeant, tamen, dum peregrinamur a Domino, neque ipsa familia religiosa locus est omnino securus, ita ut angustiis ac difficultatibus quis non praepediatur, immo et a caritate prima decidat."

102 *Constitutiones*, no. 501: "Caritas vero quae regnare debet in cordibus nostris ac dilectio decoris Ordinis totam Communitatem, Superiores ac singulos Fratres, inducere debent ad adiuvandos, quantum dederit Deus, Fratres nostros, forte in angustiis positos, illud tamen S.P. Augustini recolentes: Nos homines esse et etiam tale vitium habere potuisse, ut illam reprehensionem misericordia praecedat." See Augustine, *De serm. Domini*, 2, 19, 64; PL 34, 1298.

103 *Constitutiones*, no. 502: "Unde si quis nostrum sciat Fratrem aliquem talibus in adiunctis versari, secreto servato, propter honorem ac bonam Fratris famam, si res

CHAPTER SIX

Primarily responsibility for helping a Brother who is in some way living contrary to the Rule, Constitutions or spirit of the Order rests with the Brother who knows about the situation. The Constitutions exhort him to keep the situation secret from the others; but he is immediately to correct or admonish the wrongdoer.

If the attempt on the part of this Brother to correct the wrongdoer is not efficacious, the Prior should be notified if there is the possibility that such action will help the one in difficulty. The Prior must be informed of the situation if the matter is publicly known or about to become so.[104]

> And do not charge yourselves with ill-will when you bring this offense to light. Indeed, yours is the greater blame if you allow your Brothers to be lost through your silence when you are able to bring about their correction by your disclosure. If your brother, for example, were suffering a bodily wound that he wanted to hide for fear of undergoing treatment, would it not be cruel of you to remain silent and a mercy on your part to make this known? How much greater then is your obligation to make his condition known lest he continue to suffer a more deadly wound of the soul.[105]

---

adhuc aliis lateat, de bono spirituali eius sollicite satagat, statimque, circumstantiae id patiantur, magna cum benignitate, caritate et patientia, fraterne adliciat vel admoneat, 'ne coepta progrediatur, sed de proximo corrigatur'." (See *Regula*, c. 4.)

104 *Constitutiones*, no. 503: "Si autem bonum eius officium incassum cesserit, videat num spes affulgeat si, a Superiore adiutus, admonitus, vel correctus, Frater sublevari possit; hoc in casu Superiorem de re edoceat. Idipsum semper faciat si res ita sese habeant ut publici iuris sint vel cito fieri possint."

105 *Regula*, c. 4: "... Nec vos indicetis esse malevolos, quando hoc indicatis. Magis quippe innocentes non estis, si fratres vestros, quos indicando corrigere potestis, tacendo perire permittitis. Si enim frater tuus vulnus haberet in corpore, quod vellet occultare, cum timet sanari, nonne crudeliter abs te sileretur et misericorditer indicaretur? Quanto ergo potius eum debes manifestare, ne perniciosius putrescat in corde?"

Chapter four of Augustine's Rule, especially the passage quoted above, is more than clear, both in the obligation that rests with the Brothers to care for the member of the community who finds himself in need of healing, and in the reasons that sufficiently motivate such action as notifying the Prior when it is necessary.

While the first person responsible for seeking to aid a Brother in need is the community member aware of the situation, the weight of the responsibility rests with the Prior; once he is aware of a situation in which a Brother is in need of correction, he must act.

> The charitable duty of helping, admonishing and correcting the Brothers belongs especially to the local Prior. He should consider as especially addressed to himself the words of the Rule: "Let him admonish the unruly, cheer the faint hearted, support the weak, and be patient towards all. Let him uphold discipline while instilling fear."[106]

What action the Prior is to take depends of course upon the concrete situation: the Brother who is in trouble, the circumstances, the gravity of the situation, the risk of public disclosure and scandal. Ideally, if the Prior has been able to establish a minimum of rapport with the individual, correction or admonishment can be done in honest dialogue between them. If this is insufficient, or ineffective, the Prior does have the capacity of giving a command in virtue of the vow of obedience; in virtue of the ecclesiastical

---

[106] *Constitutiones*, no. 505: "Munus caritatis Fratres adiuvandi, admonendi, vel corrigendi ad Priorem Localem speciatim pertinet, cui immediata eorum cura committitur. Verba Regulae 'corripiat inquietos, consoletur pusillanimes, patiens sit ad omnes: disciplinam libens habeat, metum imponat' (*Regula*, c. 7), sibi praecipue dicta intelligat." See pp. 31-33, where comment is made on can. 619.

CHAPTER SIX

power of governance, the Prior can give a precept,[107] but in order to do so validly, certain conditions must be followed:

> A precept, gravely obliging in conscience either individual Brothers or all together, may be given . . . by all Superiors, local included. In order that a precept be legitimate, it must:
> 1) concern a matter that is grave, either in itself or in its circumstances, and that has to do with the Rule, the Constitutions or the Statutes;
> 2) be given in writing in a legitimate document or, in case of necessity, orally, before two witnesses;
> 3) be expressed in due form, namely: *We command or prohibit in virtue of holy obedience*, stating accurately what is to done or avoided, and the time of duration, unless the precept is to be given for an indefinite time.[108]

In addition, for the Prior validly to impose a precept on one of the Brothers, he must have the consent of his Council unless the matter is entirely secret.[109] If the Prior considers it necessary to give

---

[107] Can. 35: "Actus administrativus singularis, sive est decretum aut praeceptum sive est rescriptum, elici potest, intra fines suae competentiae, ab eo qui potestate exsecutiva gaudet, firmo praescripto can. 76, §1." See also *Constitutiones*, no. 286, text in footnote below.

[108] *Constitutiones*, no. 286a: "Praeceptum, graviter in conscientia obligans, in omnes vel singulos Fratres, possunt dare Capitula Generalia, Provincialia ac Viceprovincialia et omnes Superiores, etiam Locales. Ut vero sit legitimum, debet:
1) versari circa rem ex se vel ex adiunctis gravem ad Regulam vel Constitutiones vel Statuta attinentem;
2) in scriptis per legitimum documentum vel, in casu necessitatis, oretenus coram duobus testibus dari;
3) formula debita exprimi, sci.: *Praecipimus vel prohibemus in virtute sanctae oboedientiae*, determinando accurate quid sit faciendum aut vitandum et tempus eius durationis, nisi ad tempus indeterminatum praeceptum dari oportet."

[109] *Constitutiones*, no. 286b: "Praeceptum suam non obtinet vim, si a Priore Locali imponatur toti Communitati sine praevio consensu Superioris Maioris, vel singulis Fratribus sine consensu sui Consilii, nisi agatur de casibus omnino secretis . . ." Note, too, that a local Prior can impose a precept on the whole community. There

an ecclesiastical precept, he must follow the principles on decrees and precepts found in the first book of the Code.[110]

> In more urgent cases, when it is a matter of avoiding grave and imminent harm or scandal, the local [Prior] with the consent of his Council should deal with the Brother by commanding him to make a spiritual retreat, to leave the place, to abstain from celebrating Mass publicly, or by applying some other suitable means.[111]

If the offender is an official of the house, the local Prior with the Council can suspend him from office, provided the required admonitions have been given.[112] Canon law requires that, before a suspension is imposed, the accused must be given at least one warning in advance;[113] since the Constitutions refer to "admonitions", in the plural, it must be assumed that at least two warnings, with a suitable amount of time between each warning given

---

would obviously have to be a most grave reason for such action. Some authors think that precepts should not be used in such a way; precepts are meant for individual persons (see can. 49). In any case, the Constitutions give this authority to the local Prior, but he needs the consent of the Major Superior before imposing the precept.

110 See cann. 48-58.

111 *Constitutiones*, no. 511: "In casibus urgentioribus, ad grave damnum imminens vel ad scandalum, vitandum, Prior Localis, de consensu sui Consilii, provideat Fratri praecipiens ut exercitia spiritualia peragat, vel a loco discedat, vel a sacro publice celebrando se abstineat vel alio modo opportuno... " The official English translation has "Local Superior" in place of "local Prior"; that is not accurate, and such authority would have to be granted explicitly by the Provincial Statutes. See also can. 1319, regarding the Prior's authority to impose penalties.

112 *Constitutiones*, no. 512: "Propter causas inferius allatas et postquam monitiones requisitae facta sunt, Prior Localis, de consensu sui Consilii, officiales Domus ab officio suspendere potest, dum Superior Maior aliud provideat... " The reasons given for suspension from office are those listed in no. 513; see pp 86-87.

113 Can. 1347, §1: "Censura irrogari valide nequit, nisi antea reus semel saltem monitus sit ut a contumacia recedat, dato congruo ad resipiscentiam tempore."

for the opportunity to repent, should be given.[114] Proof of these admonitions, either in writing or by giving them in front of two witnesses, should always be retained.[115] Any time such action is taken, the Major Superior should be notified, so that he can decide if any other action should be taken to try and help the Brother in difficulty, as well as to insure the protection of the common good.[116] Moreover, any time a Prior feels unable to correct such a situation, he should refer the matter to the Major Superior.[117]

In the most serious cases of violations of the religious life, the Code establishes certain penalties.[118] Certain violations, by virtue of the act itself, are cause for dismissal from the Order: one who has notoriously abandoned the Catholic faith, and a Brother who has contracted marriage, or attempted to do so, even civilly.[119] In these cases, it is the Major Superior who must act, collecting proofs

---

114 Ibid. See also footnote no. 112: "postquam monitiones."

115 See can. 1339, §3: "De monitione et correptione constare semper debet saltem ex aliquo documento, quod in secreto curiae archivo servetur."

116 *Constitutiones*, no. 512; see footnote no. 112 above.

117 *Constitutiones*, no. 506: "Si vero suis caritatis officiis Prior Localis nihil profecerit vel casus emerserit qui modum, auctoritatem vel vires eius excedat, rem ad Superiorem Maiorem referat."

118 The Constitutions establish very few sanctions; suspension from office, as discussed above, is one of these. There are no latae sententiae penalties. The Provincial Statutes may make determinations of specific penalties according to the place and frequency of certain offenses; no. 509: "Si casus fert Statuta Provincialia determinent quaenam violationes legum nostrarum, sive ob earum frequentiam sive ob condiciones particulares temporis ac loci, maius periculum pro bono Communitatis constituant et quomodo illis occurrendum sit." But, generally speaking, corrective action is left up to the prudent judgment of the Superior: no. 508: "Ne disciplina paulatim in Ordine corruat, publicae transgressiones Regulae et Constitutionum ex prudenti Superiorum iudicio corrigantur."

119 Can. 694, §1: "Ipso facto dimissus ab instituto habendus est sodalis qui: 1) a fide catholica notorie defecerit; 2) matrimonium contraxerit vel, etiam civiliter tantum, attentaverit."

(in which the assistance of the local Prior may be required) and issuing a declaration of the dismissal.[120]

Canon law specifies a number of other violations that, in and of themselves, are considered sufficiently grave such that the law demands that the member be dismissed.[121] These offenses are: homicide, kidnapping and/or detention, mutilation or serious wounding of another, procuring of an abortion, a cleric who lives in concubinage or who remains in another external sin against the sixth commandment of the Decalogue which produces scandal.[122] The violation specified in canon 1395, §2, a cleric's committing some other offense against the sixth commandment with force or threats or publicly or with a minor below the age of sixteen, also calls for mandatory dismissal unless "the superior judges that dismissal is not entirely necessary and that the correction of the member and restitution of justice and reparation of scandal can be sufficiently assured in some other way."[123]

Four other causes are listed in the Constitutions as having the possible penalty of dismissal from the Order:

a) if one has lost the religious spirit completely;
b) if he gravely corrupts the lives of others;

---

[120] Can. 694, §2: "His in casibus Superior maior cum suo consilio, nulla mora interposita, collectis probationibus, declarationem facti emittat, ut iuridice constet de dimissione."

[121] Can. 695, §1: "Sodalis dimitti debet ob delicta de quibus in cann. 1397, 1398 et 1395, nisi in delictis, de quibus in can. 1395, §2, Superior censat dimissionem non esse omnino necessariam et emendationi sodalis atque restitutioni iustitiae et reparationi scandali satis alio modo consuli posse."

[122] These offenses are the ones specified in the enumerated canons in the footnote above. Note, however, that in the last offense (a cleric in concubinage or another external sin against the sixth commandment), the mandatory dismissal is only for a cleric; according to can. 18, laws which have penalties attached must be interpreted strictly. Thus, it is left to the discretion of the Superior whether or not to initiate the dismissal process.

[123] Can. 695, §1; see footnote no. 121, above.

c) if he causes deep dissensions in the community;
d) if, after the time granted to him for living outside the House has expired, he fails to return following the third warning by a Major Superior.[124]

While all cases of such serious offenses ought to be referred to the Provincial, the Local Superior has a particular responsibility to seek to aid the Brother before the situation becomes public or causes scandal, thereby avoiding if possible the mandatory dismissal of the member from the Order. Nevertheless, in the most urgent cases, if no other steps can be taken, the local Prior can, with the consent of his Council, expel a Brother from the house.[125] This action must then be referred to the Provincial who will decide what further action should be taken. Dismissal from the Order is not necessarily the subsequent step to be taken, unless the offense is one of those cases listed above.

In all of this discussion on protecting or safeguarding the life of the community, a couple of points must be remembered by the local Prior. He must always act very carefully, judging all the circumstances of the situation. An individual, before the penalty of dismissal is imposed, must receive several warnings;[126] but even

---

124 *Constitutiones*, no. 519: "... Causae dimissionis ab Ordine sunt quae iure canonico vel quae sequuntur:
   a) si quis spiritum religiosum omnino amiserit;
   b) si mores aliorum graviter corruperit;
   c) si profundas discordias in Communitate excitaverit;
   d) si quis, tempore ei concesso ad degendum extra domum expleto, post tertiam admonitionem Superioris Maioris non reversus fuerit."

125 Can. 703: "In casu gravis scandali exterioris vel gravissimi nocumenti instituto imminentis, sodalis statim a Superiore maiore vel, si periculum sit in mora, a Superiore locali cum consensu sui consilii e domo religiosa eici potest. Superior maior, si opus sit, dimissionis processum ad normam iuris instituendum curet, aut rem Sedi Apostolicae deferat." See *Communicationes* 13(1981)361.

126 *Constitutiones*, no. 519: "Professus votorum solemnium ab Ordine tantum dimittatur, si pluries iam monitus et correctus, contumax adhuc permaneat committendis

in other cases, the Superior should admonish the Brother, urging him to correct the difficulty before more definitive action has to be taken. If a Brother is accused of some violation, his right to defend himself must always be respected. Also, when a Superior gives consideration to the element of "scandal" which is frequently proposed as motivation for imposition of a sanction, he must be certain that real scandal is present. It is not sufficient merely to have offended the sensibilities of an individual. Finally, let the Prior keep in mind the important principle of charity, remembering that the purpose of correcting one of the Brothers is to seek his conversion and to safeguard the life of the community. Good judgment and sensitivity on the part of the Prior will insure that the best interests of all are sought, "all out of love for the person and hatred of sin."[127]

---

transgressionibus quibus comminatio dimissionis adnectitur. Causae dimissionis ab Ordine sunt quae iure canonico vel quae sequuntur . . . " (For the rest of this number, see footnote 124.) In addition, the Prior should keep in mind all of the principles found in Part I of Book VI of the Code, which discusses offenses and penalties in general.

127 *Regula*, c. 4: " . . . cum dilectione hominum et odio vitiorum."

CONCLUSION

Now that all this time has been spent on rather detailed examination and analysis of the role of the local Prior in the Order of Saint Augustine, what is there that remains to be said? The most probable response to this question is that there is yet a great deal which has perhaps been briefly mentioned here, or alluded to, or perhaps not even looked at, but which deserves more attention. Primary emphasis, throughout the entire thesis, has obviously and intentionally been placed upon the juridical aspects of the Prior's office and duties. It must be said that in the first chapter, keeping with the principle of integrating spiritual and theological principles with the law as was done in writing the new Code, some of the more spiritual and theological dimensions of the Prior's role have been presented for the reader's consideration. Nonetheless, the following chapters all took somewhat of a more strictly juridical approach, even when theological questions were brought into the discussion. (Such was the case, for example, in the entire question of the authority exercised by the local Prior, presented in the second chapter.)

There is, therefore, much which perhaps has not been said. However, this does not lessen the value of the juridical presentation which has been done here. In fact, quite the opposite is true.

CONCLUSION

Religious life, just as the Church as a whole, is a reality made up of visible, concrete dimensions and spiritual, charismatic elements as well. Frequently, it is in and through the visible dimension that the charismatic is actualized. Thus, the law has an immensely important role to play in seeking to aid the community, or in this case the local Prior, in living out the charismatic dimension of the religious life. The Prior will be well-prepared for many of his responsibilities if he has a thorough knowledge of the juridical aspects of his role, if only because in seeing all of the responsibilities that the Rule, canon law, and the Constitutions place upon him, he will quickly become aware of the much deeper reality that provides the motivation and justification for the legislation and expectations placed upon him.

In light of this, one of the most important conclusions to be made is the great care which must be taken in the nominating of a local Prior. Here, primary responsibility falls upon the Prior Provincial and his Council, although not exclusively.[1] Choosing a Prior who is not qualified can harm the life of the community. It must also be recalled that the Provincial should consult with the local community before appointing the Prior. Authority is relational, and it would be useless to appoint a man to the office of Prior if there will not be the possibility for a good relationship between him and the other members of the community.

Another conclusion drawn from this study relates to the Constitutions. Overall, the role of the Prior is fairly well specified, such that the necessary guidelines are given for him to be able to carry out his duties, while leaving, at the same time, enough freedom for a Prior not to feel too constrained, but rather to be able to develop what could be called his own personal style of

---

1 See chapter three, pp. 68-69.

leadership. However, there are a couple of points which perhaps ought to be more clearly determined by the Constitutions. These primarily relate to the relationship between the Prior and his Council, and the Prior and the House Chapter. While there are very few cases in which the Prior needs the consent of his Council in order to perform a juridical act validly, the few matters where such is required are important enough to demand greater clarity. Here, the question is related to the matter discussed above as to whether or not a Prior can vote in the Council, and whether or not he can break a tie vote, and if so, under what circumstances.[2] (The same can be said as to the Provincial and General Councils, and in these two cases, the matter is of much greater importance.) Because there does not seem to be a great deal of clarity in this area, it would be beneficial if further study were done on this question. Regarding the Prior and the local Chapter, there is for the most part a fairly good description of those matters which pertain to the Judgment of the Prior, and those which are to be dealt with by the Chapter. There may arise, nevertheless, conflict between the Prior and the Chapter, and it is not at all clear how such situations are to be handled. In this case, it might be better for the Provincial Statutes to make determinations which make clearer guidelines for such situations. Here too, at any rate, there is room for further study which would begin by evaluating the causes of such conflict between Prior and Chapter.

On another note, the Prior's role as it has been outlined must be considered as an ecclesial ministry. He is not merely an administrator within the community. The very structuring of this thesis was chosen to place greater emphasis upon this fact. Augustinian community is modeled upon the monastic

---

[2] See pp. 148-150.

community of Saint Augustine, which in turn was based upon the ideal of the early Christian community as described in the Acts of the Apostles. Thus, the Prior must be considered as a leader of a Christian community, with all that this concept entails. He is, for this very reason, empowered with the ministerial authority to teach, to sanctify and to govern those who are entrusted to his care. Moreover, in as much as the consecrated life is recognized for the witness value it has within the Church, emphasizing in a particular way the mystery of salvation, the importance of the Prior's ministry must not be underestimated.

This study has, in some way, touched upon virtually every principal moment in the life of the local community: from arranging the daily horarium to the celebration of various sacraments, from aspects of initial formation to sickness and death. While Augustinian life places great emphasis on fraternity and collegiality—shown from a juridical point of view through the House Chapter—the Prior's role as animator, leader, organizer, director, and teacher touches upon or is deeply integrated into the entire life of the community. For this reason, it would not be an exaggeration to speak of the local Prior as the principle of unity for the local community. The Constitutions and the Rule speak frequently of the communion of the Brothers, and while a great deal of responsibility for this experience of the common life rests upon each and every member of the community, it must be said that the Prior has a particularly significant role in facilitating the sharing of life that is essential to Augustinian community. Whether it be in the area of the prayer life of the community, or in his efforts to create dialogue or bring about reconciliation, or in the celebration of birthdays or other significant events in the life of the Brother, the Prior is, as primus inter pares, the instrumental figure who can create, or deepen, the fraternal bond of communion among all the Brothers. In a spirit of humility and service, and open to the help that he will need from all of the members of the community, the local Prior will be able to fulfill those duties entrusted to him, and he will therefore aid the community in fulfilling its mission in the Church and in the world.

BIBLIOGRAPHY

1. Sources

Acta Apostolicae Sedis, Commentarium Officiale. Romae: in Civitate Vaticana, 1929-.
Acta Ordinis Sancti Augustini, Commentarium Officiale, Romae: Curia Generalizia, 1956-.
Bullarium Ordinis Eremitarum S. Augustini, ed. L. Empoli, Romae, 1628.
Code of Canon Law. Translation by the Canon Law Society of America. Washington, DC: CLSA, 1983.
The Code of Canon Law. Translation by the Canon Law Society of Great Britain and Ireland. London: Collins Liturgical Publications, 1983.
Codex Iuris Canonici. Pii X Pontificio Maximi iussu Digestus, Benedicti Papae XV Auctoritate Promulgatus, Praefatione Fontium Annotatione et Indice Analytico-Alphabetico ab E.mo Petri Card. Gasparri Auctus. Romae: Typis Polyblottis Vaticanis, 1917; reimpressio, 1974.
Codex Iuris Canonici. Ioannis Pauli Papae II Auctoritate Promulgatus. AAS 75, Pars II (1983).
Communicationes. Pontificia Commissio Codici Iuris Canonici recognoscendo. Romae. From 1969 onward.
Concilium Oecumenicorum Decreta. Bologna: Istituto per le scienze religiose, 3rd edition, 1973.
Constitutiones Ordinis Eremitarum S. Augustini. Ratisbonenses, 1290, in: Aramburu Cendoya, Ignacio. *Las primitivas Constituciones de los Augustinos*. Valladolid: Archivo Augustiniano, 1966.

Constitutiones Ordinis Eremitarum S. Augustini. Romae: Typis Polyglottis Vaticanis, 1926.
Constitutiones Ordinis Fratrum S. Augustini. Romae, 1968.
Enchiridion de Statibus Perfectionis. Documenta Ecclesiae Sodalibus Instituendis. Rome: Officium Libri Catholici, 1949.
Enchiridion Vaticanum. Documenti Ufficiali del Concilio Vaticano II e della Santa Sede, 1962-1983. 8 vols. Bologna: Edizioni Dehoniane Bologna, 1981, 1982, 1984.
Informationes. Official bulletin of the Sacred Congregation for Religious and Secular Institutes, Rome. From 1975 onward.
Insegnamenti di Giovanni Paolo II. Vatican: Ed. Tipografia Poliglotta Vaticana. From 1978 onward.
Mutationes Constitutionum Ordinis Fratrum S. Augustini. A Capitulo Generali Ordinario Anno 1977 approbatae. Textus pro tempore 1977-1978. Rome, 1977.
Patrologia Latina, ed J.P. Migne. 221 vols. Paris, 1844-1864.
Regula et Constitutiones Ordinis Fratrum S. Augustini. Rome: Curia Generalizia, 1978.
Schema Codicis Iuris Canonici. Pontificia Commissio Cadice Iuris Canonici Recognoscendo. Rome: Libreria Editrice Vaticana, 1980.
Vatican Council II: The Conciliar and Post-Conciliar Documents. General editor, Austin Flannery. Dublin: Dominican Publications, 1975.
Vatican II: More Post-conciliar Documents. General editor, Austin Flannery. Grand Rapids, MI: Wm. B. Eerdmans Publishing Company, 1982.

2. Authors and Books

Andrés Guttiérrez, Domingo. *El derecho de los religiosos: comentario al Código.* Fuenlabrada (Madrid): Publicaciones Claretianas y Commentarium pro Religiosis, 1983.
Arangio-Ruiz, Vincenzo. *Istituzioni di diritto romano.* 14th edition. Naples: Casa Editrice Dott. Eugenio Jovene, 1978.
Berger, Adolf. *Encyclopedic Dictionary of Roman Law.* Philadelphia: American Philosophical Society, 1953.
Berman, Harold J. *Law and Revolution: The Formation of the Western Legal Tradition.* Cambridge: Harvard University Press, 1983.
Beyer, Jean. *I Superiori e la loro missione.* Milan: Editrice Ancora, 1983.

Bouscaren, T. Lincoln and Ellis, Adam C. *Canon Law: A Text and Commentary*. 3rd edition. Milwaukee: The Bruce Publishing Company, 1957.

Cappello, Felix. *Summa Iuris Canonici*, 3 vols. 4th edition. Rome: Pont. Universitas Gregoriana, 1945.

Castañó, José Manuel. *Ius Ecclesiae Constitutionale*, vol. 2. Rome: Pont. Universitas a S. Thoma, 1976.

Comentarios al Código de Derecho Canonico, 4 vols. Madrid: Biblioteca de Autores Cristianos, 1964.

Congar, Yves. *Jalons pour une théologie du laïcat*. Paris: Cerf, 1954.

———. *Le Concile de Vatican II. Son Église, Peuple de Dieu et Corps du Christ*. Paris: Beauchense, 1984.

Cooke, Bernard. *Ministry to Word and Sacraments*. Philadelphia: Fortress Press, 1977.

Corcoran, G. *A Guide to the Confessions of Saint Augustine*. Living Flame Series, no. 17. Edited by T. Curran. Dublin: Carmelite Centre of Spirituality, 1981.

Cox, Ronald J. *The Juridic Status of Laymen in the Writing of the Medieval Canonists*. Washington, DC: The Catholic University of America Press, 1959.

Cunningham, Richard G. *An Annotated Bibliography of the Work of the Canon Law Society of America, 1956-1980*. Washington, DC: CLSA, 1982.

Da Casola, Masseo. *Compendia di diritto canonico*. Turin: Marietti Editori Ltd., 1967.

De Andres, Heliodoro. *Ejercicio de la autoridad en la vida religiosa*. Valladolid: Estudio Agustiniano, 1968.

Der, Justin J. *The Capuchin Lay Brother: A Juridical-Historical Study*. Rome: Pont. Universitas a S. Thoma, 1983.

Dictionarium morale et canonicum, 4 vols. Rome: Officium Libri Catholici, 1962-1968.

Flannery, Austin and Collins, Laurence. *Light for My Path: The New Code of Canon Law for Religious*. Wilmington: Michael Glazier. Inc., 1983.

Forchia, Camillus A. *La cura d'anime come istituco giuridico*. Rome: Pont. Universitas Gregoriana, 1956.

Gallen, Joseph. *Canon Law for Religious*. New York. Alba House, 1983.

Gambari, Elio. *Consacrati e inviati: spiritualità e diritto della vita consacrata*. Milan: Editrice Ancora, 1979.
———. *Vita religiosa oggi*. Rome: Ed. Monfortane, 1983.
———. *Il nuovo codice e la vita religiosa*. Milan: Editrice Ancora, 1984.
Gavotto, Robert. *The Prior General: The Principle of Unity in the Order of Saint Augustine*. Rome: Pont. Universitas Gregoriana, 1973.
Ghirlanda, Gianfranco; De Paolis, Velasio; and Montan, Agostino. *La vita consacrata*. Bologna: Edizione Dehoniane, 1983.
Grossi, Vittorino and Di Berardino, Angelo. *La Chiesa antica: ecclesiologia e istituzioni*. Rome: Edizione Borla, 1984.
Gutiérrez, David. *Los Agustinos en la edad media, 1256-1356*. Historia de la Orden de San Agustin, vol. I/1. Rome: Institutum Historicum Ordinis Fratrum S. Augustini, 1980.
Hall, Brian and Thompson, Helen. *Leadership through Values*. New York: Paulist Press, 1980.
Jordan of Saxony. *Liber Vitasfratrum*. Edited by R. Arbesmann and W. Humpfner. New York: Cosmopolitan Science and Art Service Company, Inc., 1943.
Kelly, J.N.D. *Early Christian Doctrines*, revised edition. San Francisco: Harper and Row, Publishers, 1978.
Kindt, G. *De potestate dominativa in religione*. Rome: Desclée de Brouwer, 1945.
Kinney, John F. *The Juridic Condition of the People of God: Their Fundamental Rights and Obligations in the Church*. Rome: Catholic Book Agency, 1972.
Lemaire, André. *Les ministères aux origines de l'Église*. Paris: Les Éditions du Cerf, 1971.
Lozano, Juan Manuel. *La sequela di Cristo*. Milan: Editrice Ancora, 1981.
Masterman, Rose Eileen, ed. *Religious Life: A Mystery in Christ and the Church*. New York: Alba House, 1975.
Metz, Johann Baptist. *Zeit der Orden?* Freiburg im Breisgau: Verlag Herder, 1977.
Motte, Antonin. *Supériorat et renouveau dans la vie religieuse*. Paris: Éditions Saint-Paul, 1966.
Parlato, Vittorio. *La professione religiosa*. Milano: Dott. A. Giuffrè Editore, 1979.
Ramstein, Matthew. *A Manual of Canon Law*. Hoboken, NJ: Terminal Printing and Publishing Company, 1948.

Rousseau, Philip. *Ascetics, Authority, and the Church in the Age of Jerome and Cassian.* Oxford: Oxford University Press, 1978.

Schillebeeckx, Edward. *Ministry: Leadership in the Community of Jesus Christ.* Translated by J. Bowden. New York: The Crossroad Publishing Company, 1981.

Schaefer, Timotheus. *De Religiosis ad normam Codicis Iuris Canonici*, 3rd edition. Romae: SALER, 1940.

Schuler, Ralph Vincent. *Privileges of Regulars to Absolve and Dispense.* Washington, DC: The Catholic University of America Press, 1943.

Schumacher, William, ed. *Roman Replies.* Washington, DC: CLSA, 1981-1983.

Suarez, Francisco. *Operis de virtute et statu religionis*, vol. 4. Lugduni, H. Cardon, 1625.

Tierney, Brian. *Foundations of the Conciliar Theory: The Contributions of the Medieval Canonists from Gratian to the Great Schism.* Cambridge Studies in Medieval Life and Thought, vol. 4. Cambridge: Cambridge University Press, 1955.

Trapè, Agostino. "Introduzione" to: S. Agostino, *La Regola.* Milan: Editrice Ancora, 1971.

Van Bavel, Tarsicius J. *Parallèles, vocabulaire et citation biblique de la "Regula Sancti Augustini".* Louvain: Institut Historique Augustinien, 1959.

———. "Introduction and Commentary" to *The Rule of Saint Augustine.* Translated by R. Canning. London: Darton, Longman and Todd, 1984.

Verheijen, Luc. *La Règle de saint Augustin.* 2 vols. Paris: Études Augustiniennes, 1967.

———. *Nouvelle approche de la Règle de saint Augustin.* Vie Monastique, no. 8. Bégrolles en Mauges: Abbaye de Bellefontaine, 1980.

Vermeersch, A. *De religiosis.* 2 vols. Brussels: Houdmont-Bouvin, 1902.

Wernz, Francisco and Vidal, Petri. *Ius Canonicum.* De religiosis, vol. 3. Rome: Pont. Universitas Gregoriana, 1933.

Woestman, William H. *The Missionary Oblates of Mary Immaculate, a Clerical Religious Congregation with Brothers.* Rome: Oblates of Mary Immaculate, 1984.

Woywood, Stanislaus. *A Practical Commentary on the Code of Canon Law.* Revised by Callistus Smith. New York: Joseph F. Wagner, Inc., 1952.

AA.VV. *I sacerdoti nello spirito del Vaticano II*. Edited by S. Favale. Turin: Elle di Ci, 1968.

AA.VV. *Autorità e obbedienza nella vita religiosa*. Milan: Editrice Ancora, 1978.

AA.VV. *Il diritto del mistero delta Chiesa*, 4 vols. Rome: Libreria Editrice della Pontificia Università Lateranense, 1979-1980.

AA.VV. *La figura del superiore locale oggi. (Atti della XX Assemblea Generale, Conferenza Italiana Superiori Maggiori)*. Rome: Editrice Rogate, 1980.

AA.VV. *Il fratello religioso nella comunità ecclesiale oggi. (Atti del I Convegno Intercongregazionale sulla vocazione religiosa del fratello negli Istituti Clericali)*. Rome: Edizioni CIPI, 1983.

AA.VV. *Il nuovo diritto dei religiosi*. Rome: Editrice Rogate, 1984.

3. Articles

Alberigo, G. "La Juridiction: remarques sur un terme ambigu." *Irenikon* 49 (1976) 168-180.

Alonso, S. "Sentido y misión del gobierno religioso." *Vida Religiosa* 48 (1980) 405-425.

Alvarez Gómez, J. "Diversas formas de obediencia religiosa." *Vida Religiosa* 42 (1977) 422-434.

Andrés, Domingo. "Comentario al documento Mutuae relationes." *Revista Espanola de Derecho Canonico* 34 (1978) 548-657.

Andrés Gutiérrez, Domingo. "Bibliographia systematica de iure religiosorum pro ann. 1970-1979." *CpR* 62 (1981) 158-192; 237-298.

Arias Gómez, Juan. "El precepto Canónico como norma juridica o como acto administrativo." *Revista Española de Derecho Canónico* 39 (1983) 217-231.

Augé, Matias. "Autorità e obbedienza nella vita religiosa: rassegna bibliografica (1966-1976)." *Claretianum* 18 (1978) 5-34.

Barberena Iraizoz, Fermín. "Los religiosos y la pastoral parroquial. Comen tarios a unas respuestas de la Comisión de Interpretes." *Revista Española de Derecho Canónico* 36 (1980) 81-116.

Barnard, C.I. *The Functions of the Executive*. Cambridge, MA: Harvard University Press, 1938.

Baroffio, Bonifacio. "La paternità dell'abate nel monachesimo primitivo." *Renovatio* 12 (1977) 67-79.

Beyer, Jean. "Strutture di governo e esigenze di partecipazione." *Vita Consacrata* 8 (1972) 257-285.

———. "Chiarimenti sull'ufficio dei superiori nell'istituto religioso." *Vita Consacrata* 17 (1981) 393-402.

———. "De natura potestatis regiminis seu iurisdictionis recte in codice renovata enuntianda." *Periodica* 71 (1982) 93-145.

———. "Profilo del superiore locale." *Vita Consacrata* 19 (1983) 385-395.

Blat, Albertus. "De potestate superiorum in religionibus secundum Codicem I.C." *CpR* 16 (1935) 321-353.

Bonnet, Piero Antonio. "Una questione ancora aperta: l'origine del potere gerarchico della Chiesa." *Ephemerides Iuris Canonici* 38 (1982) 62-121.

Brown, Raymond. "Episkopè and Episkopos: the New Testament Evidence." *Theological Studies* 41 (1980) 322-338.

Campbell, Peter. "The New Code and Religious: Some Civil Law Considerations." *The Jurist* 44 (1984) 81-109.

Castaño, José Manuel. "De Elementis quae iuxta doctrinam concilii Vaticani II statum religiosum constituunt." *Acta Conventus Internationalis Canonistarum*. Rome, 1968, pp. 426-455.

———. "Lo 'status consecratorum' nell'attuale legislazione della Chiesa." *Angelicum* 60 (1983) 190-223.

Chittister, J. "Religious Life: The Leadership that is Needed." *Origins* 7 (1977) 209.

Congar, Yves. "Les Laïcs ont part à faire l'Église." *Les quatre fleuves: liberté et loi dans l'Église* 18 (1983) 111-120.

Connolly, Michael C. "*De munere docendi*: Some Orientations." *CLSA Proceedings*, 1982, pp. 219-232.

Cooke, Bernard. "Fullness of Orders: Theological Reflections." *Official Ministry in a New Age*. Permanent Seminar Studies, no. 3. Washington, DC: CLSA 1981.

Coriden, James A. "Rules for Interpreters." *The Jurist* 42 (1982) 277-303.

Counihan, Cyril. "The Brother in Clerical Religious Orders." Supplement to *Doctrine and Life* 16 (1976) 29-41.

Cuneo, J. James. "The Power of Jurisdiction: Empowerment for Church Functioning and Mission Distinct from the Power of Orders." *The Jurist* 39 (1979) 183-219.

Dammertz, Viktor. "Gli istituti di vita consacrata nel nuovo Codice di Diritto Canonico." *Vita Consacrata* 19 (1983) 110-136.

De Paolis, Velasio. "De significatione verborum: iurisdiction 'ordinario,' 'mandata,' 'vicaria'." *Periodica* 54 (1965) 508-516.

———. "Temporal Goods of the Church in the New Code with Particular Reference to Institutes of Consecrated Life." *The Jurist* 43 (1983) 343-360.

Dictionnaire de Droit Canonique, vol. 6, s.v. "Juridiction ecclésiastique." By A. Dumas. Paris: Libraire Letouzey et Ané, 1957.

Dizionario degli Istituti di Perfezione, vol. 2, s.v. "Clericalizzazione della vita religiosa." By J. Leclercq. Rome: Edizioni Paoline, 1975.

Dizionario Patristico e di Antichità Cristiane, vol. 1, s.v. "Autorità nella Chiesa." By Ch. Munier, Casale Monferrato (AL): Casa Editrice Marietti, 1983.

Ennis, Arthur J. "The Spirit of the Present Constitutions: An Attempt to Recapture the Elements of our Original Charism." *Second Annual Course on Augustinian Spirituality*, Rome, 1976, pp. 146-155.

———. "The Historical Development of the Constitutions of the Order as Seen Chiefly through an Analysis of the Ratisbon Text of 1290." *Second Annual Course on Augustinian Spirituality*, Rome, 1976, pp. 133-146.

Fontinell, Eugene. "Authority and Freedom in the Christian Community: Expressed in the Structures of the Institution." *We the People of God: A Study of the Constitutional Government of the Church*. Edited by J. Coriden. Huntington, IN: Our Sunday Visitor, Inc., 1968.

Fransen, Gérard. "Juridiction et pouvoir législatif." *Acta Conventus Internationalis Canonistarum*, Rome, 1968, pp. 212-220.

Fuertes, J. "Ad pastores: an superiores religiosi sint veri pastores." *CpR* 60 (1979) 127-162; 222-260; 351-391.

———. "Auctoritas." *CpR* 54 (1973) 193-212.

Fürst, Carol Gerold. "Il progetto di diritto penale elaborato dalla commissione per la riforma del Codice." *Concilium* 11 (1975) 1178-1188.

García Martín, J. "Exemptio religiosorum iuxta Concilium Vaticanum Secundum." *CpR* 60 (1979) 281-330; 61 (1980) 9-36; 67-130; 62 (1981) 193-206; 289-302.

Garvey, Thomas. "The Religious Brother in the Clerical Community." *Review for Religious* 31 (1972) 206-209.

Gorricho, C. "Reelección de los superiores locales para un tercer trienio." *Vida Religiosa* 26 (1969) 375-376.

Goyeneche, S. "Potestne superior suo voto paritatem suffragorium dirimere?" *CpR* 8 (1927) 31-32.

Greeley, Andrew. "Leadership and Friendship: A Sociologist's Viewpoint." *The Jurist* 31 (1971) 265-279.

Gutiérrez, Anastasio. "De superiore et consilio triplex quaestio." *CpR* 54 (1973) 122-134.

———. "Facultas superioris dirimendi partitatem in actibus consilii." *CpR* 63 (1982) 35-38.

———. "I canoni riguardanti gli Istituti di vita consacrata e le società di vita apostolica collocati fuori della parte ad essi riservata." *Vita Consacrata* 20 (1984) 61-78.

Gutiérrez Vega, L. "Renovación doctrinal y práctica de la obediencia religiosa." *Claretianum* 11 (1971) 139-209.

———. "Misión fundamental del gobierno religioso." *Vida Religiosa* 34 (1973) 97-111.

Hill, Richard. "Authority and Obedience in Consecrated Life." *CLSA Proceedings*, 1983, pp. 221-229.

Hite, Jordan. "Church Law on Property and Contracts." *The Jurist* 44 (1984) 117-133.

Holland, Sharon. "Internal Governance in Consecrated Life." *CLSA Proceedings*, 1983, pp. 37-48.

———. "The New Code and Religious." *The Jurist* 44 (1984) 67-80.

Huizing, Peter. "Reflections on the System of Canon Law." *The Jurist* 42 (1982) 239-276.

Kelly, M. Thaddea. "Collaboration: Key Concept for Religious and Bishops in the Diocese." *CLSA Proceedings*, 1983, pp. 92-99.

Kilmartin, Edward J. "Lay Participation in the Apostolate of the Hierarchy." *Official Ministry in a New Age*. Permanent Seminar Studies, no. 3. Washington, DC: CLSA, 1981.

Kneal, Ellsworth. "Interpreting the Revised Code." *The Jurist* 42 (1982) 304-310.

Knut, Walf. "Disciplina ecclesiastica e vita della Chiesa d'oggi." *Concilium* 11 (1975) 1125-1139.

Komonchak, Joseph A. "Church and Ministry." *The Jurist* 43 (1983) 273-288.

Konidaris, G. "De la prétendue différence des formes dans le régime du christianisme primitif: ministres et ministères du temps des Apôtres à la mort de saint Polycarpe." *Istina* 10 (1964) 59-92.

Kress, Robert. "Membership and Leadership in the Church." *The Jurist* 42 (1982) 29-69.

Larraona, Arcadius. "Commentarium Codicis: can. 489." *CpR* 4 (1923) 134-139.

———. "Commentarium Codicis: can. 501." *CpR* 7 (1926) 30-36.

———. "De potestate dominativa publica in iure canonico." *Acta Congressus Iuridici Internationalis*, vol. 4. Rome, 1934, pp. 145-180.

Lawless, George. "Psalm 132 and Augustine's Monastic Ideal." *Angelicum* 59 (1982) 526-539.

———. "The Monastery as Model of the Church." *Angelicum* 60 (1983) 258-274.

———. "Augustine's Burden of Ministry." *Angelicum* 61 (1984) 295-315.

Lazcano, Rafael. "Notas sobre la obediencia y la caridad en san Agustín." *Revista Agustiniana* 25 (1984) 219-236.

Leonard, Joan de Lourdes. "The Vow of Poverty and the Temporal Goods of Religious according to the Proposed Code." *CLSA Proceedings*, 1982, pp. 207-218.

Lesage, Germanus. "De collegialitate in regimine ordinario religiosorum." *Acta Conventus Internationalis Canonistarum*. Rome, 1968, pp. 460-477.

Linscott, Mary. "The Service of Religious Authority: Reflections on Government in the Revision of Constitutions." *Review for Religious* 42 (1983) 197-217.

Lozano. J. M. "Notulae de ortu vitae monasticae." *CpR* 53 (1972) 302-311; 54 (1973) 3-11; 135-148.

Maroto, Ph. "Studia canonica: Ea quae constitutionibus inhaerent." *CpR* 18 (1937) 244-269.

Marques, José A. "Función pastoral y poder en la Iglesia." *Ius Canonicum* 15 (1975) 159-185.

McDermott, R. "Schema of Canons on Institutes of Life Consecrated by Profession of the Evangelical Counsels: Revision or Update?" *CLSA Proceedings*, 1980, pp. 124-131.

Modde, Margaret Mary. "Governance in Institutes of Consecrated Life: New Law, New Praxis." *CLSA Proceedings*, 1981, pp. 184-193.

Moersdorf, Nicolaus. "Munus regendi et potestas iurisdictionis." *Acta Conventus Internationalis Canonistarum*. Rome, 1968, pp. 199-211.

Moingt, Joseph. "Authority and Ministry." *Authority in the Church and the Schillebeeckx Case*. Edited by L. Swindler and P. Fransen. New York: Crossroad Publishing Company, 1982.

Morán, J. "Sacerdocio y vida común en la perspectiva conciliar y en la Augustiniana." *Augustinianum* 7 (1967) 5-25.

Munier, Charles. "Disciplina penitenziale e diritto penale ecclesiale." *Concilium* 11 (1975) 1100-1112.

O'Connor, David. "The Changing Role and Image of Brothers in Clerical Institutes." *Review for Religious* 41 (1982) 286-298.

O'Rourke, Kevin. "Obedience and Subsidiarity in Religious Life." *Review for Religious* 25 (1966) 305-313.

Onclin, W. "The Power of Decision in the Church at the Supradiocesan Level." *Communicationes* 2 (1970) 197-212.

Örsy, Ladislas. "Government in Religious Life." *The Way*, Supplement, 6 (1966) 90-107.

Pasquier, J. "Models of Leadership." *The Tablet* 228 (1974) 1203-1205.

Peinador, A. "Finalidad de los consejos locales." *Vida Religiosa* 26 (1969) 215- 218.

Pennington, Basil. "The New Code of Canon Law and the New Legislation of the Religious Institute." *The Jurist* 42 (1982) 192-196.

Power, David N. "The Basis for Official Ministry in the Church." *Official Ministry in a New Age*. Permanent Seminar Studies, no. 3. Washington, DC: CLSA, 1981.

Rubio, J. "Estructuras y libertad en la vida religiosa." *Revista Agustiniana de Espiritualidad* 11 (1970) 385-407.

Said, Mark. "Particular Law of Institutes on the Renewal of Consecrated Life." *Review for Religious* 36 (1977) 924-947.

Souto, José Antonio. "El *munus regendi* como función y como poder." *Acta Conventus Internationalis Canonistarum*. Rome, 1968, pp. 239-247.

Sticker, A. "De potestatis sacrae natura et origine." *Periodica* 71 (1982) 65-91.

Turrado, A. "¿Servicio o autoridad de los ministerios en la Iglesia de Cristo?" *Revista Agustiniana de Espiritualidad* 16 (1975) 9-53.

Urru, Angelo. "Principio di sussidiarietà e diritto dei religiosi nel nuovo Codice di Diritto Canonico." *Vita Consacrata* 19 (1983) 501-511.

Van Luijk, Benigno. "L'Ordine agostiniano e la riforma monastica." *Augustiniana* 18 (1968) 173-202; 19 (1969) 14-32; 349-383.

Verheijen, Luc. "Saint Augustin: un moine devenu prêtre et évêque." *Estudio Agustiniano* 12 (1977) 281-334.

Subject Index

A

Acta Ordinis Sancti Augustini, 2–3nn8–10, 7–8nn18–20, 55n67, 120n27–28, 122nn35–36

AG. *See* Second Vatican Council

Andrés Gutiérrez, Domingo J., 20n26, 62n85, 72n20

Anointing of the Sick, 30n60, 137–39

apostolate, 9, 20–21, 24, 35, 54, 85, 95, 100, 102, 107–11, 115–16, 127, 141

auctoritas, 22n33, 37n9, 45n28, 47n37, 48n39, 82n49

Augustine, 16, 40n18, 92–94

    authority according to, 12, 16–17, 40n18, 69n13

    community life according to, 12, 24–25n41, 28, 30–33, 119, 126, 159–60, 176–79, 190

    Confessions, 42n18

    De civitate Dei (*City of God*), 39n14

    De magistro (*On the Teacher*), 89n1

    De sermone Domini in monte (*Our Lord's Sermon on the Mount*), 177n102

    Enarratio in psalmum (*Expositions on the Psalms*), 13n6, 38n12

    letters of, 41n18

    ministry according to, 23

    obedience according to, 12, 38

    Rule of. *See Regula S. P. Augustini*

B

baptism, 18

Bellah, Robert, 6n17

Bombin, L.M., 44n26, 48n41

C

canon, etymology of, 16n17

canon law, 3, 9–11, 40, 55n67, 67, 82, 88, 143, 153–54, 172, 175, 181–83, 188

Castaño, José Manuel, OP (dissertation director), 9n23, 45n28, 49n43

CD. *See* Second Vatican Council

Chapter. *See* General Chapters; Local (House) Chapters

charism, xx, xxv, 50–51

    Augustinian charism, 93

charismatic, 5, 42n18, 188

charity, xxii, xxxiv, 12–13, 61, 113, 177, 185

civil law, 173, 175

common good, xxi–xxv, xxx, xxxiii–xxxiv, 5–6, 21. 36, 90, 123, 182

common law, 44, 55n67, 62, 144, 149

confession. *See* penance

Cuneo, J. James, 51n52, 53n60

cura animarum (care of souls), 104–7, 114–17, 137. *See also* pastoral care

D

DH. *See* Second Vatican Council

dignity, 4, 18, 38, 116, 130

discipline, 31n62, 130, 154, 164n59, 176, 179, 182n118

dispensation, 128n56, 163

E

education. *See* study

ES and ET. *See* Pope Paul VI

SUBJECT INDEX

Eucharist / Holy Communion, xxviii–xxx, 114, 116n12, 119, 125–28, 139, 189n89
  as Viaticum, 138–39
Eucharisticum mysterium (Sacred Congregation of Rites), 125n44, 127n53
exempt orders/exemption, 15n15, 48n40, 55n67, 77n32, 105

F

finances, xxxi, 153, 168–76
budget, 170, 174–75
formation, 35n2, 61, 77n32, 95–104, 110–11, 119, 127, 145, 157–58, 170–71, 190
  director of, 96–100
fraternity / brotherhood, 17, 20, 155
equality, 11, 13, 16n16, 17, 56, 145, 155–56
freedom, 4–6, 12, 19, 38–39, 50, 108, 130, 131, 188

G

Gallen, Joseph, 72n20, 77n32, 81n43, 131n62
Gambari, Elio, 44n26, 49n44, 113n1, 150n14
General Chapters, 2–3, 7, 55n67, 75, 77n32, 79, 122n36, 124n41, 189n56, 151n17, 156–57, 160
governance, 51–63, 70–72, 106, 134, 135n78, 142, 156, 159–60, 180
  as jurisdiction, 43n18, 44, 51–53
  and obedience, 12, 35, 59, 69–70
  by religious superior, 12, 14, 18, 35–38, 51–55

Gutiérrez, Anastasio, 62n85, 95n13
Gutiérrez, David, 54nn65–66
Gutiérrez, D.J.A. *See* Andrés Gutiérrez, Domingo J.

H

Holy Orders, 40n18, 55n67, 60nn78–79, 95
House Chapters. *See* Local (House) Chapters.
House Council, 68, 78, 83, 84–88, 96n15, 120, 125, 128n56, 143–55, 159, 163, 171, 181, 184, 188–89
House Treasurer, xxxi, 116, 142, 144n6, 153, 168–69, 172–73, 175
humility, 15, 26, 38, 191

J

Jerome, 41n18
John Paul II, Pope, 3, 4n12, 92, 94n10
John XXIII, Pope, 1n3, 3,
Jordan of Saxony (Augustinian)
  Liber Vitasfratrum (Vfr.), 12n2, 59n76, 168n75
judgment, 37, 86, 99, 144, 152, 182n118, 183, 185, 189
jurisdiction. *See* power
The Jurist, 49n43, 51n52, 173n95

L

Larraona, Arcadius, 77n32, 100n24, 101n29
Lawless, George, 23n37, 24n41
laity, 49n43
  lay brothers, 40n18, 55n67, 110–11
  lay societies, 110n52

liturgy, celebration of, 22, 25–26, 118, 125

Local (House) Chapters, 66, 99–100, 103, 142, 145, 154, 155–71, 189

    authority of, 160–63

    matters to be discussed by, 167–69

    membership, 157–59

    procedures, 163–66

local Prior, 35–36, 51–63, 65–89, 90, 106–7, 134

    distinction from local superior, 65–66

    relationship with Director of Formation, 97, 99

LG. *See* Second Vatican Council

love, xxiv, xxx, 5, 11–12, 18, 20, 22, 24–25, 30, 32–33, 38, 59, 93–94, 102, 110, 113, 118, 122n36, 136, 177, 185

    fraternal, 11, 30, 59, 102, 136

M

magister, xxvii, 89, 91, 94–95, 104

marriage / matrimony, 85, 182

Moingt, Joseph, 90

MR. *See* Sacred Congregation for Religious and Secular Institutes

N

natural law, 44

O

obedience, 1, 4, 7, 12, 14, 18, 26, 35–40, 44–46, 48, 58, 69–70, 102, 179–80

ordination. *See* Holy Orders

Örsy, Ladislas, 17n20, 19n23, 19n25, 91n5

OT. *See* Second Vatican Council

P

papacy, 50, 90, 139

    papal infallibility, 90n3

pastoral care, 40n18, 57, 98, 108, 137

    for the sick, 22, 30, 136–39

pastoral ministry, 54, 59, 102, 107

pastoral office (*munus pastoral*), 60

patience, 32, 177

Paul VI, 5nn14–15, 6n16, 118

    Ecclesiae sanctae (ES), 2, 23n35, 157n35

    Evangelica testificatio (ET), 22, 36, 37n9, 55n69, 57n74

PC. *See* Second Vatican Council

penance, 62n85, 124n41, 129–35, 139

    seal of confession, 134–35

Peter and keys as source of authority in the Church, 49, 52

Pius XI, *Ad catholici sacerdotii*, 98

Pius XII, 1–2, 46–47

Pope (office). *See* papacy

power:

    abuse of, 7, 16–17, 58

    of chapters that are not general, 159–60

    of (ecclesial or ecclesiastical) governance, 44n22, 51–55, 58, 62n85, 106, 134–35, 159–60, 180 of jurisdiction / jurisdictional, 15n15, 44, 47, 55n67, 101; definition of, 40n18, 52–53; alteration by Vatican II, 53, 67n6; supreme, 47

of the keys, 52

of legislation, 160–61

of orders, 67n6

potestas dominativa, 15n15, 40n18, 44, 45n29, 46

potestas ecclesiastica regiminis / potestas regiminis, 51, 53nn61–62, 55n67, 62n85, 67n6, 106n42, 134n75, 156n32, 160n42, 175n98

potestas iurisdictionis, 40n18, 45, 51n51, 55n67, 62n85

potestas ordinis, 40n18, 67n6, 133n73

prayer, 35n2, 122n36

individual, 118–19

life of the community, 119–20, 122, 139

Liturgy of the Hours, 119–21, 170

preaching (preach), 90, 95, 104–9

priesthood. See Holy Orders

Prior General, 71, 73–74, 76, 78, 96n15, 120, 139

Prior Provincial, 19, 68, 79, 81, 84, 120, 164, 188

proper law, 36, 43, 70, 75, 77, 80, 146–47, 149–50, 153, 156, 160

Provincial Chapter, 68

Provincial (Province) Statutes, 10, 27, 66, 80, 96n15, 97, 99–100, 108, 123, 128, 144–45, 150, 155, 157–61, 167, 170, 189. *See also* termination

R

reconciliation, sacrament of. *See* penance

Regula S. P. Augustini, 9n22, 69n13

c. 1, 12n5, 24n40, 25n42, 28n53, 93n8, 119n22

c. 3, 28n54

c. 4, 31n63, 177n103, 178n105, 185n127

c. 5, 30n58

c. 7, 12n4, 13nn7–8, 31n61, 31–33nn64–66, 179n106

c. 8, 33n69, 38n13, 40n18

removal / privation of office, 81–88

retreat, 14, 119, 121–25, 181

reverence (*reverentia*), 14n13, 18, 114n5, 115n7, 130n60

Rousseau, Philip, 40n18

Rule of St. Augustine. *See Regula S. P. Augustini.*

S

sacrament, 113, 117. *See also* Anointing of the Sick; baptism; Eucharist / Holy Communion; Holy Orders; matrimony; penance

Sacred Congregation for Religious and Secular Institutes (SCRSI), 35, 47, 55n67, 57n74, 120n27, 128n56, 132n66

"Essential Elements in the Church's Teaching on Religious Life as Applied to Institutes Dedicated to the Works of the Apostolate," 35–36nn1–7, 56n70

Mutuae relationes (MR), 48, 60–62, 89–90nn1–2, 101–2nn28–30, 103n33, 113n2, 141

SUBJECT INDEX

Sacristan, 129

SC. *See* Second Vatican Council

Second Vatican Council, 1, 3, 9, 14, 15n15, 21, 45, 52, 53n61, 97, 116n12

   Ad gentes divinitus (AG), 102n31

   Christus Dominus (CD), 48n40, 61–62

   Dignitatis humanae (DH), 4n13, 5n14

   Lumen gentium (LG), 23n35, 38n12, 48n40, 50–52, 60, 125n44, 127n53

   Optatam totius (OT), 97–99

   Perfectae caritatis (PC), 1–2, 14, 21, 23n35, 38n11, 39n16, 47, 57n74, 101, 102n31, 114, 117, 118n21, 126, 130nn59–60

   Presbyterorum ordinis (PO), 67n6, 114n6, 125n44, 126n47, 127n53

   Sacrosanctum Concilium (SC), 121n30, 125n44

   Unitatis redintegratio (UR), 125n44

Schillebeecx, Edward, 40n18

   case of, 90n4

service, 6, 10, 11–16, 23–33, 36, 38–40, 47, 59, 60n78, 65, 89, 96, 101–2, 113, 118, 132, 141, 156, 160, 191

sexual sin (against the sixth commandment), 183

spiritual direction, 29, 60, 89, 118

status, 49n43

St. Augustine Societies, 111

study, xvii, xxv, xxvii–xxviii, 29, 54, 91–96, 101–3

Suarez, Francisco, 45n27, 46n33

submission, 4, 38, 40n18

T

Tack, Fr. Theodore (Prior General), 7

teach, 40n18, 52, 60, 89–95, 104, 109, 190

transfer, 84–85

Trapè, Fr. Agostino (Prior General), 2n9, 55n67

Treasurer. *See* House Treasurer

U

universal law, 43–44, 146

UR. *See* Second Vatican Council

V

vacancy, 71, 84–85, 87–88

Van Bavel, Tarsicius J., 69n13

Verheijen, Luc, 24n41, 40n18

Villanova, PA, xvin2, 2

virtue, xvi, xxiv, xxvi, 26–27, 32

   cultivation of, 22, 26

vocation(s), 29, 94, 97, 101, 105, 168

   director of, 168n76

   discernment of, 96

Vows, 35n2, 110n52, 156–57

   profession of, 18, 26, 29, 46, 76, 77n32, 100, 170

   renewal of, 125, 170

Scripture Index

Psalms
99   13n6
132   24n41
132:1   93n9

Matthew
10:1–4   40n18
20:25–27   40n17
25:36   30n59

Mark
3:14–18   40n18
10:35   16n16
10:42–44   40n17

Luke
6:13–16   40n18
12:41–43   16n16
18:1   119n24
22:25–27   40n17

John
13:12–15   16n16
17:11   97n17
20:24   40n18

Acts
4:32   119n22, 126n48
4:32–35   25n41, 28n53
11:28–30   40n18
16:4   40n18

I Corinthians
4:1   113n1
15:5   40n18

II Corinthians
2:5, 6   171n88

Philippians
2:3   69n13
2:5–11   16n16
2:8   38

I Thessalonians
5:12–13   40n18
5:14   14n9

I Timothy
3:1–7   40n18
5:17   40n18

Hebrews
13:7   40n18
13:17   40n18, 114n3
13:24   40n18

James
5:14   40n18

I Peter
5:1   40n18
5:3   26n48, 118n20

Canonical Index

Code of Canon Law (1983)

Can. 2	138	Can. 155	163	Can. 589	53n62
Can. 10	77n31, 152–53n20–21	Can. 158	88n68	Can. 591	48n40
Cann. 17–19	107n45	Can. 166	145, 146n8, 147, 147n9, 163n55	Can. 592	103
Can. 18	183n122	Can. 170	164n63	Can. 596	15n15, 43–44, 44n22, 45n30, 51, 53n62, 103n33, 106n42, 160
Can. 35	180n107	Can. 171	164n63		
Can. 48	51n53	Can. 172	165n64		
Cann. 48–58	181n110	Cann. 184–196	81	Can. 608	65–66, 126n50
Can. 49	51n53, 180n109	Can. 186	81–82	Can. 617	36, 43n20
Can. 76	180n107	Can. 187	82nn47–48	Can. 618	14–22, 30n57, 33, 36, 47–48, 106n43, 114, 114n5, 115, 130n60
Can. 102	134n74	Can. 188	84n54		
Can. 103	134n74	Can. 189	82–84nn49–53		
Can. 119	147n11, 148–49	Can. 190	84n55, 84n57	Can. 619	13, 22–28, 30–33, 31n61, 33n64, 34n65, 104, 106n43, 114n6, 115, 118n20, 179n106
		Can. 191	84n58		
Can. 127	146–47, 147n11, 149, 152n20, 166n71	Can. 193	86n62		
		Can. 194	85–86		
Can. 129	51n51, 52n56, 55n67	Can. 196	86n64	Can. 622	43n21
		Can. 197	45	Can. 623	75, 77
Can. 131	46n30, 52n55, 55n67	Can. 199	45	Can. 624	70nn14–15, 72n19, 85n59
		Cann. 206–209	45		
Can. 133	45n30	Can. 207	49n43	Can. 627	143
Cann. 137–144	45n30	Can. 463	115n11	Can. 629	80n42
Can. 137	52n55	Can. 517	57n73	Can. 630	130, 130n61, 132nn67–68, 133n71, 134, 134n75
Can. 145	67	Can. 534	129		
Can. 146	68	Can. 573	46n32		
Can. 147	68	Can. 576	50	Can. 631	156
Can. 149	75	Can. 578	27n51, 91–92, 94n11, 167n74	Can. 632	157, 160, 160n43
Can. 150	115n11			Can. 633	156, 157n34
Can. 151	115n11	Can. 587	77n32	Cann. 634–640	172n90
Can. 152	78n33	Can. 588	49n43, 54	Can. 634	171n88

Can. 635	172n89, 172n91	Can. 749	90n3	Can. 970	135n78
		Can. 753	90n3	Can. 974	134n74
Can. 636	172nn92–93	Can. 757	104–5, 107n44, 115n11	Can. 983	133n72
Can. 638	151n16, 153n22			Can. 984	133n72
		Can. 762	105n38	Can. 986	115n11
Can. 661	100–101, 103n32	Can. 764	106	Can. 1003	115n11, 137
		Can. 765	106–7, 107n44	Can. 1276	173n95
Can. 663	119n25, 122n35, 124n42, 127n51	Can. 767	109	Can. 1284	173–74, 175n98
		Can. 771	115n11		
Can. 664	131n65	Can. 778	110	Can. 1290	175n98
Can. 670	29	Can. 833	79n36, 79n39	Can. 1319	181n111
Can. 677	111n55	Can. 897	125	Can. 1339	182n115
Can. 678	115n7, 115n11	Can. 905	127n53	Can. 1347	181n113, 182n114
Can. 694	183nn119–20	Can. 911	138n89		
Can. 695	183n121, 183n123	Can. 922	115n11	Can. 1395	183, 183n121
		Can. 966	133n73	Can. 1397	183n121
Can. 699	151n16	Can. 967	134n74, 135	Can. 1398	183n121
Can. 703	154nn23–24, 184n125	Can. 968	134–35, 135n77	Can. 1547	175n98
				Can. 1752	117n16
Can. 738	115n11	Can. 969	135n77		

Codex Juris Canonici (1917)

V. can. 11	152n20	V. can. 505	70n14, 72n18	V. can. 1328	105n39
V. can. 101	147n10, 148n12			V. cann. 1337–1348	105n39
		V. can. 508	80n42		
V. can. 105	152nn18–19	V. can. 514	138n87	V. can. 1337	105n39
V. can. 145	67n6	V. can. 516	53n63, 57n74	V. can. 1338	105n39
V. can. 170	165n67			V. can. 1406	79n38
V. can. 189	83n52	V. can. 593	23n35	V. can. 1653	152n19
V. can. 488	53n63	V. can. 595	23n35, 131nn63–64		
V. can. 501	44, 44nn23–24, 55n67	V. can. 813	79n36		
		V. can. 938	138n87		

Constitutiones of the Order of St. Augustine

No. 4	53n62	No. 98	121n29	No. 227	99–100n23–24, 171n84
Nos. 7–17	92n7	No. 10	122n34, 122n36		
No. 10	24n38, 77, 107n46, 155–56	No. 102	122n35	No. 229	96n15
		No. 105	121–22	No. 231	76n28, 100n25
No. 12	128n56, 156	No. 106	122n32	No. 232	100n25
No. 13	156n32	No. 107	122n33	No. 233	171n85
No. 14	115, 117n15, 162n50	No. 108	123n37, 123n39, 124n42, 125n43	No. 237	96–97
				No. 238	97, 99n22
No. 15	11–12, 59n76			No. 240	56
No. 16	21	No. 109	123–24	No. 242	79n36, 80n40, 144
No. 32	25	No. 111	139nn90–92		
No. 39	20	No. 113	77n32, 143n2, 161n44, 169–70	No. 243	51n53, 52n54
No. 43	25n43			No. 244	56n72, 66
No. 43	25n43	No. 116	170n82	No. 245	66nn3–4
No. 48	110n53	No. 117	77n32	No. 246	66n2
No. 49	110–11	No. 118	77n32	No. 274	9n22
No. 66	25	No. 120	168n75	No. 276	51n53
No. 68	29n55	No. 121	88n67	No. 280	154n27, 164n59
Nos. 75–81	38n10	No. 122	30, 136	No. 282	51n53
No. 75	38–39	No. 147	95	No. 286	51n53, 155n28, 180
No. 76	39	No. 148	170n83		
No. 78	39	No. 151	96n14	No. 292	69
No. 82	118	No. 154	103n34	No. 293	145n7, 157n35
No. 86	123n38	No. 159	96n14	No. 294	159n38
Nos. 87–91	126n49	No. 161	108	No. 295	164
No. 89	127n52	No. 166–67	104n36	No. 296	165n66, 166n68
No. 91	126n49	No. 177	108		
No. 92	132–33, 132n66	No. 188	96n14	No. 299	166
No. 94	136–37, 139	Nos. 200–239	96n14	No. 300	166n69
No. 95	119	No. 200	168n76	No. 301	157n35, 161n45
No. 96	120, 121n30	No. 201	168n76	No. 302	154n25, 163n51, 163n54
No. 97	120, 170n80	No. 204	96n14		
		No. 218	104n36		

213

CANONICAL INDEX

No. 303	154n26, 158n37, 163n52	No. 339	171n86	No. 499	175n97
		No. 349	76n29	No. 500	177
No. 304	163n56, 164	No. 350	79n37	No. 501	177
No. 305	159nn39–40	No. 361	68n10	No. 502	177
No. 306	167	No. 363	68n11, 144n6	No. 503	178n104
No. 308	165n65	No. 366	78n35	No. 504	116n14
Nos. 310–316	8n21	No. 383	164n60	No. 505	179
No. 311	26, 118n20	No. 384	78n34	No. 506	182n117
No. 312	26, 128	No. 391	150n15	No. 508	182n118
No. 314	68n9, 71, 73, 76n27, 77n30, 83n50, 84n56	No. 392	78n33	No. 509	182n118
		No. 423	76n29	No. 511	181
No. 315	80n41	No. 468	116n14, 150n15	No. 512	155n29, 181n112, 182n116
No. 316	82n45, 87n67				
No. 317	144n6	No. 486	171n88	No. 513	87
No. 319	144	No. 489	175–76	No. 514	82n46, 86n63, 87n66
		No. 492	153n22		
No. 320	129n58	No. 494	168n77	No. 519	183–84, 184n126
No. 321	116n13, 42, 172n92	No. 496	171n87		
		No. 498	169n78	No. 522	94n12

Constitutiones (1926)

No. 125	131n64	No. 894	166n72	No. 1093	105n39, 107n45
No. 646	115n10	Nos. 896–901	164n61		
No. 891	157n35			No. 1097	105n39

Constitutiones (1290)

C. 31, no. 231   115n9